Tasting
Chile

THE HIPPOCRENE COOKBOOK LIBRARY

Afghan Food & Cookery
African Cooking, Best of Regional
Albanian Cooking, Best of
Aprovecho: A Mexican-American Border
  Cookbook
Argentina Cooks!
Australia, Good Food From
Austrian Cuisine, Best of, Exp. Ed.
Belgian Cookbook, A
Brazilian Cookery, The Art of
Bulgarian Cooking, Traditional
Burma, Flavors of,
Cajun Women, Cooking With
Calabria, Cucina di
Caucasus Mountains, Cuisines of the
Chile, Tasting
Colombian, Secrets of Cooking
Croatian Cooking, Best of, Exp. Ed.
Czech Cooking, Best of, Exp. Ed.
Danube, All Along The, Exp. Ed.
Dutch Cooking, Art of, Exp. Ed.
Egyptian Cooking
Eritrea, Taste of
Filipino Food, Fine
Finnish Cooking, Best of
French Caribbean Cuisine
French Fashion, Cooking in the (Bilingual)
Greek Cuisine, The Best of, Exp. Ed.
Gypsy Feast: Recipes and Culinary
  Traditions of the Romany People
Haiti, Taste of
Havana Cookbook, Old (Bilingual)
Hungarian Cookbook
Hungarian Cooking, Art of, Rev. Ed.
Icelandic Food & Cookery
Indian Spice Kitchen
International Dictionary of Gastronomy
Irish-Style, Feasting Galore
Italian Cuisine, Treasury of (Bilingual)
Japanese Home Cooking
Korean Cuisine, Best of
Laotian Cooking, Simple

Latvia, Taste of
Lithuanian Cooking, Art of
Macau, Taste of
Mayan Cooking
Middle Eastern Kitchen, The
Mongolian Cooking, Imperial
New Hampshire: From Farm to Kitchen
Norway, Tastes and Tales of
Persian Cooking, Art of
Poland's Gourmet Cuisine
Polish Cooking, Best of, Exp. Ed.
Polish Country Kitchen Cookbook
Polish Cuisine, Treasury of (Bilingual)
Polish Heritage Cookery, Ill. Ed.
Polish Holiday Cookery
Polish Traditions, Old
Portuguese Encounters, Cuisines of
Pyrenees, Tastes of
Quebec, Taste of
Rhine, All Along The
Romania, Taste of, Exp. Ed.
Russian Cooking, Best of, Exp. Ed.
Scandinavian Cooking, Best of
Scotland, Traditional Food From
Scottish-Irish Pub and Hearth Cookbook
Sephardic Israeli Cuisine
Sicilian Feasts
Slovak Cooking, Best of
Smorgasbord Cooking, Best of
South African Cookery, Traditional
South American Cookery, Art of
South Indian Cooking, Healthy
Spanish Family Cookbook, Rev. Ed.
Sri Lanka, Exotic Tastes of
Swiss Cookbook, The
Syria, Taste of
Taiwanese Cuisine, Best of
Thai Cuisine, Best of, Regional
Turkish Cuisine, Taste of
Ukrainian Cuisine, Best of, Exp. Ed.
Uzbek Cooking, Art of
Warsaw Cookbook, Old

Tasting Chile

A Celebration of Authentic Chilean Foods and Wines

Daniel Joelson

HIPPOCRENE BOOKS, INC.
NEW YORK

This book is dedicated to all of those close to me whom
I could not be with in the past few years because
I was far away in distance, though not in spirit.

It is in loving memory of two dear people whose last days
I could not share, Grandma and Uncle Allan.

Book and jacket design by Acme Klong Design Inc.
Photography by Daniel Joelson.

For more information, address;
HIPPOCRENE BOOKS, INC.
171 Madison Avenue
New York, NY 10016

ISBN 0-7818-1028-0
Cataloging-in-Publication Data available from the Library of Congress.
Printed in the United States of America.

Contents

¡-------

As a celebration of authentic Chilean food, this book owes itself to Chile and its people. It could not have been written were it not for all of those Chileans who kindly opened up their kitchens and bestowed upon me some of their culinary knowledge. The list of those who did so would be endless, but I would like to give special thanks to Elcira Parra, Isabel Olivares, Francisco Correa, and Juan Espinoza for sharing their time and intimate understanding of the local cuisine.

I also would like to thank all of those who helped bring this book to press, enabling me to reveal this important and overlooked cuisine. A special thanks goes to Chris Spanos, for his invaluable assistance in opening up my ideas about Chilean cuisine to the book publishing world. I am also grateful to Barbara Haber, Darra Goldstein, Josh Horowitz and Deborah Krasner for their kind advice about cookbook publishing. Enriqueta Carrington deserves a special mention for fine-tuning my translation of Pablo Neruda's poem, *Oda al Caldillo de Congrio*. I learned different book marketing approaches from Rob Kerns and his fellow students in the MBA program at Johns Hopkins University, to whom I am most grateful. Patricio Mas deftly designed a Website for the book in English and Spanish, for which I am also deeply thankful. Additionally, I would like to thank the Chilean historian Hugo Ramírez for helping shed light on the roots of Chilean cuisine.

Hippocrene Books provides the vital service of publishing cookbooks that are less mainstream, focusing on cultures such as Chile that have much to offer the culinary world. I would like to thank Hippocrene for championing this important endeavor, which enables home chefs to truly understand and enjoy world cuisine, rather than merely the handful or two of cuisines commonly brought to the fore. My editors Rebecca Cole and Anne McBride have been terrific in offering all of their knowledge, kindness, and experience to help see this project through, and I am most grateful. Additionally, I would like to thank the copy editor, Iris Bass, and the designer Katareya Wilson Godehn for their invaluable work on the book.

Among the last, but not the least, I would like to thank my wife Anny for her patience and support of this project, for cooking with me, and for having the zeal to sample all of my creations, which only ended when our swelling stomachs commanded it. I would also like to thank her family for their warmth and their support. Finally, I give a loving thank you to my father Mark, my mother Anastasia, and my sisters Helen and Marisa for

Acknowledgements

standing by me and pushing me forward. A special thank you goes to my mother for sparking my love for cooking and my interest in exploring exotic and lesser-known cuisine. Besides being enormously energetic in trying my recipes, she shared all of her knowledge of food, something she has done ever since she stationed me as a young boy in the kitchen as designated chef.

Daniel Joelson

When I first arrived in Chile as part of a two-month South American voyage to choose a site in which to perch for a while, the nation's ubiquitous farmers' markets tantalized me with their colorful medley of fresh fishes, meats, fruits, vegetables, nuts, and berries. The golden conger eel stared at me; the mammoth, cut-up, orange *calabaza* pumpkins beckoned to me; and the winding cable of a sea creature called the *cochayuyo* intrigued me. Each time I stumbled upon another market I had no recourse but to race into a restaurant in hopes of getting my hands on some of the traditional dishes sprouting from this fresh food bonanza.

Once inside, however, I almost invariably found that all those vegetables and fishes in the market were suddenly nowhere to be seen. To where had the avocado, the pumpkin, the cabbage, and all those fabulous fish fled, I wondered. I would soon find out. After peregrinations through Peru, Paraguay, and Argentina, Chile won me over by its beautiful mountains and valleys, by its wonderful beaches, and by its exquisite red wine. I decided to settle in Valparaíso, a fascinating port city seventy miles west of the capital, Santiago, knowing that I would be able to avail myself of streams of different fish and a cornucopia of wine at more than reasonable prices.

It was in part the visceral joy of suddenly having such easy access to the bustling farmers markets and boundlessly enthusiastic fishmongers of "la Perla del Pacífico" ("the Pearl of the Pacific"), as Valparaíso is known, that led me to think more seriously about Chilean food. But a perhaps still greater stimulation for my curiosity were the unsettling images around me: the proliferation of fast-food restaurants, the dominance of international cuisine, the banality of the same types of joints offering the same puny assortment of dishes, and children and their parents gorging on *completos* (hot dogs with an outrageous amount of condiments).

Without question each of these offerings deserves its place in the market, and there are many restaurants—particularly in Santiago—that are creating outstanding international fare. But why should the nation's classic cuisine be the one squeezed out? Where can I find truly local food? I asked myself.

When I mentioned this to the Chileans I encountered, I was met with nods and sighs. Some told me that they mourned the fact that *chatarra* (junk food), international "family-style restaurants," and prepared foods were starting to swallow up their native culture. Their heritage, they said, should be treated with pride, not summarily dismissed as even many of their own compatriots do. Yet they would often conclude the conversation with a resigned shrug, as though this erosion of customs was inevitable. This not only signified a loss of tradition, but also of dishes that are *para chuparse los dedos*—finger lickin' good—which I found after finally being invited into Chilean households.

An undeniable electricity and sincerity surrounded food whenever I set foot in the homes of ordinary Chileans. Suddenly the national cuisine began to show itself in spades, displaying all of the fruits and vegetables from the markets that I had salivated over earlier. The kaleidoscope of colors and aromas was extraordinary, and the hospitality of Chileans was much greater than I could ever have expected. I discovered that when I spoke up about my keen interest in Chilean cuisine, some people reacted almost giddily, talking at length about their favorite foods and dining experiences, and sharing not only their own recipes, but also those of their mothers and grandmothers.

A cookbook soon started to emerge from my frequent get-togethers with Chileans, with whom I discussed food tirelessly and in whose gracious hands I threw myself headlong. Over the next four years I traveled throughout the country by car or bus in order to unearth the best-kept recipes in Chile. I talked about cuisine with merchants selling vegetables and other produce at farmers markets, with shopkeepers who prepared their own pastries, with vendors selling strawberries and zucchini on intra-city roads, and with almost anyone who was willing to stop for a few seconds and exchange local vignettes and recipes. I even knocked on a few strangers' doors in small towns, unbeknownst to who or what awaited me (pleasant surprises were the norm). I also learned that one could discover restaurants offering varied traditional cuisine if one was scrupulously shrewd about eating out, so given the opportunity, I chatted up the waiters and owners who championed the Chilean kitchen. More often than not I tried to talk with elderly women—or grandmothers (*abuelitas*)—who retain a strong sense of what constitutes typical Chilean cuisine and who displayed a keen interest in sharing their knowledge.

The endeavor was extremely enjoyable, as it gave me a terrific excuse to eat like a king, something I did far more often than I deserved. However, the task was also utterly serious. I collected and tailored recipes in painstaking fashion, a process both overwhelming and exhausting. I traveled throughout the enormously long country (see map on page 19), scribbling down recipes from the Chileans who invented them or who received them via oral tradition. I dismissed those recipes that people acquired from books or from cooking classes (which in Chile focus on international food).

And what was the chief result of all of this research? For my part, I developed a colossal appreciation for Chilean cuisine, as well a great respect for the Chilean people. It became clear to me that each country holds gastronomical gems just waiting to be mined. And it struck me that, at a time when Latino food is tickling the tongues of Western nations, it is a pity that the proud cuisine of Chile is being greatly overlooked. However, it need not stand silent and play second fiddle to the more exposed food found north of the border in Peru or to the cuisine of Mexico that has permeated the U.S.

Just as an initial exploration of Chilean food left me longing to discover more, the tantalizing array of wine offered in Chile, at prices that are truly eye-popping, prodded me to leap into a pond I had only dipped my toes into. When I left the U.S., the typical tag on Chilean wines was that there were some goods ones out there, but that they were a gamble and were not for the true wine connoisseur. However, Chilean wineries have made tremendous strides in just the past three or four years, a fact that has gone unnoticed to too many people outside of Chile.

For home chefs armed with a French cookbook, it is only natural to go to your local wine store and pick up a Châteauneuf-du-Pape or a Beaujolais Nouveau. With the cassoulet simmering and the bottle breathing, you smile as your guests drool with anticipation, and you then transport them for the evening to a cozy bistro in the Côte d'Azur or Paris.

Sadly, guests even at Latino-style dinners are rarely transported in a similar way to the quaint town of Puerto Varas in the south of Chile or to the breathtaking ocean-side resort of Zapallar. One of the treasures of living in or visiting Chile is being able to enjoy terrific native cuisine along with exquisite wine without fear of punishing your pocketbook. When one leaves Chile that experience becomes but a memory.

But as U.S. and Chilean commerce continues to increase and competition among Chilean wines grows fiercer every month, a dizzying selection of fine Chilean wines has entered the States and is beckoning for wine lovers to explore them more fully. Little was known of Carmenère in the U.S. when I arrived in Chile, yet by 2003 the signature grape of Chile—which has avoided the wrath of the vine-worshiping phylloxera insect—was generating newsworthy buzz.

It is my sincere hope that with this book and with the large and ever-increasing variety of Chilean wines in U.S. stores, you will be able to enjoy the complete Chilean dining experience in your home. This book aims to offer you, the home chef, a glimpse of the rich color and life of Chile and to savor tastes that are rarely experienced outside of that remote country.

And should you have the opportunity to make it to Chile and to one of its farmers markets, sidle up to one of the women or men haggling over the prices of the tomatoes or arguing over how best to prepare smelt. The best thing that can happen is that they will take you home and feed you to your heart's content.

The Thrill of the National Cuisine

Dozens of pelicans are squawking and bustling amongst themselves for a few handouts of hake at Caleta Portales, the cove that rests between the coastal cities of Valparaíso and Viña del Mar. Just beyond them a new shift of boats is mooring with the day's catch, fresh from the Pacific, as men sit on cardboard boxes deftly maneuvering their knives to slice up fish for customers. There I stand amidst the pelicans, which shoot me a stiff look as I step forward towards the stalls where more fishmongers clean, scrape, and cut. The birds cluck at me stridently, "Hey, we were here first, *señor!*" My affront is unmistakable.

Heading away from the ships and pelicans on the shoreline, I duck under the roof where a glorious array of fish, from conger eel, swordfish, and sole to yellow mackerel, pomfret, and salmon, present themselves. Here too is an enticing rainbow of shellfish: there are the more commonplace oysters, clams, mussels, shrimp, and scallops, and then stacks of more exotic creatures, such as thorny sea urchins and rock-like giant barnacles. The shower of energy is contagious, with fishmongers belting out their best prices, beckoning you closer to see and poke at their wares, or hacking open the tough shells of sea urchins. Just-prepared plates of *ceviche* and *mariscal frio* are served at the market's entrance, where

Consumers yield the right-of-way to a group of pelicans at a fish market in Valparaíso.

savvy salesmen look to complement your fish purchase by offering fresh cilantro and lemon, or maybe a few piping-hot *sopaipillas* if you can't wait to get home to eat.

This market in Puerto Montt is among the most dazzling of Chile's many fish markets.

It's 10:00 am on this inlet on the central coast of Chile, and many tourists who come here feel sad to leave it behind for other points on their itinerary. But this is a scene that will repeat itself every morning and early afternoon of the week throughout the country, from places like Puerto Montt in the south to Valparaíso and Los Vilos in central Chile to Coquimbo up in the north.

This is daily life in the long and lean South American country that straddles the Pacific Ocean at every turn. Chile is merely a fine perpendicular sliver on the far reaches of the globe, but it swells with pride. It is a nation that lives off of the fresh fish and produce around it and that thrives on human interaction, which is as warm as the country's northern waters, central valleys, and southern brick ovens. This fraternal sensibility nourishes, and in turn is fed by, the native cuisine. There is much *cariño*—or warmth—and love of food in the air.

This is vividly seen not only in fish markets but also in the farmers' markets that dot small towns and cities across the country. For although Chile is best

known to the rest of the world for its fish, as well as its wine, it too has quite a breadbasket to boast. Because whether you find yourself in one of its infinite *ferias* (street markets) or *mercados* (covered markets), a mélange of avocados, tomatoes, potatoes, apples, cherries, cheeses, olives, hot peppers, and much more brim over in individual lots for blocks on end. For some, the trip to

Fishmongers at the Angelmo cove in Puerto Montt await the day's rush of foot traffic.

the market is a daily social event—a chance to gossip with a neighbor selling raisins, or maybe cuts of beef, out in the open air. Some talk about the economic rigors of the moment, or perhaps exchange recipes. But everyone always takes a few minutes to ask about each other's families.

The legwork of examining tomatoes and eyeballing prices is done to prepare for a still greater social occasion: *el almuerzo*, the large afternoon meal. Chile is a country deeply steeped in tradition that exalts the family high above all other institutions. As children grow up, they seldom strive to move away from their family, but rather live near their parents, if not in the same house. Large families unite weekly, or even daily, to share their tales and experiences over the afternoon meal. Stores are generally shuttered between 2:00 pm and 4:00 or 4:30 pm during the week and all day on Sunday nationwide, except in much of Santiago.

A Cross-Country Journey

Traveling across the country, you can't help but see the importance of cuisine and yearn to taste it, because it literally leaps out at you. Driving on the highway near the central Chilean town of La Ligua, women aptly dubbed *palomitas*—or little doves—spring before you in their white aprons and wave at you frantically with their white handkerchiefs so that you wind up bringing along a couple of homemade sweets nestled beneath white cloth in embroidered baskets. Have no fear if you fail to slam on the brakes quickly enough because lines of others will pop out at you in the ensuing few miles. With all of the white flags fluttering about you may feel like you are at the Indianapolis 500, with *chilenitos*, *alfajores*, and other sugary delicacies as the grand prize.

The first time I drove on the highway near Chillán in southern Chile, the sight of dozens of men and women bobbing fishing rods on the side of the paved road was more than I could comprehend. That "fisherman" after "fisherman" seemed to be motioning for me to stop made matters even more inexplicable. Were they hitchhikers, or some sort of weirdoes who thought they could hook in a Mercedes and call it their own? Finally I stopped and saw that they were selling crawfish (*camarones del fango*); only a tourist wouldn't know what their gesticulations signified.

A man in Pomaire toots the horn of his peanut-mobile to catch the attention of passersby.

More often than not, Chilean roadway salesmen have exactly what your gastronomic achings demand. They know you can't resist. As Chileans say, *"Guatita llena, corazón contento"*—"A full stomach, a contented heart." If the litany of roadside peddlers selling walnuts or honey in Cajón del Maipo, near Santiago, cannot meet your needs, hold on a little longer and you might find someone cradling hot crescent-shaped beef turnovers called *Empanadas de Pino*.

If you want a more intimate experience, watch for little signs by the side of the road or in front of houses in the small towns. You might want to venture into the one selling the delicious fruit called *alcayota*, or the one next to it that has different varieties of avocado. Or why not go down to the end of the path and knock on the door of the house with a sign that reads, *"huevos de codorniz"*? There you will be greeted by someone who sells quails' eggs.

You hardly need to travel by car to witness the sights and smells of Chile leaping, wafting, and shouting in the air around you. Sit on one of the country's stunning beaches and someone is liable to come by with *churros rellenos con manjar*, pastries filled with a caramel-like cream, known in other countries as *dulce de leche*. Or, hop on a bus and you'll soon see a parade of vendors jockeying to sell you nuts, homemade bread (*pan amasado*), or perhaps some pineapple or *lúcuma* ice cream. On foot, you are likely to come across the occasional grocery store, but what you will mostly see are small houses converted into makeshift stores that specialize in vegetables, fruits, breads, or meats. It's the mom-and-pop business with the freshest goods money can buy. And it is what moves Chile.

Many a soul has found the local cuisine to be nothing short of passionate. The Chilean-born writer Isabel Allende, finds nostalgic titillation through the sea urchin, while the beauty of Chilean cuisine fascinated the nation's famed poet, Pablo Neruda. The legendary writer, memorialized in the film *Il Postino*, wrote numerous poems that extolled the splendors of such foods as artichokes, tomatoes, corn, tuna, lemons, chestnuts, and salt, as well as the typical national dish, conger eel chowder. Neruda's ode to this chowder is found on page 134.

Chile in Brief

Chile is a country in South America of approximately 15 million people that lies along the Pacific Ocean. In spite of its remoteness, Chile has caught the eye of Westerners for years now. Part of its international resurgence came in the '70s and '80s, when military ruler Augusto Pinochet pioneered the country's move to free-market economics. Many hailed Pinochet's economic experiment, calling it the prototype for Latin America and a way to bring Chile into the international community. Yet, although his neoliberal policies led to strong economic growth, the growth was unbalanced and Pinochet suppressed dissent, torturing and killing political opponents. This polarized Chile, led many nations to condemn it, and ultimately the general was pressured into calling for free elections. He lost those and relinquished power in 1990.

Political and economic life is centered in Santiago. Pictured is the presidential palace, La Moneda, located downtown.

Since that time, Chile has continued along the road of economic growth and has further opened itself to the rest of the world. Its recognition abroad has bloomed, due in large part to its wine exports, but also because of its reputation as a peaceful and beautiful oasis in Latin America. While countries around it have suffered from terrorism, civil war, authoritarianism, and financial collapse, Chile has witnessed increased peace and prosperity (though it has hardly been immune to turmoil).

Today Chile is striving to lead Latin America in tourism and international trade. With the turn of the millennium it has signed free trade agreements with both the U.S. and the European Union that are expected to greatly expand trade between the blocs and give Chile a larger name in the global forum. Chile views itself as a gateway to the rest of the continent.

Such generous attractions have led many tourists to choose Chile as their vacation spot in Latin America, and have encouraged many international businesses to concentrate their regional investments in the nation. While entrepreneurs are drawn by Chile's openness, stability, and transparency, and tend to focus their attention on Santiago, tourists' passions are stoked by a broad variety of activities and landscapes that shoot them far and wide across the country. Birdwatchers, mountain and rock climbers, skiers, and water sports fanatics find their way to Chile, as do hobby fishermen, astronomers, and anthropologists. Beach lovers discover paradise here, as *playas* line Chile from north to south, alluring people from all over the world, including droves of Argentines, Bolivians, and others from the region. Adding to Chile's charm is the fact that all can be done at very affordable prices, especially for U.S. and European travelers.

Spanning the country, the geographical and climatic shifts paint a study in stark contrasts that may be unrivaled in the world. Northern Chile is mountainous, hot, and almost never "stricken" by even a few drops of rain (fortunately, because people often build homes unable to withstand a visit from the Big Bad Wolf). It is also home to the Atacama, the world's driest desert, and save for a few major cities, towns and humans are nowhere to be seen for vast stretches at a time, although one does occasionally come across contractors mining for the nation's most important mineral, copper.

Icebergs glisten in Torres del Paine in southern Chile.

Travel from Arica, on the Peruvian border, for more than three thousand miles south and it is hard to believe that you are still in the same small country. Suddenly, the scenery is not mountainous fortresses and desert sand, but leafy forests, icebergs, and penguins: Patagonia. Not far from the town of Puerto Natales is one of Chile's gems, Torres del Paine, an enormous wildlife park said by some to be the most extraordinary of all in South America.

Many find a happy medium between the southern frost and northern haze in central Chile. This area, which has four marked seasons, is littered with cities and towns bursting with political and economic activity. Santiago is home to the president, the financial markets, and one-third of all Chileans, while nearby Valparaíso hosts the national Congress and a series of the nation's most fashionable beach towns. Yet, while its climate is largely Mediterranean, the region defies a simple label: skiers feast on snow-capped mountains just a couple of hours east of Santiago, near the Argentine border.

As one heads south it becomes wetter, with abundant rainfall and myriad lakes; here, fish and timber exports, not minerals, move the economy. Scores of small villages and the country's largest ethnic group, the Mapuche, abound in this region. Not only here in the south-central part of Chile, but throughout the country's coastal areas, houses—some tattered and roofless, others almost as magnificent as those of Hollywood Boulevard—spiral around zigzagging layers of hills that overlook the sea.

Chile's Landscape

Chile's long and lean shape largely explains its diet. You can wander off just about anywhere in the country, yet you are always just a few hours from the sea. It is no secret that Chile is blessed with fantastic seafood. Fresh fish and shellfish—from conger eel, sea bass, and hake, to crabs, mussels, and sea urchins—are plentiful throughout the country.

In recent years Chile has used its maritime position to increasingly reach out to Asia, Europe, and the U.S., and has become a leading exporter worldwide of products such as fresh salmon, which is extensively farmed in Chile. Chilean sea bass is hardly an odd sighting on the menu of a fine restaurant in the U.S.

Chile's gastronomic riches, however, are hardly confined to fish, thanks to the hodgepodge of climates and variegated topography that the nation possesses. In the major cities of Valparaíso and Santiago in central Chile, a largely Mediterranean diet prevails, due to the region's fairly mild winters and hot summers. Land is fertile, with *huasos* (farmers) raising pigs, chickens, cows, fruits, and vegetables, and winegrowers planting acres upon acres of grapes. Spareribs, casseroles (such as *Pastel de Choclo*), and beans are staples there.

A *huaso* couple ride their chariot on a highway in Central Chile.

As you make your way north, you approach La Serena, Antofagasta, Iquique, and finally Arica, where it is hot year-round and scorching during the summer. The diet changes as well, with such fruits as mango and papaya flourishing, and the food sizzling like the terrain. While hot peppers are found throughout Chile, in the north many dishes incorporate hot green peppers (*ají*) or *rocotos*, spicy red peppers also found in Bolivia and Peru. Many in the region with indigenous Aymara and Quechua roots incorporate this pepper in such dishes as *Picante de Pollo* and *Patasca*.

Given the often cold and rainy climate, southern Chileans have crafted rich and hearty dishes that warm the soul, including such stews as *Curanto*, soups, such as *Ajiaco*, and such filling desserts as *Picarones*. Seasoned by an historic influence from the Mapuche and other indigenous groups such as the Chonos and Huiliches—in addition to being less internationalized than central Chile—southern towns like those in the archipelago of Chiloé lay claim to having best preserved many of the country's culinary traditions.

The native taste, however, is textured with foods and flavors from all over the world. For despite the fact that some refer to Chile as "the edge of the earth," the national cuisine hardly sprung up in a vacuum: For centuries this has been an open country heavily reliant on exports shipped out of its numerous ports. Other cultures have helped shape the nation throughout its history.

Because Spain colonized Chile hundreds of years ago and Chile has fought wars and traded with the bordering countries of Peru, Bolivia, and Argentina, the intermingling of these countries' cuisines was inevitable. The interchange between Chile and its neighbors is laid bare when observing that both Chile and Peru boast *Pastel de Choclo*, *ceviche*, and Pisco Sour, with each staunchly claiming authorship over these creations. Chile and its eastern neighbor Argentina also have several dishes in common, though they generally prepare them in distinct fashions. Like the Argentines, Chileans are fond of *parrilladas*—a slew of barbecued meats—as well as such offal as tripe, blood sausage, and tongue.

The conquistadors may have arrived in Chile with big appetites, but they certainly didn't come empty-handed. The Spaniards brought the *cazuela*, the empanada, and other dishes with them to Chile, which finally won independence in 1810. Snugly hidden inside the most typical empanada, the *Empanada de Pino*, are olives, which the Spaniards also brought to Chile. In northern Chile lie olive trees dating back more than a century. And olives are commercially prominent throughout Chile—you can't go to a *feria* or *mercado* without seeing an olive salesperson. Resting partly on the pillars of the fruits of Spain, Chilean cuisine continues to evolve: the nation is beginning to produce premium olive oils, for export, as well as to appease the domestic market. At home the penchant for olives continues to bloom: Chileans doubled their consumption of olives between 1990 and 1998.

Yet, the Spanish weren't simply philanthropists bestowing upon their colony the seeds to help create new dishes for the future. Corn enchanted the Conquistadors, who didn't hesitate to bring the ubiquitous marvel back to their home country. Chilean produce stirred the Spanish, as well as other Europeans. As this book's chapter on wine describes, on occasion the Spaniards indulged in wine without any inhibitions, and in the 1800s

Grecia Vargas and Armando Campos like to sing praises of Chile's olives. Among the best come from their hometown of Tiltil in central Chile.

and 1900s the French used their savvy to refine the local winemakers' techniques.

The Italians, too, came to Chile, though their footprint on neighboring Argentina is much more pronounced, with its torrent of pizza and pasta establishments and Italian surnames. But Germans and English immigrants swarmed to Chile and instilled culinary habits from back home. For instance, Chile's *Pastel de Papas* resembles shepherd's pie; and old haunts such as El Hamburg and Bar Inglés in Valparaíso attest to the strong legacy of these nations.

A Middle Eastern dynamic is also conspicuous in Chile today. Many of those who arrived in Chile from Spain were not Castilian, but rather from the southern Spanish region of Andalucia. The Andalucians, who lived under the rule of the Moors for 700 years, brought with them their Arab-influenced culture. That influence is perpetuated today, as Chile has a sizeable Arab population, including the largest number of Palestinians in South America. The Moors' influence on the food of Andalucia, including its desserts, was marked, and that same love for sweets is the most pronounced contribution the Arabs have made to Chilean cuisine.

Some Chileans start the day with oatmeal (called *avena* or simply *quaker*), and Chileans religiously *"toma once."* The Chilean *once* is similar to an English afternoon tea, although it wasn't always that way. Chileans say that in the old days in the mineral-rich north, miners were accustomed to drinking the strong liquor, *aguardiente*, in the afternoon when they were given time off to eat. The miners' bosses, however, became fed up with this unruly behavior and forbade it. The miners, though, were not easily dissuaded and during the day would signal to fellow miners that it was time to take a break for *"once." Once*, meaning "eleven" in Spanish, referred to the number of letters in the word *aguardiente.*

As for the Germans, for generations people of this extraction have lived in southern Chile in such towns as Frutillar, Puerto Varas, Osorno, and Valdivia. Over the years they have fostered traditions in the Chilean culture of preparing such dishes as kuchen and sauerkraut (*chucrut*) and using tasty sausages in dishes such as *curanto*. Indeed, throughout Chile various locales have come to specialize in producing different foods and plates, as the map on page 19 indicates.

Yet, though there are some regional food variations, by and large Chileans throughout the country have a similar repertoire of recipes to which they turn.

Only When in Chile

When in Chile, the best way to enjoy typical cuisine is to dine in a family home. While there are some traditional restaurants, few rescue the national cuisine as loyally as do those who cook at home. However, if you do not have the luxury of staying with an acquaintance when in Chile, there are some restaurants that faithfully preserve the nation's classic cuisine. Among the best places to dine are the large indoor markets or the central market, which you'll find by asking for the *mercado* or *mercado central*. These are found in most towns and cities throughout Chile, happily cohabitating with vendors of fruits, vegetables, meat, and fish. For example, *el mercado central* in the southern city of Concepción is just one that offers wonderfully fresh fish in typical Chilean guises at very fair prices. The quality and cleanliness of these establishments can vary, so be prudent, but across-the-board they are hotbeds of native cuisine.

Those staying at the finer lodgings of Chile will generally find that their hotel restaurant serves international cuisine. If you are a bootstrapper or seek a more "native" experience, then you will find that many of the modest hotels, called *hospedajes* or *hosterías*, serve food, which is often home-cooked. And it's not a faux pas to ask if they might make something for you (which I did with success in Chiloé).

I wish it were possible to prepare Chilean cuisine in the U.S. *exactly* as it is done thousands of miles away. However, since Chile has an extraordinary variety of climates and does not do a robust trade in its more exotic foods, some foods traditionally used for this book's recipes simply will not be found in your local stores. For example, a wealth of Chilean fruits are not commonplace abroad, including *mosqueta*, *mutilla*, *chirimoya* (cherimoya), and *calafate*. It is in Chile that you will appreciate the wonderful buttery flavor of an *alcayota* and walnut jam, a creamy *chirimoya* yogurt, or a mouth-watering *lúcuma* ice cream cone. Nor is it likely that you will find in your local fishmarket the frog-like fish called *pejesapo*, or such fresh shellfish as *locos* (abalones), *piure*, *lapas*, or *picorocos* (giant barnacles). Too few people have had the luxury of nibbling on the juicy rhubarb-like *nalca*, with a bit of salt and perhaps a sprinkling of spicy *merquén*. That is how it is consumed in places like Puerto Varas in southern Chile. Due to these realities, you will not be able to fully appreciate Chilean food in all of its manifestations unless you set foot on the country's soil yourself. However, this cookbook covers a great deal of gastronomical ground that takes into account the resources that you will likely find at your local store.

Nalca looks like little more than a chubby stick from the outside, but is a fleshy juicy delight inside.

Thankfully, for the most part it *is* possible to replicate the Chilean experience in your home, because the most common ingredients used in the Chilean kitchen are found all over the world. I have also indicated numerous substitutes that can be used in place of Chilean products so that you can easily prepare the dishes in this book at home. For example, *merquén* is a crushed hot pepper used in Chile to give many dishes a punch. Though it is unavailable in the U.S. (and even throughout Chile), hot red pepper flakes are a fine replacement. These can be found in Turkish and Middle Eastern or Asian food stores, under such names as *kirmizi biber*.

However, conjuring up the ingredients for a few dishes, like frogs' legs and blood sausages, will be challenges. But since those who desire a taste of Chile often have a penchant for the exotic, this book includes some adventurous recipes for adventuresome chefs.

Essential Ingredients of the Chilean Kitchen

The Chilean kitchen is what they call *sencillo*—it doesn't require any bells or whistles. The chief necessities are the purest and freshest raw ingredients available, a love for the task at hand, and at times a good dose of planning and patience. Often, meats are marinated or beans are soaked overnight. While some dishes are light and airy, others call for thickeners that add flavor and richness, such as cornstarch, cornmeal, or moistened bread. For the latter, the crusts of fresh white bread are removed, and the bread is soaked in milk or water until the liquid is fully absorbed and the bread becomes creamy. Sometimes *crema espesa*, also called Crema Nestlé (from the Swiss manufacturer), is used. It is thicker than the heavy cream found in the U.S.

A wide range of fats are used, but I have generally called for extra-virgin olive oil because of its taste, healthfulness, and growing appeal in the Chilean culture.

Historically Chileans did a lot of cooking with animal fat, also called lard, but they have moved to less rich fats, such as vegetable shortening, margarine, and butter. While *manteca*, or animal fat, is still sometimes used to make breads and pastries, much more common is *manteca modificada*, or vegetable shortening, which I have usually summoned instead for the recipes in this book. Chileans also have a predilection for confectioners' sugar, which is frequently used instead of granulated sugar for desserts and drinks.

Furthermore, there are a couple of items that every Chilean has on hand. One is a wooden spoon, the essential instrument to properly mix all the stews and

Stands brimming with fresh vegetables line farmers markets throughout Chile.

beans that brew in their *ollas* (pots). The second are earthenware products known as *gredas*. Finely sculpted out of clay, they take the form of everything from bowls and plates to pots and mugs. They not only are aesthetically pleasing and provide a traditional touch to each meal, but also are extremely practical. You can eat salads and casseroles in them or cook in them in the oven or on the stove. Just a few of this book's recipes that you can use them for include such casseroles as *Pastel de Choclo* and *Pastel de Papas*, and such sautéed dishes as *Ostiones al Pilpil*.

Chile's manufacturing center of *gredas* is Pomaire, just an hour southwest of Santiago. This tiny town has dozens, if not hundreds, of stores that sell oodles upon oodles of these earthenware products. A few artisan pieces can be found in Pomaire, but the bulk of the town's products are for industrial purposes, so visitors usually stock up on *gredas* and grab a meal at one of the many traditional restaurants before moving on towards points elsewhere.

While most of Chile's cooking techniques are standard, others are relatively unorthodox. For the dish *Tortilla de Rescoldo*, a dough is covered in hot ashes in the ground until fully cooked, at which point the ashes are brushed off. The aforementioned *curanto*, prepared in southern Chile, is now usually cooked on the stovetop (*Curanto en Olla*) rather than over hot rocks outside (*Curanto en Hoyo*). However, it is also prepared by some Chileans in the traditional fashion: They dig a hole in the ground, insert rocks and start a fire, allow it to heat up for several hours, then blow out the fire and remove the ashes and rocks so that the hole is as hot as an oven. They then insert the largest leaves available, such as those of the nalca plant, and each of the ingredients, and cover them with more leaves.

In the kitchen many Chileans use a *tostador*, which is like a small skillet with various ridges and holes that enables the heat from the stovetop below to enter. This baby barbecue-like device is used to toast the bread people eat daily, but it also is placed below other pots like a "flame-tamer" in order to cook their contents at a very slow simmer. Some Chileans have even found the hair dryer to be a very effective cooking instrument. Various people I encountered ignited their home barbecue by reaching for their hair dryer, plugging it into the nearest electric source, and then blowing it over the coals. One woman told me she holds her hair dryer over a saucepan to ensure that, as her milk and sugar congeal to form a creamy *manjar* and the mixture does not thicken too quickly.

In terms of ingredients, there is no set repertoire in the Chilean kitchen, however, here are some of the essentials:

Avocados. Chile has wonderfully aromatic and rich avocados, so they are exported in great quantities. In fact, Chile is among the world's largest exporters and producers of avocados in the world. Known in Chile as *palta* rather than by its more traditional Spanish name, *aguacate*, they come in numerous varieties, including the dark purple, pear-shaped *palta La Cruz* and the similar but smaller *palta champion*. But by far the most popular is the ovular *palta Haas*, which is fragrant and creamy. Avocados are used for stuffed dishes, in sandwiches, and in simple mixed salads along with celery or tomatoes.

To give a basic barometer of the avocado's culinary importance, fast food chains like McDonald's provide their Chilean units with canisters of pureed avocado for their burgers, placed alongside those of ketchup and mustard. Chilean avocado firms are undertaking great efforts to transport their avocado fascination to the U.S., having boosted spending on promotion to US$3.5 million in 2003, from US$1 million two years earlier. Chile's avocado industry hopes Americans will find avocados as practical and versatile as Chileans do, to the point where Americans won't think twice before draping their hamburgers and hot dogs with avocado.

Calabaza/Zapallo. The most common type of pumpkin in Chile is the *camote zapallo*, or *camote* pumpkin. Unlike the U.S. pumpkin that is sweet and used for desserts and Halloween, Chile's *camote* has a more subtle taste and adds flavor and color to Chilean stews, as well as the fried treats called *sopaipillas*. It can often be found in grocery stores or Latin markets in the U.S., generally under the name *"calabaza,"* so I have called it thus in the book's recipes. Though it has a hard exterior and a stiff interior, upon cooking it becomes soft over time, and even creamy. If you cannot find *calabaza* at your local store, butternut squash is a good substitute because its taste is somewhat similar and it also becomes soft and tender upon cooking.

Celery Leaves. Though celery leaves are forgettable for most Americans, Chileans put them to ample use in stews, soups, and rice and bean dishes. They also boil the leaves in water to make a tea that serves as an antidote for the sick, for the species of celery found in Chile is chockfull of aromatic leaves and nutrients. The recipes in this book usually call for just a few leaves to augment flavor, so the small crest of the celery at your local supermarket should have enough horsepower. However, you can find bountiful leaves on Chinese celery, which is also excellent for soups and stews. It can be found in Asian stores.

Corn. Corn plays a very versatile role in the Chilean kitchen, which uses it in far more dishes than do most countries. In Chile there are two main types of corn: pie corn and sweet corn. This latter type is like that found in the U.S.: it is sweet and yellow when cooked. Chileans eat it on the cob with butter, put it in stews, and strip its whole kernels for bean dishes, among others. While pie corn is the same length as sweet corn, it is double its width. Chileans grind this thicker corn to a paste and use it as a base for hot casseroles, such as *Pastel de Choclo*. This corn variant also has big sturdy husks that are ideal for wrapping *humitas*. Chile's pie corn is scarce in the U.S., so you will probably have to use sweet corn for the casserole recipes in this book. Consequently, I have omitted sugar from recipes such as *Pastel de Choclo* that in Chile call for pie corn and sugar. Additionally, add a bit of cornstarch to these dishes to make them as rich as they are in Chile and to enable them to hold together better, as pie corn does.

Cornmeal. Both corn and the mortar and pestle are vital in Chile, so it naturally follows that *chuchoca*, or cornmeal, took on an important role in the country's cuisine. The most traditional way of making *chuchoca* is by pounding sundried corn kernels to a powder with a mortar, but food processors are today's practical shortcut, or a trip to the store to scoop up a packaged brand. Fresh cornmeal is at its finest in stews, enhancing their richness, depth, and intensity. Cornmeal is particularly prevalent in southern Chile; in fact, those in the town of Cauquenes are so fond of it that some simply refer to these folks as the *Chuchoqueros* (Chuchoca people).

Garlic. Garlic is said to be an aphrodisiac in Chile, so maybe that is why Chileans add it to a dizzying array of dishes. It is essential in salsas, bean, vegetable, and meat dishes, as well as in the empanada. Having a good mortar and pestle on hand is recommended, especially if you plan on making the salsa *Chancho en Piedra*. Mortars and pestles found in southern towns like Chillán and Talca can dwarf those of the U.S., as copious amounts of sauce are to be ground and served in them.

Lemons. Chileans can be fast and furious when it comes to using lemon. Nowhere is this more clear than in *ceviche* and *mariscal frío*. In these dishes, raw fish "cooks" in a sea of lemon juice. However, in many other fish dishes, lemon is used sparingly. Lemon also serves as the base of Chile's national drink, Pisco Sour. The better restaurants typically provide a bowl of lemon wedges at the table, not only for fish, but also for squeezing on salads of lettuce, avocados, and more. Many Chileans have taken their passion for lemon into their own hands, as evidenced by the prodigious lemon trees growing in their yards.

Olives. Olives are used in myriad ways in Chilean cuisine, as they're picked at for hors d'oeuvres, mixed into salads, tucked into casseroles like *Pastel de Choclo* and *Pastel de Papas*, and sealed inside the national empanada, the *Empanada de Pino*. My personal regret is that the majority of olives found in Chilean markets are of the same black variety and lack a strong personality. However, this can be a boon for the aforementioned dishes, which have many ingredients and spices that do not want to be upstaged. Chile does have exceptional olives bursting with flavor that can be enjoyed by the handful, and these hail from towns, such as Tiltil in central Chile and from the valley of Huasco in the north.

Soon, though, Chile is destined to be awash with olives. At the turn of the twenty-first century the nation intensified the conversion of its olives into extra-virgin oils, and olive oil tastings are popping up like wine tastings throughout the country. Leading the extra-virgin olive oil field is the Canepa family, which began cultivating olives in the wine mecca of Curicó in 1953. José Canepa, from Genova, Italy, passed on his olive oil passion to his daughters, Gilda, Antonieta, and Edda, who have since spawned acclaimed brands such as TerraMater. Foreign companies too are looking to take advantage of Chile's fertile land to cultivate olives. These include the Spanish firm Aceite Borges, one of the world's largest olive oil producers, which began cultivating Chilean olives in 2002.

Onions. Many tears are shed to create Chilean cuisine, so onion lovers feel quite at home here. Chileans prove their fondness for this regal reeker by adding it in relatively modest portions to bean and meat dishes. Onions are vital in empanadas: they are added in great quantities so that at first sight they might seem overbearing. They never are, however, because of the way they are treated. For example, in empanadas, the onions cook for at least fifteen minutes, greatly reducing in size and brute strength until they finally act as a very agreeable complement. In *Escabeche de Cebollas*, they are submerged in vinegar for a week or so before eaten. And in *Ensalada a la Chilena*, the onions are treated with salt, washed, and squeezed several times before they are combined in plentiful amounts with sliced tomatoes. Chileans frequently finely slice, wash, and squeeze onions for other dishes so that they can be enjoyed to their utmost without reservation.

A typical method of preparing onions is by cutting them in *cuadritos*, or little squares. One simply peels off the onion's skin, removes its core, and using a sharp knife, cuts slightly into the flesh of one side, making numerous rows. One then rotates the onion and again cuts to make numerous rows, crisscrossing the rows already cut. This creates a kind of checkerboard that allows tiny bits of onion to fall into the plate below. One repeats the procedure until the entire onion is chopped. The onion "nuggets" are then sprinkled into salads or fried with herbs and added to other dishes.

Peppers. In general, Chilean food is less spicy than that of its northern neighbor, Peru, and significantly less so than Mexican food. Yet, Chile does summon an important variety of peppers for everyday cooking and thus makes valuable contributions towards the Latin American segment of hot cuisine. What most commonly crops up is *pebre*, the hot sauce often eaten with bread as an appetizer. Hot peppers also animate fish and chicken dishes and give some dishes their name, such as *Picante de Pollo* (Spicy Chicken) and *Ostiones al Pilpil* (Spicy Sea Scallops). For many Chileans, a meal is not complete unless they have a little hot green pepper (*ají verde*) that they can nibble on throughout.

Hot pepper varieties in Chile include *ají verde*, *ají rojo*, *cacho cabra verde*, *cacho cabra rojo*, *cacho cabra rojo seco*, *rocoto*, and *puta madre*. Several Chilean companies also plant, process, and export *jalapeño* peppers, which are perceived by many as part of Mexico's domain. Several exporters said these peppers have not caught on in Chile because they are not native, and Chileans typically like peppers that are less spicy than the *jalapeño*. For more on hot peppers, see, "Sauces, Herb Mixes, and Salads" (page 21).

Mild bell peppers are also mainstays in the Chilean kitchen, dressing up stuffed avocados, enhancing casseroles, and bringing color and flavor to bean dishes and stews. Red bell peppers are more popular than their green counterparts, but both are treasured.

Pisco. Chile's national liquor, Pisco is a grape brandy produced in the north of the country. A special part of the drinks section of this book is dedicated to Pisco recipes, which is slowly but surely making a name for itself throughout the U.S. and Europe. Thirty-five– or forty–proof Pisco is usually used.

Potatoes. Chilean potatoes are said to originate in the southern archipelago of Chiloé, and some even argue that Chiloé is where the world's potatoes originated. If true, this bodes a very rosy future for typical Chilean cuisine because it is known across the country for fiercely preserving traditions. Chiloé is one of the places where the stew *Curanto* is still prepared in the old-fashioned, complex fashion. Cooked in a pit in the earth, *Curanto* not only includes various layers of meats, shellfish, and vegetables, but also two potato pancake–like variations: *Chapaleles* and *Milcao*. But you need not rip up earth in Chile to enjoy its "apples" (as the French call this vegetable). Rather, simply try the invariably fresh French fries or sautéed potatoes, where you can taste that the potatoes are just-harvested.

Tomatoes. Throughout Chile tomatoes are central to the home-cooked meal. Perhaps the most famous in the country come from Limache, a town in Chile's central region that produces big, meaty spheres. Found in salads, stews, casseroles, and just about anything, tomatoes are usually peeled in Chilean recipes. An easy way to do this is to put them in boiling water for ten to fifteen seconds, which allows for their jackets to slip off easily when pulled at by a knife or your fingers. Chileans also often slice tomatoes into thin rings. Rather than slicing them lengthwise, they slice finely from the top to the bottom of the tomato. (This is also often done for onions.)

Vinegar. Chileans are fond of marinating meats overnight, which usually calls for the use of vinegar. This softens the meat, kills germs (especially useful for the just-killed meats found throughout Chilean markets!), and enhances flavor. For maximum results, use the best red wine vinegar that you can find for the recipes in this book. Pickling is also quite popular, and Chileans use vinegar to pickle onions, hot peppers, cucumbers, and more. Those foods that are soaked or cooked in wine or wine vinegar are called *escabeches* in Chile.

Herbs and Spices

Aliño Completo. This is a combination of the most common dried spices in the Chilean household, so it often incorporates all of the ingredients in this "Herbs and Spices" section, apart from basil, cinnamon, and cloves. This combination of spices such as oregano, cumin, and paprika is believed to have gained currency in Chile in the early times because of its ability to preserve foods in the absence of refrigerators.

Basil. Fresh basil is usually ground and mixed with corn in such dishes as *Pastel de Choclo*, *humitas*, and *Porotos con Mazamorra*. It is like the basil found in the U.S.

Cilantro. Chileans use cilantro as other cultures use parsley: to add color and a touch of flavor. However, so that the taste of cilantro does not overtake a dish's inherent flavor do not be overly generous with the amount you sprinkle on for the recipes in this book. As Chileans do, you can also substitute flat-leafed parsley (rather than curly-leafed parsley) for cilantro in some cases. Cilantro is not only a typical component in Chilean stews, but also in its salsas and salads.

Cinnamon. Cinnamon is invaluable for Chilean desserts, both in the stick and powder form. Ground cinnamon is sprinkled on puddings and cakes and the mixed drink, *Vaina*, and cinnamon sticks are simmered in rich dessert sauces. Cinnamon is also enjoyed in the after dinner drink called *Canelita*, when it is combined with *aguardiente*.

Cloves. Cloves are cinnamon's bedfellow in Chile. A few cinnamon sticks beg for several cloves in recipes such as *Sopaipillas Pasadas*. They are usually used whole to give a slight nuance to a dish.

Cumin. Like India, Chile makes wonderful use of cumin. The spice is frequently sprinkled on meats and stews and makes up the lion's share of the Chilean spice *Aliño Completo*. Unless otherwise specified, the recipes in this book call for ground, rather than whole, cumin.

Oregano. Sprinkled on fish, stews, bean dishes, and barbecued meats, in Chile oregano is almost always used in dried flakes rather than ground. It is so commonly used that you can buy a cup of oregano from vendors ambling through markets for just fifteen cents.

Paprika. Aptly referred to as "*ají de color*," or "colored hot pepper," paprika is used to color dishes or provide a subtle spice. It is also often mixed with hot oil and ladled over bean dishes.

The Chilean Meal

Typically Chileans start the day with *el desayuno*, a small breakfast that consists of bread, jam, and cold cuts, along with coffee or tea. Sometimes the day begins with a banana drink called *Leche con Plátano*, *Paila Huevo* (scrambled eggs), or *Paila Jamón* (scrambled eggs with ham). The main meal of the day comes in the early afternoon and is called *el almuerzo*. In this family-oriented society, *el almuerzo* is the time for parents and their children—be they youths or adults—to come together to discuss life and the week's affairs. The meal usually starts with fresh bread and a saucer of spicy *pebre*, into which the bread is dipped. Then follows the main course with a side dish and salad. Salads are much more common than hot vegetables as an accompaniment, as Chileans usually incorporate vegetables into stews or casseroles, rather than eating them alone. Often, Chileans start the meal with a Pisco Sour and have *vino* (wine) or a *bebida* (soft drink) with the meal. They might conclude the meal with a digestive known in Chile as a *bajativo*. Wine suggestions are made throughout the book. If your wine store doesn't have the recommended wine, try another Chilean wine from the same grape, or even a different one. Whatever tickles your fancy!

While in the late evening some Chileans eat a hot dinner, or *cena*, most instead *toma once* in the early evening, as aforementioned. This typically cold meal consists of bread, cold meats, pâté, eggs, cheeses, and salads, or other light fare, such as a few *sopaipillas*.

During the holidays, Chileans often celebrate in a special way. For example, on Independence Day, known as "*el 18 de septiembre*," they have friends over or attend festivals where they consume healthy—or gluttonous—quantities of empanadas, *choripan* (sausage sandwiches), *anticuchos* (shish kebabs), and *alfajores*, and drink a sweet grape wine called *chicha* that is sometimes served in a bull horn (called *Chicha en Cacho*). At such fiestas, carts and carts of *mote con huesillo* (shelled wheat and peach nectar) are pushed around by vendors.

On Christmas and New Year's Eve, Chileans exchange *Pan de Pascua* (fruitcakes) and drink a type of eggnog that is radically different from ours, called *Cola de Mono*.

Chileans also show their devotion to the national cuisine on other special occasions. In southern and northern Chile, towns commemorate saints on different days via large stews, such as *calapurca*. In Chiloé, for example, the *derretimiento* feasts are capable of bringing entire villages together during the cold winter months. In these sometimes macho affairs, women labor over the stove, preparing accompaniments such as *sopaipillas* and *roscas*, while the men roast a pig on a spit, cooking it for an entire day and "melting" it (*derretimiento* means "the melting") in order to produce animal fat and *chicharrones*. Meanwhile, groups in the village form to share in the preparation of the rest of the feast. Some prepare *longanizas* (mild or spicy sausages) and *prietas* (blood sausages), while others make *costillares* (spareribs), *chuletas* (pork chops), and *jamón* (ham).

Word Games

There is one caveat for the Chilean recipe names in this book: be careful not to over-analyze them. Often confusing or downright illogical, they may add little clarity to the dish you will be preparing. But their goofy eccentricity is also what makes them distinctly Chilean.

Some of these names and English translations are:

calzones rotos: ripped underwear
chancho en piedra: pig in stone
humitas: bow ties
machos ahogados: drowning fellows
navegado: traveled
niños envueltos: wrapped babies
palta reina: queen avocado
papas duquesas: duchess potatoes
picarones: flirtatious men
porotos con riendas: beans with reins

For those mindful scholars who take issue with any editorial shortcomings or translations on my part, such as in the way of spelling, in my defense Chileans themselves often differ over such matters. For example, if you go to a grocery store or market in Chile you will find that one butcher will say a chicken leg is a *tuto*, while the next will call it a *trutro*. A package of pasta for one typical Chilean dish might be spelled *Pancutra*, and the same product by another brand is called *Pantruca*. Such gaffes can be fun, but they can also make someone who is dyslexic, paranoid—or someone who is paranoid, dyslexic.

Chileans not only invert letters, but also differ on a single word for a food. A small crunchy bread that resembles a small baguette is called *pan francés*, *marraqueta*, or *pan batido*, depending on where you are in Chile. Similarly, if you are traveling inside Chile and want to order a cold crab salad that you savored earlier, be mindful that it could suddenly be called *escarapachos*, *carapachos*, or *jaiba mayo*.

There are flat-out misnomers here as well. Go to the meat market and order *pollo ganso*. Translated into English this is "chicken goose," but what you're requesting is not a fowl, but rather a cut of beef. No butcher I met could explain this linguistic enigma. Or, if you ask for *choclillo*, you might expect to get a little piece of corn, as the name suggests (*choclo* is corn), but you will instead get another cut of beef. In this case, though, it makes some sense, because the meat is shaped like an ear of corn.

Listening to Chileans inventing and revising the nomenclature on local foods, selling everything under the sun in buses and on highways, or simply rustling up cabbages, apples, and hake in the market to prepare for the big *almuerzo* is just where the fascination begins in this far-flung country with hidden treasures.

More information about the food and wine of Chile, as well as the local "dialect," can be found at www.tastingchile.com. Please feel free to contact the author at comments@tastingchile.com.

Chile

Regional Food Specialties

Arica

Iquique

limes (Pica)

Antofagasta

Copiapo

olives, olive oil, raisins (Huasco)

La Serena

papaya (La Serena)
goat (Vicuña)
goat cheese (Ovalle)
Pisco (Valle del Elqui, Limari)
Valparaíso   pastries (La Ligua)
avocados, chirimoya (Quillota)
Rancagua   tomatoes (Limache)
olives (Tiltil)
Talca   pastries (Curacarí)
Concepción   watermelons (Paine)
cow cheese (Chanco)
sausages (Chillán)
sea bass (Talcahuano)

Temuco

kuchen, strudel, other German foods
cold cuts (Llanquihue)

Puerto Montt

salmon (Puerto Montt)

potatoes, curanto (Chiloé)

Coihaique

lamb, king crab
(Punta Arenas, Puerto Natales)

Punta Arenas

● **Santiago**

Salsas, Aliños, y Ensaladas

hile is alight with hot peppers, boasting numerous types, such as:

Ají verde
Ají rojo
Cacho cabra verde
Cacho cabra rojo
Cacho cabra rojo seco
Rocoto
Puta madre

The most common pepper is *ají verde*, which is fairly mild, light green in color, and shaped like a small banana. *Ají rojo* is the same as ají verde, except for its color and it is often dried.

A spicier green pepper is called *cacho cabra verde*, which is similar in shape and form to *ají* peppers but is olive green. The red pepper version of this is known as *cacho cabra rojo*, which can be dried to make *cacho cabra rojo seco*. This dried red pepper is often coarsely chopped and added to give a kick to dishes such as *Ostiones al Pilpil*. It also is crushed (sometimes with paprika) to make *merquén* powder, which can be purchased in many Chilean markets, particularly in the south. The tasty *merquén* salsa derived from this is delightful in salads, rice dishes, and soups.

The lightning hot, red pepper, *rocoto* or *locoto*, as others call it, can be found in northern Chile. It is shaped like a very small bell pepper and is used in such dishes as *Picante de Pollo*. Northern Chileans also often substitute this for *ají verde* when making pebre and other salsas.

Finally, there comes the very small red pepper called *puta madre*. It resembles a jalapeño pepper and its name derives from its ferocity. When you try even a whisker of it, you're tempted to shout, *"¡Puta madre!"* which translated into English is something to the effect of, "Your mother is a whore!"

It is important to wear plastic or rubber gloves while handling hot peppers to protect your skin from the peppers' oils. Additionally, protect (and don't touch!) your eyes. Wash your hands thoroughly after handling hot peppers.

When preparing recipes that call for peppers I suggest that you gradually add the peppers as the final ingredient, because everyone's love for—and tolerance

Sauces, Herb Mixes, and Salads

of—spicy foods differs, and you may not be able to obtain the exact pepper called for in the recipe. Additionally, the spiciness of even the same kind of pepper varies wildly. In general, the smaller the pepper, the hotter it is. The heat of the pepper comes not from its exterior but, rather, from the white "veins" and seeds inside; thus, one way to adjust the spiciness of the dish is to decide what part of the pepper to use. If you just want to add a bit of spice and some color to the dish, then just use the pepper's skin and discard its insides.

There are a few peppers that you can substitute in place of Chile's most common peppers, *ají verde* and *cacho cabra rojo seco*. *Pasilla* hot peppers, which are light green and fat, and *cubanelle* peppers, which are green and large, and are longer than *pasilla* are both able to stand in place of *ají verde*. Yellow Caribe chili peppers may also be the name of the pepper in your grocery store that approximates *ají verde*. Relatives of *cacho cabra rojo seco* can be found as Puya chili pods, California chili pods, or New Mexico chili pods.

Hot peppers frequently add zest to Chilean salads, which are included in this chapter. In Chile, salads lean heavily on the use of tomatoes, lettuce, avocados, onions, cabbage, and celery. Further, a native green called *penca*, which is similar in appearance and water content to celery, is a Chilean salad favorite.

Traditional Spicy Salsa

Pebre   2 cups

Hot sauce, or pebre, is a veritable jack-of-all-trades at the Chilean dinner table; almost every meal starts with pan y pebre. It is found in restaurants all over the country, used as a dip for bread. In the home, it is even more popular, where it adds energy to cazuelas, seasons boiled potatoes and serves as a sidekick to Humitas (page 42). Pebres often include tomatoes, garlic, onions, or cilantro, but the essential ingredient of every pebre is a good hot pepper. From there the variations become limitless.

1 large tomato (10 ounces), peeled and finely chopped
5 tablespoons finely chopped hot green pepper
5 tablespoons finely chopped onion
5 tablespoons finely chopped fresh cilantro
2 cloves garlic, finely chopped
¼ cup vegetable oil
1 tablespoon plus 1 teaspoon freshly squeezed lemon juice
Salt to taste

1. In a nonreactive bowl, combine the tomato, hot green pepper, onion, cilantro, garlic, vegetable oil, and lemon juice.

2. Slowly mix in the salt to taste. This salsa is best fresh, but keeps for one week when refrigerated.

Spicy Cilantro Mayonnaise

Pebre de Cilantro   1½ cups

Some Chilean salsas, such as this one, take on a delightful green color due to an abundance of cilantro. After chopping the ingredients, process them in a blender to create a light and smooth, creamy sauce. You can dip bread in this salsa, as you do with pebre *(page 23), or use it as a sauce for side dishes. A wonderful meal is fried fish, with boiled potatoes, a tomato salad, and this spicy salsa.*

2 juicy red tomatoes (10 ounces), peeled and quartered
½ cup coarsely chopped fresh cilantro
¼ cup coarsely chopped onion (about ⅓ small onion)
3 tablespoons coarsely chopped hot green pepper, seeds and veins removed
2 cloves garlic, coarsely chopped
¼ cup Mayonnaise (see recipe, page 29)
1 tablespoon vegetable oil
Salt to taste

1. Put the tomatoes, cilantro, onion, hot pepper, garlic, mayonnaise, and vegetable oil in a blender or juicer. Blend to a paste. You may instead want to blend in 1 tablespoon of hot peppers at a time, sampling it for flavor each time, to ensure that the peppers you purchased do not overpower the rest of the ingredients.

2. Add salt to taste and serve.

Pure Hot Pepper Salsa

Salsa de Ají Rojo y Salsa de Ají Verde   1 cup

The most common hot pepper in Chile is a light green pepper called ají verde. Some Chileans enjoy it so much that they always have one or two of the peppers on their plate that they eat raw with salt. Since it is not as hot as other peppers this is actually believable. To enjoy ají verde, or ají rojo—the same pepper but more mature—in a salsa, simply mix it with the ingredients below. It is terrific for eating with bread, humitas, or stuffed cabbage leaves called Niños Envueltos. Though you can remove all the seeds, I keep several to make the sauce even hotter and because the white seeds and cherry-red color of the salsa make a nice contrast in the bottle. A similar commercially-made sauce is sold in Asian and Middle Eastern stores, under such names as Chinese chili sauce.

10 ounces hot red or green
   peppers
4 cloves garlic, halved
1 tablespoon vegetable oil,
   plus extra for storing
About ¼ teaspoon salt

1. Wash the hot peppers well. Seed them, but do not remove their veins. Put the pepper and garlic in a blender and blend until almost a puree, about 30 seconds.

2. Mix in the vegetable oil, 3 tablespoons water, and salt.

3. Put the salsa in a small bottle and add a bit of oil on top of the sauce once the jar is full to maintain the color and freshness. Be sure to fill the bottle completely, sealing it tightly so that there are no spaces of air to cause the salsa to spoil quickly. It stays good for one to two weeks. If you do not open the bottle it stays good for several months. When making large quantities of the sauce, store it in tightly-sealed glass jars.

Stoneground Tomato Salsa

Chancho en Piedra *is eaten primarily in southern Chile, including in Talca, the city where it is said to have been created. It is used as a dip for everything from bread and roast meats to Fried Frogs' Legs (see recipe, page 144). When the* Chancho en Piedra *arrived at my table in the restaurant El Chancho con Chupalla in the town of Machalí I knew it was authentic. My waiter presented it in a gargantuan mortar and pestle made of stone. True to custom, it was served in the stone in which most of the ingredients were ground. Its vibrant colors and fragrance quickly made me grab a* sopaipilla *for dipping. I immediately realized that the combination of soft, mild* sopaipillas *and the spunky* Chancho en Piedra *was a match made in heaven. Rarely is coriander seed or cilantro included in the* Chancho en Piedra *found in southern Chile today, but in the past many included it and it is a tasty alternative. Coriander seed may have fallen out of favor, in part, because cilantro is so popular that Chileans typically purchase the seed (called* semilla de cilantro, *or cilantro seed) in order to plant it.*

¾ teaspoon salt (approximately)

4 cloves garlic, halved

1 pound juicy tomatoes (2 to 3), peeled and quartered

2 tablespoons finely chopped hot green peppers, such as cubanelle

Ground coriander seeds to taste (optional)

1. Put the salt and garlic in a large pestle and grind thoroughly with the mortar.

2. Add the tomatoes and grind with the mortar. Or coarsely grate the tomatoes into the pestle.

3. Mix in the hot pepper and the coriander seeds, and serve.

Salsa of Dried Red Peppers

Salsa de Merquén   ¹/₂ cup

Merquén *derives from* cacho cabra, *the dried red hot pepper found primarily in southern Chile. In the U.S., a fine substitute is hot red pepper flakes, or kirmizi biber, found in Turkish stores. Sometimes it is combined to make a sauce that is ideal for drizzling over* Arroz Chileno, *for dipping on barbecued meats, or for generating heat in salads. The amount below is more than enough for four to six people to use in any Chilean meal.*

1¹/₂ tablespoons *merquén* powder or hot red pepper flakes
3 teaspoons freshly squeezed lemon juice
1 small clove garlic, finely chopped
¹/₂ teaspoon vegetable oil
Salt to taste

1. Use a fork to mix the merquén, lemon juice, garlic, and vegetable oil in a bowl. Add about 4 tablespoons of water and salt to taste. Store in a small jar.

2. Refrigerate after opening.

Mixed Herbs

Aliño Completo *is to the Chilean chef what herbes de Provence are to the French chef or garam masala is to the Indian chef. It is a mixture of locally popular, dried spices that are packaged under a single name.* **Aliño completo,** *which means "complete seasoning," is added to meats, bean dishes, and much more. Since it is often a potpourri of the most abundant spices in the home chef's cabinet, its composition varies according to the chef, and in Chilean stores it is also sold under various guises. While its mainstays are cumin and black pepper, it can also include oregano, coriander, paprika, and dried garlic.*

3 tablespoons ground cumin
1¾ tablespoons paprika
1¾ tablespoons ground
  coriander
1½ tablespoons ground
  black pepper

1. Mix all the ingredients together thoroughly in a small bowl.

2. Place them in a jar and store in a cool, dry place. The herb mixture stays fresh for more than one year.

Mayonnaise

Mayonesa

2¼ cups

I am immediately encouraged when a saucer of **pebre** *and another of homemade mayonnaise arrives at my table in a Chilean restaurant. A simple dip for bread, mayonnaise has enormous appeal in Chile and comes in handy for many of this book's recipes.* **Palta Reina** *(Stuffed Avocado, page 39) and* **Escarapachos** *(Crab Salad, page 137) are just some of the Chilean dishes that incorporate mayonnaise; also, the delicious Chilean* locos *(abalones) are dipped in mayonnaise alone. I find Chilean mayonnaise less sweet than its bottled counterparts found in U.S. grocery stores, so the recipe below is well suited for the dishes in the book.*

6 egg yolks, at room
temperature
1¾ cups vegetable oil or
light olive oil
1 tablespoon freshly
squeezed lemon juice
Salt to taste

1. Whisk the egg yolks in a bowl until light and creamy.

2. Gradually add the oil, continuing to whisk.

3. Mix in the lemon juice and a bit of salt. Refrigerate the mayonnaise when not using. It keeps, refrigerated, for about four days.

Cornmeal

It's not every day that you see ears of corn hanging from a rope in a common home. That's what I saw when I visited Elcira Parra in Rancagua. Elcira tries to buy as little canned or bottled food as possible so that everything she prepares is all-natural. Dangling red and green hot peppers and yellow corn, and glass jars of pickled onions and marinated olives, make for a beautiful house, but also for a very busy culinary schedule for Elcira. The hanging corn, she told me, is used to make fresh cornmeal, called chuchoca. *Chileans often call upon* chuchoca *for such stews as* Cazuela de Chancho. Chuchoca *is best prepared in the summer, with the cobs of corns soaking in the sun, so that hot, dry heat desiccates them. Otherwise, cold or moistness are liable to give you moldy corn.*

4 ears of corn

1. Bring a pot of water to a boil over high heat. When boiling, add the ears of corn, reduce the heat to medium, and cover. Cook the corn until tender, about 15 minutes.

2. Remove the ears from the pot. Wrap string around the ears and tie them to a line (such as a clothesline outside). Let dry for 7 to 10 days.

3. When the corn has dried, remove the kernels (by scraping with a knife or vigorously rubbing two ears of corn against each other). Cut off and discard any white stems that remain. You should have approximately 2½ cups of kernels.

4. Place the kernels in a food processor and grind until a powder forms. Store the cornmeal in a covered glass jar. It keeps for several months.

Tuna and Giant White Corn Salad

Ensalada de Atún y Maíz Pelado   4 to 6 servings

Commonly used in northern Chile, giant white corn is delicious in soups and salads. These kernels are about the size of a penny and expand further on cooking. Raquel Mamani, from the town of Mamiña, in northern Chile, told me she cooks giant white corn in a beef broth so that it absorbs the beef flavor. You can find giant white corn in some U.S. stores—the company Goya sells it—and you can find it in Latin stores under their Spanish name, maíz pelado. *Consult with the instructions on the package because cooking time can vary. Below I indicate how to cook the type that needs to be soaked and cooked thoroughly.*

2 cups giant white corn
1 raw beef bone
¾ cups finely chopped green onions
2 cans (totaling 12 to 14 ounces) tuna in vegetable oil
2 tablespoons finely chopped fresh parsley
1½ tablespoons freshly squeezed lemon juice
Salt to taste

1. Soak the corn in water overnight.

2. Boil the corn in 6 cups of water with the beef bone, adding water when necessary to fully submerge the corn. When the kernels are tender and begin to break open, after about 1 hour and 15 minutes, strain, and discard the bone.

3. Combine the hot corn with the green onions and tuna (including its oil).

4. Mix in the parsley, lemon juice, and salt to taste. Chill and serve.

Spicy Cabbage and Cilantro Salad

4 servings

Glorious green cabbages abound in markets and proliferate in restaurants in Chile They are favorites in many dishes, particularly salads and somewhat less so in casseroles. This dish can be made in seconds when using a food processor. In Chile, I use merquén to add spice to this dish, but hot red pepper flakes are a perfectly good substitute. A handful of fleshy black olives is also delightful in this dish.

4 cups finely chopped green cabbage (about ½ cabbage)
½ to ⅔ cup finely chopped fresh cilantro
3 tablespoons freshly squeezed lemon juice
2 tablespoons vegetable oil
½ teaspoon hot red pepper flakes
½ teaspoon salt
½ to 1 cup whole black Kalamata olives (optional)

1. Mix the cabbage and cilantro in a bowl.

2. Add the lemon juice, vegetable oil, hot red pepper flakes, and salt. Mix thoroughly. Layer with black olives, if desired.

Tomato and Onion Salad

Ensalada a la Chilena   4 servings

In Valparaíso, Yenny Montecinos taught me how to make this most typical of Chilean salads. It is brimming with onions and tomatoes yet is neither overbearing nor acidic. First, slice an onion in thin rings. Put the rings in a colander and, with the water running, squeeze the onion. Do this several times, helping rid the onion of its strong juices. Generously sprinkle salt on the sliced onions and set them aside to drain for ten minutes, then rinse the salted onions. The onions are now ready to mingle in abundance with the tomatoes.

3 medium tomatoes
  (1½ pounds), peeled and
  cut into slices
1 large onion (12 ounces),
  prepared as indicated
  above
2 tablespoons extra-virgin
  olive oil
Salt to taste
2 tablespoons finely chopped
  fresh cilantro
1½ tablespoons finely
  chopped hot green
  peppers, such as *cubanelle*

1. Mix the tomatoes, onions, oil, and salt to taste.

2. Add the cilantro and hot peppers, stir briefly, and serve.

Summer Salad

This is a terrific way of taking advantage of tomatoes and corn when they are in season. The roasted onion gives the salad a nice tang. I like bringing it along for picnics and barbecues.

1¼ pounds small onions, both ends removed, but unpeeled
2 ears of corn
1 pound small tomatoes
2½ tablespoons extra-virgin olive oil
Salt and freshly ground black pepper

1. Wrap the onions in aluminum foil and cook them on a grill until they are moist and tender, about 30 minutes. A sharp knife should easily penetrate the center of the onions. Otherwise, put the onions in the oven and cook at 400° F until brown outside and soft inside (about 50 minutes). When the onions are cooked, peel off one or two layers and quarter the onions.

2. Bring a pot of water to a boil. Add the corn. Remove it when cooked, about 15 to 20 minutes and allow to cool. Remove the corn kernels from the cobs (you will have about 1½ cups).

3. Peel and quarter the tomatoes.

4. In a bowl, mix the onions, corn, tomatoes, olive oil, and salt and pepper to taste.

Broad Bean Salad

Broad beans are big, rich beans that make wonderful salads. They are especially good accompaniments for spareribs, steak, and other grilled meats. While the recipe below calls for fresh peas, canned peas can also be used, and should be added to the pot after the broad beans.

6 pounds fresh broad beans (in their pods)

9 ounces fresh peas (in their pods)

½ lemon, plus 1 tablespoon freshly squeezed lemon juice

½ cup finely chopped green onions

3 tablespoons extra-virgin olive oil

Salt

1. Bring a large pot of lightly salted water to a boil.

2. Remove the beans and peas from their pods. You will now have approximately 1¾ pounds of broad beans and 3½ ounces of peas.

3. Add the beans, peas, and the lemon half to the boiling water. Cook over a high flame until the beans and peas are cooked and tender, about 10 minutes.

4. Rinse the beans and peas in cold water, and strain.

5. Put the beans and peas in a bowl. Mix in the lemon juice, green onions, olive oil, and salt to taste. Serve cold.

Entradas, Agregados, y Sandwiches

I still remember the first time I came to Valparaíso and tried the fish. Yet, what I remember almost as vividly is the French fries—so fresh, so crispy. The experience would repeat itself again and again. For many Chileans, potatoes need little more than salt. The very popular *Papas Cocidas* are nothing more than boiled potatoes, and many eat them alone, without butter, though perhaps with a bit of hot sauce.

However, side dishes can also be somewhat more exotic here. The penny-sized giant white corn, or *maíz pelado*, found in northern Chile, is similar to an overgrown popcorn seed. Few countries have the imagination of Chile when it comes to dolling up the avocado. The sometimes staid white rice found in other countries is transformed in Chile into a tasty golden brown grain with a potpourri of minced vegetables and alluring aromas. And mashed potatoes will never be the same again for you once you try *Puré Picante*, whose flaming orange color and striking scent ignite the nasal passages and warm the belly.

Stuffed Avocado

The avocado, or palta, *is exquisitely tender and fragrant in Chile, so unsurprisingly it does brisk business in the exporting trade. Frequently included in sandwiches, such as* **Ave Palta** *(chicken and avocado), the avocado also plays a royal role in the* **Palta Reina** *("queen avocado"), which is shredded chicken, blended with mayonnaise, nestled in the dimple of a halved avocado. With an olive placed atop this robust ovular form, the end product looks a bit like a crowned queen resting on her throne. Sumptuous variations of the stuffed avocado include* **Palta Calbuco,** *which is cooked mussels inside the avocado: Just mix the ingredients below, substituting mussels for the chicken. The same applies for* **Palta Cardenal** *(shellfish medley),* **Palta York** *(with ham), and southern Chile's* **Palta Victoria,** *in which avocado is filled with king crab* (centolla).

4 medium avocados
  (1½ to 2 pounds)
10 to 12 ounces boneless
  chicken breast, cooked
  and shredded
¼ cup Mayonnaise (see
  recipe, page 29)
Salt and freshly ground
  black pepper
2 tablespoons finely chopped
  red bell pepper
8 black olives
3 cups coarsely chopped
  lettuce
Lemon wedges

1. Cut the avocados in half lengthwise. Discard the pits. Use a spoon to gently remove the entire avocado half from the skin without breaking it. Set the avocados aside.

2. In a bowl, mix the cooked chicken breast and mayonnaise. Mix in salt and black pepper to taste.

3. Place about 2 tablespoons of the mixture into the dimple of each halved avocado. Sprinkle with the bell pepper, then place an olive on top.

4. Place the avocados upon a bed of lettuce. Serve with lemon wedges and a saucer of homemade mayonnaise for the group.

Pickled Onions

Innumerable recipes bear witness to the fact that Chileans are very serious about beans. There are scores of bean varieties in the indigenous Mapuche community, and because they are low cost and high-protein, beans have been ingrained in the national culture for centuries. Chileans are equally serious that the beans be accompanied properly, and that usually means having ample Escabeche de Cebollas. *While this is the most popular form of pickled vegetables in Chile, others, such as pickled bell peppers, hot green peppers, and cucumbers, are quite common. Throughout the country, markets and stores proudly display jars in full view for you to choose the* escabeche *of your pleasure. Chileans often eat the pickled onions straight from the jar, but they are also delicious with cilantro and a touch of oil and salt. For other variations of* escabeche, *simply add small amounts of green onion, hot green pepper, bell pepper, or cucumber to the bottle of onions that you are pickling. I always have several onions or peppers steeping in a bottle of vinegar labeled with the date when I made them. This way, any time I want a bean, lentil, or other dish that calls for* escabeche, *it is already prepared.*

2 medium onions
(1¼ pounds), peeled and
quartered
2⅓ cups red wine vinegar
Finely chopped fresh cilantro
Vegetable oil
Salt

1. Place the onions in a glass jar.

2. Add vinegar to fully submerge the onions. Set aside for 5 to 8 days at room temperature. You can store *escabeche* for four to six weeks at room temperature.

3. When you are ready to eat the *escabeche*, remove the onions and chop them coarsely. Put them in a bowl with a bit of the vinegar. Sprinkle on cilantro, a bit of oil, and a dash of salt. Amounts will depend on how much pickled onion you extract from the jar. Mix thoroughly and serve.

Stuffed Tomatoes

Tomate Relleno

Stuffed tomatoes are found in many parts of the world, but the stuffed tomato below is purely Chilean, calling upon the nation's most commonly found ingredients. Stuffed tomatoes are generally served as an appetizer in Chile, and regional variations include **Tomate Victoria,** *which in Puerto Natales and other parts of Patagonia uses the abundant king crab.*

2 cans (totaling 12 to 14 ounces) tuna, drained
⅔ cup cooked corn kernels
1/4 cup mayonnaise (see recipe on page 29)
2 tablespoons freshly squeezed lemon juice
2 tablespoons finely chopped fresh cilantro
Salt
8 tomatoes (1¾ pounds), peeled
Lettuce
Lemon wedges

1. In a bowl, mix the tuna with the corn, mayonnaise, lemon juice, and cilantro. Mix in salt to taste.

2. Cut a 2-inch hole from the top to the base of each tomato, removing the inner part to allow room for stuffing.

3. Stuff 3 to 4 tablespoons of the tuna mixture inside each tomato. The mixture should protrude out of the tomato.

4. Place 1 or 2 tomatoes on a bed of lettuce, dab additional mayonnaise on top, if desired, and serve with lemon wedges on the side.

Spicy Basil-scented Corn Rolls

Humitas (Picantes)

A humita *is literally a "bow tie." Yet, despite the fact that Chileans tend to dress conservatively, you will find many more people eating* humitas *than wearing them.* Humitas *are one of Chile's classic dishes: ground corn and herbs rolled up in a cornhusk, which is then tied with a bow and boiled.* Humitas *come in slightly different guises, such as* picante *(spicy), which includes ground hot red peppers (*merquén*) or chopped* ají verde*;* dulce *(sweet), which includes sugar;* salada *(this lacks both sugar and hot peppers); and* chicharrones*, which calls for fried pork (that is chiefly fat).*

2 small onions, finely chopped
4½ ounces (1 stick plus 2 tablespoons) butter
6½ cups corn kernels, stripped coarsely with a knife from about 6 cobs; reserving the husks
½ cup loosely-packed fresh basil leaves
Salt
2 hot green peppers, chopped finely
Dash sugar
Cornstarch
Kitchen string

1. Fry the onions in a skillet over a high flame. There is no need to add oil because you will be stirring constantly so that the onions do not stick to the pan. When the strong odor of the onions has reduced, after about 6 to 8 minutes, remove the pan from the heat. Stir in the butter, letting it melt into the onions. Set aside.

2. Bring a large pot of water to a boil.

3. Puree the corn kernels and basil in a food processor. Cook the pureed corn mixture in a pot over a medium flame for 10 minutes, stirring constantly so that the mixture does not stick to the bottom of the pan. Stir in the onions and add salt to taste.

4. Mix in the hot green pepper and a dash of sugar. Dissolve a few tablespoons of cornstarch in ½ cup water and gradually stir it into the mixture, until thick and creamy.

5. Wrap the corn mixture in the cornhusks like bow ties. Do this by using 2 or 3 large, clean corn husks for each *humita*. Arrange the leaves so that they overlap a bit. Place about ¼ cup of the corn mixture in the middle of the leaves. Fold the leaves lengthwise over the corn mixture, then fold them widthwise to fully cover the mixture. Tie by wrapping around once widthwise with the string. Repeat with remaining corn mixture and husks.

6. Submerge the *humitas* in the boiling water by laying them flat (rather than standing up). Cook covered, over a high flame for approximately 20 minutes. Carefully remove the humitas with a metal spatula so that they do not unravel and none of the corn mixture escapes. Serve immediately.

Serving Suggestion

Serve as an appetizer, or as a meal with a salad of chopped tomatoes.

Sweet Basil-Scented Corn Rolls

Humitas (Dulces)   6 *humitas*, or 4 to 6 servings

Many Chileans love sweet corn and have two ways to enjoy it: by eating corn-on-the-cob in the traditional sense known to Americans, or by sweetening a larger, non-sweet variety of corn not available in the U.S. This corn is ground, cooked and then sweetened with sugar in dishes such as **Pastel de Choclo** *(page 92), which also has a creamy corn and basil base. It is recommended that even if you have a penchant for sweet corn, do not add more sugar than the amount provided below when preparing these* **humitas**. *Rather, as Chileans do, provide a canister of sugar to diners, who can sprinkle additional sugar to acquire the balance they choose. As you prepare this recipe several times, you will find the ideal balance according to the sweetness of your corn.*

2 small onions, finely
  chopped
4½ ounces (1 stick plus
  2 tablespoons) butter
6½ cups corn kernels,
  stripped coarsely with a
  knife from about 6 cobs;
  reserving the husks
½ cup loosely-packed fresh
  basil leaves
Salt
½ cup sugar
Cornstarch
Kitchen string

1. Fry the onions in a skillet over a high flame. There is no need to add oil because you will be stirring constantly so that the onions do not stick to the pan. When the strong odor of the onions has reduced, after about 6 to 8 minutes, remove the pan from the heat. Stir in the butter, letting it melt into the onions. Set aside.

2. Bring a large pot of water to a boil.

3. Puree the corn kernels and basil in a food processor. Cook the pureed corn mixture in a pot over a medium flame for 10 minutes, stirring constantly so that the mixture does not stick to the bottom of the pan. Stir in the onions and add salt to taste.

4. Mix in the sugar. Dissolve a few tablespoons of cornstarch in $\frac{1}{2}$ cup water and gradually stir it into the corn mixture, until thick and creamy.

5. Wrap the corn mixture in the cornhusks like bow ties. Do this by using 2 or 3 large, clean corn husks for each *humita*. Arrange the leaves so that they overlap a bit. Place about $\frac{1}{4}$ cup of the corn mixture in the middle of the leaves. Fold the leaves lengthwise over the corn mixture, then fold them widthwise to fully cover the mixture. Tie by wrapping widthwise with the string. Repeat with remaining corn mixture and husks.

6. Submerge the *humitas* in the boiling water by laying them flat (rather than standing up). Cook covered, over a high flame for approximately 20 minutes. Carefully remove the *humitas* with a metal spatula so that they do not unravel and none of the corn mixture escapes. Serve immediately.

Chilean Rice Pilaf

Arroz Chileno

This is Chile's flavorful answer to white rice, incorporating some of the vegetables most commonly found in the local market, along with the ubiquitous cumin. I like how it is served in Chile, in the home and restaurant alike the cook molds the rice in a coffee cup or small bowl, which is overturned on the plate. Sprinkling a bit of hot pepper sauce (see recipe for Salsa de Merquén on page 27) on the rice at the end gives it a wonderful bite.

3 tablespoons extra-virgin olive oil
1/3 cup finely chopped onion (about 1/3 medium onion)
2 cloves garlic, coarsely chopped
2 cups white rice
1 small carrot, coarsely grated
1/4 medium red bell pepper, cut in thin julienne strips
1/2 teaspoon ground cumin
4 cups hot water
1 1/4 teaspoons salt

1. Heat the oil in a medium pot over a medium flame. When the oil is hot but not smoking, add the onion and garlic.

2. When the onion is translucent and the garlic is golden, reduce the heat to medium-low and add the rice. Using a wooden spoon, stir the rice frequently, for about 5 or 6 minutes, until the rice becomes bright white.

3. Add the carrot, bell pepper, and cumin and cook for 3 minutes, stirring occasionally.

4. Add the hot water and salt. Stir so that nothing sticks to the bottom of the pot. Reduce the heat to low and cover. Let cook for about 15 more minutes, or until the water is fully absorbed and the rice is fluffy and tender. Add more water while cooking, if necessary. When it is cooked, add salt to taste, remove it from the heat, and serve immediately.

Serving Suggestion ━ ━ ━ ━ ━ ━ ━ ━ ━ ━ ━ ━ ━ ━ ━ ━ ━

This is an ideal accompaniment to roast chicken (giving you the Latin mainstay, *Arroz con Pollo*).

Spicy Mashed Potatoes

Puré Picante

4 to 6 servings

*Mashed potatoes are a favorite in Chile because people use fresh potatoes and mash them by hand, the only way to do it, my father always told me. Chile inflames the potatoes a bit in this spicy version called **Puré Picante**, in which the potatoes take on a light orange, almost pinkish hue with the addition of hot red pepper sauce. While ideally you use a homemade sauce, such as the one in this book, you can also use bottled hot red pepper sauces found in Latin, Asian, and other ethnic stores. For a milder variation of mashed potatoes that is sometimes eaten in southern Chile, instead of using hot pepper sauce, substitute calabaza. Simply boil one pound of calabaza and when it is tender, mash it along with the potatoes and stir in the milk, butter, and salt, as described below.*

4 pounds baking potatoes, such as russets, peeled
$2/3$ cup milk (approximately)
$1/4$ cup butter
$1/4$ cup Salsa de Ají Rojo (see recipe, page 25)
Salt

1. Boil the potatoes in a pot of salted water until tender. When cooked, drain and mash the potatoes thoroughly.

2. Mix in $1/3$ cup milk, the butter, and 2 tablespoons of the hot pepper sauce. Gradually add more milk and hot pepper sauce until you have creamy mashed potatoes with a nice bite. Mix in salt to taste and serve immediately.

Potato Salad with Beef Cubes

Salpicón   6 servings

In southern Chile, potato salad is frequently eaten with roast chicken. It also constitutes a light meal when the salad includes beef, as in the recipe below. Some recipes substitute chicken cubes for beef cubes.

2 pounds small new potatoes
3 tablespoon extra-virgin olive oil
10 ounces boneless beef, cut into ³⁄₄-inch cubes
Salt
1 cup coarsely chopped lettuce
3 hard-boiled eggs, coarsely chopped
½ onion, finely chopped
¼ cup mayonnaise
3 tablespoons finely chopped fresh cilantro
Freshly ground black pepper

1. Boil the potatoes in a pot of water. When they are tender, remove from the pot and drain them. Let them cool, then peel and discard their skins. (Do not peel the potatoes before boiling because they will crumble when cooked, instead of being good and sturdy.) Chop the potatoes into approximately 1-inch cubes.

2. While the potatoes are cooking, heat 2 tablespoons of the oil in a skillet over medium-high heat. When the skillet is hot, add the beef, sprinkle on a bit of salt, and cook until it has browned on all sides. Remove the beef from the skillet.

3. Put the potatoes, beef, lettuce, eggs, and onion into a large bowl. Add the remaining 1 tablespoon of olive oil, mayonnaise, and cilantro. Mix thoroughly, sprinkling in a bit of salt and pepper to taste. Serve cold.

Potato Puffs

Papas Duquesas *(Duchess Potatoes) are the refined potato accompaniment of Chile, often offered on menus at the nation's finest restaurants to go with fish and meat dishes. The slightly crunchy exterior and wonderfully moist interior is irresistible, but be careful because these little rollers are filling. There are two other variations that are appealing side dishes or even hors d'oeuvres. In the first, you include a bit of cheese in each potato puff. Just follow the directions below, but in Step 2, before dipping balls in the egg yolks, split them open and insert tiny slivers of cheese. Then roll the potato in your hands again, enclosing the cheese. Follow the same procedure to make shrimp potato puffs, but place a tiny cooked shrimp or small bits of cooked shrimp in each potato puff.*

This dish certainly owes its origins to the French **Pommes Duchesse**, *having found its way to Chile with the waves of French that hit its shores, bringing some of the French customs and tastes along with them.*

1¼ pounds baking potatoes, such as russets, peeled
Salt and freshly ground black pepper
⅓ cup flour (approximately)
3 egg yolks, lightly beaten
⅔ cup finely ground dried breadcrumbs
2 cups vegetable oil for deep frying

1. Boil the potatoes in lightly salted water until very tender, remove. Drain and mash the potatoes, making a puree. Set the potatoes aside to cool, then add salt and pepper to taste and use your fingers to gently mix in ¼ cup flour. Do not overmix or the potatoes will become mushy and will not come together when forming balls. Add a bit more flour in order to make a dough that is slightly sticky, but barely sticks to your hands.

2. Roll the potato mixture in the palms of your hands to create 1-inch balls. Dip each ball into the egg yolks, then roll them in the bread crumbs. Set aside for cooking.

3. Heat the oil in a skillet over a medium-high flame. When the oil is hot but not smoking, add the potatoes and cook until golden, about three minutes. Repeat with remaining balls.

4. Remove the potato balls and place them on paper towels to absorb excess oil. Serve immediately.

Stuffed Potatoes

Papas Rellenas   6 stuffed potatoes (3 to 4 servings)

This is a cousin to the **Pastel de Papas** *(see page 91), except rather than a fill-ing casserole you have a snack or appetizer. The stuffed potatoes can also be eaten as a main course, with a side salad of chopped, fresh tomatoes.*

1¾ pounds baking potatoes, such as russets, peeled

Salt

2 tablespoons flour, plus extra for dredging (about ½ cup)

1 egg, lightly beaten

2 tablespoons vegetable oil, plus about another 1 cup for deep-frying

1 cup finely chopped onion (about ½ onion)

10 ounces boneless chicken breast (about 1 large breast), cooked and shredded; or 10 ounces ground beef

½ teaspoon paprika

1. Boil the potatoes in a pot of water. When they are tender, drain and mash them. Mix in salt to taste. Set aside to cool, then lightly stir in the flour and the egg. Do not overmix or the potatoes will become mushy and will not stick together.

2. Heat 2 tablespoons of oil in a nonstick skillet over a medium flame. When it is hot but not smoking, add the onions and cook until translu-cent, about 3 to 4 minutes. Gently stir in the chicken, paprika, and about ¾ teaspoon of salt and remove from heat. If using beef instead of chicken, cook the onions and beef together until the onions are translucent and the beef is cooked. Then mix in the paprika and salt to taste.

3. Using your fingers, form about ¼ cup of the mashed potatoes into a long oval (the shape of a thin hot dog bun). Working on a lightly floured surface, flatten the oval to about 1-inch thick.

4. Place a slightly heaping ¼ cup of the chicken or ground beef mixture on top of the potatoes, leaving about ½ inch at each end.

5. Using your fingers, form another ¼ cup of the mashed potatoes into another long oval. Flatten and place on top of the chicken or beef mixture.

6. Using your fingers, seal the sides of the stuffed potato so that the chicken or beef mixture cannot fall out. The stuffed potato should now look like a thick, stuffed, hot dog bun.

7. Put a generous amount of flour on a large plate. Roll the stuffed potato in the flour, covering it lightly.

8. Repeat with remaining potato and chicken or beef mixtures.

9. Pour the remaining vegetable oil into a deep skillet and heat over a high flame. When the oil is hot but not smoking, reduce the heat to medium and add two or three of the stuffed potatoes. Fry the potatoes on both sides until golden, about 3 minutes on each side. Remove and place on paper towels to absorb excess oil.

Potatoes Sautéed in Garlic and Cilantro

Papas Salteadas   4 servings

Garlic and cilantro frequently collaborate in Chile, working together to give mussels, chicken, and other dishes outstanding flavor. Here they provide potatoes with a zest that belies their simplicity.

2 pounds firm, smooth-skinned potatoes
¼ cup extra-virgin olive oil
Salt
3 cloves garlic, finely chopped
3 tablespoons fresh chopped cilantro

1. Boil the potatoes in a pot of water over high heat until slightly tender, about 25 to 30 minutes. Drain the potatoes, peel them, and cut them into 1-inch pieces.

2. Heat the oil in a large skillet over a medium-high flame. When the oil is hot, but not smoking, add the potatoes and add salt liberally.

3. Stir frequently, using a metal spatula to scrape off any potatoes that stick to the base of the skillet. When the potatoes are almost cooked, add the garlic. Continue mixing for 3 to 4 minutes. A minute before removing the skillet from the heat, mix in the cilantro. Serve immediately.

Potato Fritters

Chapaleles are typically eaten with **curanto** *(see recipe, page 70), a hearty, multimeat and shellfish stew. When preparing them along with* **curanto,** *simply stop after step 3 below and include the* chapaleles *in one of the layers of the pot of* curanto. *Otherwise, continue on to step four and enjoy them alone.*

---

2 to 2½ pounds baking potatoes, such as russets, peeled
¾ cup flour (approximately)
Salt
Vegetable oil for frying

1. Boil the potatoes in a pot of water. When the potatoes are tender, drain them, and then mash them thoroughly.

2. Mix in ¾ cup flour and salt to taste, using a spoon, and then your hands. Add more flour, if necessary, to make a dough that is stiff, and not sticky.

3. Form the mixture into patties that are about 4 inches in diameter.

4. Cover the base of a large skillet with about ¼ cup vegetable oil and heat over a medium flame. When the skillet is hot, add the patties. Fry them until they are golden brown on both sides. Remove them and place them on paper towels to absorb excess oil. Serve hot.

Potato Pancakes Stuffed with Pork

Milcao Relleno con Chicharrones   8 pancakes

Milcao *is Chile's answer to potato latkes (pancakes). Often added to curanto, they are also eaten alone, or stuffed. In the recipe below, they are filled with chicharrones, a high-cholesterol treat. These tiny, crunchy bits are basically finely chopped pork fat—or a fatty bacon—which is then fried. Butchers in Chile often sell* **chicharrones** *to their clients, who nibble on them like popcorn. More power to you if use fried pork fat in this recipe, but I have substituted pork meat to keep the calorie count under reasonable control. In southern towns such as Bulnes, many people eat* **milcaos** *with honey, instead of in the salty fashion with* chicharrones.

1¼ pounds boiling potatoes, peeled, then grated finely
1¼ pounds baking potatoes, such as russets, peeled and thoroughly boiled
Salt and freshly ground black pepper
1 tablespoon extra-virgin olive oil
14 ounces pork, chopped into small (about ¼-inch) cubes
Vegetable oil for deep-frying

1. Put the grated potatoes into a strainer. Press the potatoes so that their juices go through the strainer. Set the potatoes in the strainer for several more minutes so that more of their juices fall through. Discard the potato juices.

2. Mash the boiled potatoes.

3. In a bowl, mix the two types of potatoes with a spoon. Add salt and pepper to taste and mix thoroughly.

4. Form the mixture into 4-inch patties.

5. Heat the olive oil in a skillet over a medium flame. When the oil is hot, add the pork. Fry until golden brown on all sides.

6. Remove the pork bits and place them inside each of the formed patties. I do this by putting them on top of the patty, then folding opposite sides of the pancakes toward the center, covering the pork bits. Then I re-form the potato pancake.

7. Add a few tablespoons of vegetable oil to the skillet and heat over a medium flame. Fry the stuffed potato pancakes until golden brown on both sides. Eat hot or cold.

Spicy Beef and Green Bean Sandwich

Chacarero

Sandwiches are very important in Chile, in part because of the culture's love of fresh bread, meats, and cold cuts. This sandwich usually includes quick-fried steak, but some people substitute **Carne Mechada** *(see page 165). This is a delicious alternative because it uses a juicy, vegetable-laced meat that perfectly complements the texture of the green beans, the heat of the hot peppers, and the coolness of the tomatoes. The dish's name derives from the word* **chacra,** *the land on which Chileans plant vegetables, such as green beans.*

¼ cup green beans, halved lengthwise
1 (3 to 4 ounce) slice of *Carne Mechada* (see recipe, page 165) or quick-fried steak
1 Kaiser or hamburger roll
Salt and freshly ground black pepper
½ tablespoon hot green peppers
2 slices tomatoes
Mayonnaise (optional)

1. Boil the green beans until thoroughly cooked. Drain and set aside.

2. If you are not using carne mechada, fry the steak in butter until cooked.

3. Put the steak or carne mechada and a bit of its sauce on the roll. Sprinkle with salt and pepper. Add the beans, hot peppers and tomatoes. Add mayonnaise to the sandwich (mayonnaise is not necessary when using carne mechada and its sauce). Serve hot.

Sirloin Steak Sandwich with Avocado and Melted Cheese

Barros Luco   1 sandwich

Ramón Barros Luco, who served as president of Chile from 1910 to 1915, loved a *special kind of sandwich. He didn't hesitate to make his mind known at restaurants, and waiters quickly caught on. Some simply started shouting to the cooks: "Give me a Barros Luco!" The name stuck on the sandwich to this day. The sandwich is delicious made using fresh Chilean mayonnaise and homemade bread.*

1 tablespoon butter
1 thin strip of boneless steak sirloin (5 ounces)
Salt and freshly ground black pepper
1 to 2 strips of Swiss cheese (3 ounces)
1 tablespoon Mayonnaise (see recipe, page 29) (optional)
1 hamburger bun or similarly-shaped roll
½ avocado (3 to 4 ounces), cut into thin slices

1. Heat the butter in a medium skillet over a medium-high flame. When it has melted, add the steak. Lightly sprinkle with salt and pepper. When the steak browns, turn it over and top with the cheese. Cover and remove the steak from heat when it is cooked.

2. Spread the mayonnaise on the bun. Add the cheese steak and avocado, cut the sandwich in half, and serve it immediately.

Empanadas

Chile has shaped the empanada into a national institution. Probably Chile's most popular food, it is eaten as a snack, light meal, or, when it is the size of its bite-sized counterparts from Argentina, as an hors d'oeuvre. Empanadas have been part of the Spanish diet since the thirteenth century and were eaten elsewhere in Europe, but Chile made them its own by baking the turnovers and filling them with a mixture of meat, onions, eggs, olives, and raisins.

While beef is the most popular type, you can also easily happen upon chicken, shellfish, and cheese empanadas. Sweet empanadas are also in vogue in some places, including El Molle in the northern Elqui Valley, and near Rancagua in central Chile. There, bakeries make empanadas filled with *alcayota*, papaya, pear, and even rice pudding. I find empanadas to be the most consistently delicious—and ubiquitous—dish in Chile, perhaps because so many people cook them day in and day out, sell them from their home or sit patiently on a street corner with them jutting out of baskets.

There are three basic types of empanada dough − − − − − − −
1. Dough for oven-baked empanadas, like those filled with beef or chicken
2. Dough for fried, salty empanadas, like those filled with cheese and/or shellfish
3. Dough for sweet empanadas

The chief differences are that the oven-baked empanadas have a heavier dough than fried ones, so that they do not stick to the baking pan in the oven. Sweet empanadas are fried or oven-baked, but sugar is added to the dough.

Empanadas are often prepared by a team of two, since the duo can equally divide responsibilities and cut preparation time in half. For example, in the Musso household in the town of Quilpué, Gloria makes the empanada filling, called the *pino*, while her father, Jaime or her brother Andrés, forms and kneads the dough. A tip that Gloria offers—and one that many Chileans swear by (though others consider an old wives' tale)—is to add a touch of sugar to the filling in order to cut the strength of the abundant onions. It also is important to have a juicy filling so the empanadas are moist following cooking. Furthermore, if you do not want to use all of the dough at once, you can store it for up to two days in a plastic bag in the refrigerator. In this case, pick up from Step one below on "How to form the empanadas." Generally, cooks prepare the empanada filling before the dough, so that the latter can cool and thus will not tear the dough when added. Some set the filling in the refrigerator overnight so that the flavors can mingle.

How to form the empanadas - - - - - - - - - - - - - - - - - -

1. Place about ¼ cup of the filling in the center of the flattened pieces of dough.

2. Dip your fingers in water and pat them over the surface of the dough, around the filling. This is done so that when you fold the dough it sticks shut firmly.

3. Fold the dough from the side farthest from you to the side closest to you, covering the filling.

4. Press down firmly with your fingers on the area directly surrounding the filling in order to seal it in, creating a semicircle. With your fingers, you are making indentations in the empanadas that will ensure that the filling does not escape from its shell upon cooking.

5. Use a cookie cutter to trim the three sides of the empanada shell (but not the side that covers the filling). This is done both to make the sides even for folding and to ensure that the empanada is not too doughy. Set this excess dough aside. You can use it later to form an additional one or two empanadas, or you can incorporate it into the balls you have already formed.

6. Again, dip your fingers in water and pat the surface of the dough around the enclosed filling.

7. Seal in the empanada filling completely by turning the dough corners in toward the meat mixture and again using your fingers to press down and make indentations on the dough.

8. Proceed to cook the empanadas as described in the recipes that follow.

Cheese Turnovers

Empanadas de Queso   14 to 16 empanadas

These are delicious, moist turnovers, but don't rank high on the calorie-fighting list. This is especially the case if you add a bit of heavy cream along with the cheese in the filling, as some do. You can use this recipe as the basis to create many other recipes for fried empanadas. These include empanadas with ham, ham and cheese, spinach, or pizza filling (tomato sauce, cheese, and oregano).

The dough
4 cups flour
$\frac{1}{2}$ teaspoon baking powder
2 teaspoons salt
$3\frac{1}{2}$ ounces vegetable short-
    ening, at room temperature
$\frac{1}{4}$ cup milk
$\frac{3}{4}$ cup lukewarm water
    (approximately)

The filling
$1\frac{1}{2}$ pounds mild cheese,
    such as *provolone*

2 cups vegetable oil for
    deep-frying

For the dough
1. Mix the flour, baking powder, and salt in a deep bowl. Add the vegetable shortening, mixing it in thoroughly.

2. Mix in the milk, then slowly add about $\frac{3}{4}$ cup lukewarm water. Use your hands to form a thick dough that is a bit sticky. Add a bit more water, if necessary. Knead the dough for 10 to 15 minutes.

3. Cut the dough into twelve to fourteen pieces, and form smooth balls.

4. On a lightly floured board, use a rolling pin to roll out the balls. Turn the dough over so you have thin circles of dough that are lightly floured on both sides.

5. Form the empanadas, as described on page 58. For this type of empanada, put about $1\frac{1}{2}$ ounces of cheese in the middle of each piece of dough.

To make the empanadas
1. Heat the vegetable oil in a skillet over a medium-low flame. When the oil is hot but not smoking, add the empanadas without crowding them. The empanadas should be partly submerged in oil.

2. Cook them over medium-low heat until golden brown on both sides, 3 to 4 minutes total.

3. When the empanadas are cooked, remove them and place them on paper towels to remove excess oil. Make additional empanadas, adding more vegetable oil for deep frying, when necessary. Serve hot.

Beef Turnovers

In most of Chile you'd be hard-pressed to walk a few blocks without finding a restaurant, bakery, or little food shop that offers a variation of the Empanada de Pino. Pino usually refers to a ground beef and onion mixture, though it can also be a combination of other chopped or ground meats, vegetables, and spices that are fried together to make up a filling, for dishes such as empanadas, Pastel de Papas, or Pastel de Choclo.

The Empanada de Pino is typically graced with olives, ground beef, and onions. Many Chileans find it taboo to mix salty and sweet ingredients, so they omit raisins from their Empanadas de Pino (and they take pains never to cross the two flavorings in any recipe). However, I find the combination delightful: the raisins dance well with the ground beef–onion mixture, giving the empanadas a pleasant zing.

Olives, too, are a Chilean staple. While Chile produces outstanding olives, many of those sold in markets and stores are very mild. This allows them to perform a nice, subtle role in the creation of the Empanada de Pino and such dishes as Pastel de Papas.

Gloria Musso taught me how to make beef empanadas that are moist and tasty inside with a thin, crispy crust. Gloria, who prepares beef empanadas for her family once a week, learned the recipe below from her mother, now deceased. Making her mother's Empanadas de Pino is just a small way she keeps family tradition alive.

The filling

- 2 tablespoons extra-virgin olive oil
- 4 cloves garlic, finely chopped
- 1 pound ground or coarsely chopped boneless beef
- Salt
- 2½ pounds onions (5 onions), finely chopped
- ½ cup raisins
- 1 beef bouillon cube
- 2 teaspoons paprika
- 1 teaspoon ground cumin
- 1 teaspoon dried oregano
- 1 teaspoon flour
- ½ teaspoon sugar

For the filling

1. Heat the oil in a skillet over a medium flame. When it is hot but not smoking, add the garlic and cook until golden. Add the beef and salt to taste, and cook for a few minutes, stirring occasionally.

2. Add the onions, raisins, bouillon cube, paprika, cumin, oregano, flour, and sugar. Cover, reduce the heat to medium-low, and continue cooking, mixing occasionally with a wooden spoon. Cook the mixture for about 15 minutes to mingle flavors and reduce the onions' strength. Test the mixture for seasoning, add salt to taste, remove from heat, and let cool.

The dough

7½ cups flour
9 ounces vegetable shortening or unsalted margarine,
   at room temperature
1 tablespoon salt
1 teaspoon white vinegar
1½ to 1⅔ cups water

For the dough – – – – – – – – –

1. Put the flour and salt in a deep bowl. Add the vegetable shortening. Mix everything together with your hands.

2. Add the vinegar and gradually mix in enough lukewarm water to form a dough. It should not be sticky. Knead the dough for 10 to 15 minutes to make it soft and pliant.

3. Cut the dough into eighteen roughly equal pieces and form into smooth balls.

4. On a lightly-floured board, use a rolling pin to flatten each ball as thinly as possible into 8-inch circles.

4 hard-boiled eggs, chopped
   very coarsely
2 cups whole black olives,
   pitted or whole
1 egg yolk, lightly beaten

5. Form the empanadas, as described on page 58. For this type of empanada, add ¼ cup of the beef mixture to the middle of each circle of dough and then top with a couple slices of the chopped egg and one or two olives.

To make the empanadas – – – – – – – – – – – – – – – – –

1. Preheat the oven to 350° F.

2. Lightly flour a baking pan and place the empanadas on top without crowding them.

3. Brush the top of each empanada with the beaten egg yolk.

4. Put the pan into the oven. Remove it when the empanadas are golden brown, about 25 minutes. Serve hot. You can also make the empanadas and then freeze them for four to five months.

Shellfish Turnovers

Perhaps nothing is better in Chile than arriving at a seaside restaurants and starting your meal with a Pisco Sour and a shellfish turnover, as waves break below you. Throughout the nation's coastline you can find a vast assortment of empanadas filled with shellfish. Some, such as the traditional recipe below, combine a mix of mussels, clams, and other shellfish. Others contain just one type of shellfish. Empanada varieties include **Machas con Queso** *(Clams with Cheese),* **Camarones con Queso** *(Shrimp with Cheese),* **Locos** *(Abalones),* **Jaibas** *(Crabs), and* **Ostiones** *(Sea Scallops). The dough for the following recipe is the same as that for* **Empanadas de Queso,** *since these are also fried. For a variation on empanadas with shellfish and/or cheese, add a bit of cream to the filling.*

The filling

¼ cup extra-virgin olive oil
1 pound onions, finely chopped
4 cloves garlic, finely chopped
½ teaspoon ground cumin
½ teaspoon dried oregano
½ teaspoon salt
1½ pounds shelled mixed shellfish, such as equal parts shrimp, mussels, and littleneck clams, chopped very coarsely
2 tablespoons finely chopped fresh parsley

For the filling

1. Heat the oil in a large skillet over a medium flame. When it is hot but not smoking, add the onions, garlic, cumin, oregano, and salt.

2. Continue cooking the mixture, stirring frequently. After the mixture has reduced in size and the onions' strength has diminished, add the shellfish. Turn the heat up to medium-high. Stirring frequently, cook the shellfish until they are thoroughly cooked, about 3 to 4 minutes. Mix in the parsley and additional salt to taste, remove from heat, and let cool.

The dough

4 cups flour
½ teaspoon baking powder
1½ teaspoons salt
3½ ounces vegetable shortening, at room temperature
¼ cup milk
¾ cup lukewarm water
  (approximately)

2 cups vegetable oil for deep-
  frying

For the dough — — — — — — — — — — — — —

1. Mix the flour, baking powder, and salt in a deep bowl. Add the vegetable shortening, mixing it in thoroughly.

2. Stir in the milk, then slowly add about ¾ cup lukewarm water. Use your hands to form a thick dough that is a bit sticky. Add a bit more water, if necessary. Knead the dough for 10 to 15 minutes.

3. Cut the dough into twelve to fourteen pieces, and form smooth balls.

4. On a lightly floured board, use a rolling pin to roll out the balls. Turn the dough over so you have thin circles of dough that are lightly floured on both sides.

5. Form the empanadas, as described on page 58. For this type of empanada, place 2 tablespoons of the shellfish mixture onto each piece of dough. Include just a touch of the pan juices. You can do this by straining the shellfish into a container, and drawing on a bit of these juices.

To make the empanadas — — — — — — — — — — — — — — — — — —

1. Heat the vegetable oil in a skillet over a medium-low flame. When the oil is hot but not smoking, add the empanadas without crowding them. The empanadas should be partly submerged in oil.

2. Cook them over medium-low heat until golden brown on both sides, 3 to 4 minutes total.

3. When the empanadas are cooked, remove them and place them on paper towels to remove excess oil. Make additional empanadas, adding more vegetable oil for deep frying, when necessary. Serve hot.

Rice Pudding Turnovers

This is a traditional recipe that is a favorite among Chilean grandmothers. The dough is lighter and sweeter than the others, and it can either be baked or fried. The sweet creamy rice that you make for this recipe can be eaten alone, but try to hold back since when it is wrapped in empanada dough it is truly distinctive.

The filling
1 cup uncooked rice
4 cups milk
¼ cup plus 1 tablespoon
  granulated sugar
1 cinnamon stick
Peel of 1 orange

For the filling

1. Put the rice, milk, sugar, cinnamon stick, and orange peel in a pot. Mix thoroughly.

2. Bring to a boil, then cover and reduce the heat to low and cook until the rice is tender and the milk has been absorbed, about 20 minutes. Add more milk if necessary. It should be moist and creamy, but not watery.

3. Remove the pot from the heat, uncover, and discard the orange peel and cinnamon stick.

The dough

4 cups flour
3 tablespoons sugar
2 egg yolks
1½ teaspoons vegetable
  shortening
½ cup water (approximately)
¼ cup plus 1 tablespoon
  milk

2 cups vegetable oil for
  deep-frying
Confectioners' sugar

For the dough – – – – – – – – – – – – –

1. Mix the flour, sugar, and egg yolks in a deep bowl. Add the vegetable shortening, mixing it in thoroughly.

2. Gradually mix in the milk, then slowly add about ½ cup lukewarm water. Use your hands to form a thick dough that is a bit sticky. Add a bit more water, if necessary. Knead the dough for 10 to 15 minutes.

3. Cut the dough into 12 to 14 pieces, and form smooth balls.

4. On a lightly floured board, use a rolling pin to flatten the balls individually. You should now have thin circles of dough that are lightly floured on both sides.

5. Form the empanadas, as described on page 58. Place about 3 tablespoons of rice pudding in the middle of each empanada.

To make the empanadas – – – – – – – – – – – – – – – – – – –

1. Heat the vegetable oil in a medium skillet over a medium-low flame. When the oil is hot but not smoking, add the empanadas without crowding them. The empanadas should be partly submerged in oil.

2. Cook them over medium-low heat until golden brown on both sides, 3 to 4 minutes total.

3. When the empanadas are cooked, remove them and place them on paper towels to remove excess oil. Make additional empanadas, adding more vegetable oil for deep frying, when necessary. Serve hot. Alternatively, you can bake these empanadas in the oven, as you do *Empanadas de Pino* (see page 60).

Sopas y Cazuelas

Many envision Chile as a country riddled with beaches where people spend hours upon hours frolicking in the sun. While that may sometimes be true, it also can be a very cold country, in central Chile during the winter evenings, and particularly in southern Chile. In fact, while there are many theories as to where Chile got its name, one of those most staunchly defended holds that it came from the indigenous Quechua, who found the country to be *chiri*, meaning cold. The word "Chile" is a variation of that.

Whether or not this is the true origin, there is no question that it can get pretty nippy in Chile, and it is then that people huddle inside and wait for the *cazuela* to roar off of the stove. This hearty stew derived hundreds of years ago from Spain's *Olla Podrida*, a large pot of broth with a range of meats and seasonal vegetables. Chile has literally converted this single plate into a slew of stews, each with its own identity. Each stew has the flavor of the most popular foods present in the regions offering them. Contributions to the *cazuela* might be greatest in the south, where many wake up and have soup for breakfast to ward off the frost.

Most of the recipes below are suitable for four to six people, depending on appetites. General rules are to have a large pot on hand and to include two cups of water for each person you plan on serving. Also provide a number of slices of meat (which are often shanks) according to how many you plan on serving. All *cazuelas* cook for at least forty-five minutes to an hour in order for the meats to become extremely tender like osso buco (which is also the name of the preferred cut in Chile) and to allow the flavors to meld. After the *cazuela* is cooked, I usually let it rest, covered, for twenty to thirty minutes, in order to imbue a still deeper flavor. Serve *cazuela* in large individual bowls, but also provide a plate. If people wish, they can take corn from the stew and nibble on it off the plate, or cut their meat on the plate. *Cazuelas* are also excellent the next day. Just add a bit more water when reheating.

When chicken or turkey is used in *cazuelas*, you may prefer to remove the skin before adding it to the pot since upon cooking it will become soft and fatty rather than crispy and tasty.

Chileans are also fond of lighter soups and anything that can warm them up on a frosty day (though *cazuelas* are consumed copiously year-round). As testament to either Chile's love for soups or its love for inventing, contorting, and using different words, it counts these as just some of its terms for soups and stews: *sopa*, *crema*, *consomé*, *cazuela*, and *caldillo*.

Pork Stew

------ *The* cazuela *is one of Chile's central dishes: there is* Cazuela de Pavo *(turkey),* Cazuela de Gallina *(chicken),* Cazuela de Chancho *(pork),* Cazuela de Vacuno *(beef) and others. Two of Chile's stalwarts,* calabaza *and corn, play starring roles in this very satisfying soup. The* calabaza *of Chile, which can weigh as much as forty-five pounds, is both dense and dazzling. In markets, vendors use small, fine-toothed saws called* cerruchos zapalleros, *created specially for cutting* calabazas *because they are so sturdy when raw. Vegetable vendors can carve off pieces for shoppers only by cutting from the center of the* calabaza *towards them, rather than vice versa. When it cooks, this hard-as-a-rock vegetable rapidly metamorphoses into something tender and succulent that almost melts in your mouth.*

2 to 2½ pounds pork-on-the-bone such as pork neck bones, cut into 4 to 8 pieces
½ large onion, finely chopped
2 medium carrots, finely grated
1 red bell pepper, coarsely chopped
4 cloves garlic, finely chopped
2 celery leaves
4 medium-size boiling potatoes (1½ pounds), peeled and halved
2 small ears of corn, halved
1 to 1½ pounds calabaza or butternut squash, cut into 4 to 6 pieces
⅓ cup cornmeal
Salt and freshly ground black pepper
2 tablespoons finely chopped fresh cilantro

1. Bring 8 cups (two quarts) of lightly salted water to a boil over high heat. Add the pork and reduce the heat to low. Simmer for 15 minutes, skimming fat from the surface and replacing the lost volume with additional water.

2. Add the onion, carrots, bell pepper, garlic, and celery leaves and simmer, partly covered, for 15 more minutes.

3. Add the potatoes.

4. After 10 minutes, add the corn and *calabaza*, and continue simmering until the *calabaza* and potatoes are tender, about 15 to 20 minutes. In the last few minutes, add the cornmeal to thicken the soup, as well as salt and pepper to taste. When serving, sprinkle cilantro on top of each bowl.

Wine Suggestion - - - - - - - - - - - - -
Marqués de Casa Concha Merlot

Pork and Shellfish Stew

Curanto en Olla

This is one of my favorite Chilean dishes, one that is traditionally made in southern Chile, particularly on the island of Chiloé. It is a wonderful treat for a winter day along with a hearty wine, and it is even better reheated a day or two after preparation. While there are many variations of curanto, some of which include rabbit, the version below includes the most common combination of red meat, chicken, and shellfish.

The most traditional version of curanto is prepared over hot rocks— curantu *means "abundance of rocks" in the Mapuche language of Mapudungun—in a burning pit in the ground. Also called* Curanto en Hoyo, *this dish features layers of ingredients separated by large leaves, such as those of a cabbage or native* nalca *plant. In the recipe below, rather than digging up a big hole in your backyard you need only get your hands on a large pot. This more practical dish is given a different name,* Pulmay, *or else* Curanto en Olla (Curanto in a Pot). *Curanto is so beloved in Chile that there's even a popular ditty, particularly sung in Chiloé that includes the phrase "*Quiero comer curanto con chapelele,*" which means, "I want to eat* curanto with *cha-palele." This book also contains recipes for both* chapaleles *and* milcaos, *in the event that you want to include these potato dishes in or alongside your* curanto. *Some Chileans are also fond of having the salsa of* pebre *with* curanto.

Salt and freshly ground black
  pepper
$\frac{1}{2}$ chicken (1$\frac{1}{2}$ to 2 pounds),
  cut into 4 pieces
1 pound pork chops (about 3
  medium chops), cut into
  several pieces
3 tablespoons extra-virgin
  olive oil
12 ounces semi-spicy
  sausage, cut into two-inch
  pieces
1 small onion, finely chopped
  into thin one-inch strips
1 medium carrot, peeled and
  grated
1 small red bell pepper, finely
  chopped; or half green bell
  pepper, half red bell pepper
4 cloves garlic, finely
  chopped
$\frac{1}{4}$ cup fresh celery leaves
2 cups white wine
8 mussels, in their shells,
  cleaned and scrubbed
8 littleneck clams, in their
  shells, cleaned and
  scrubbed
$\frac{1}{3}$ cup finely chopped fresh
  parsley
Milcaos (optional) (see recipe,
  page 54)
Chapaleles (optional) (see
  recipe, page 53)

1. Sprinkle salt and pepper on both sides of the chicken and pork chops. Heat half of the oil in a large pot over a medium flame. When hot, add the chicken pieces and lightly brown them on both sides. Remove the chicken from the pan and lightly brown the pork slices on both sides. Remove the pork and then brown the sausages on both sides.

2. Remove most of the fat from the pot, reserving 2 to 3 tablespoons. Return the chicken, pork, and sausages to the pot and add the onion, carrot, bell pepper, garlic, celery leaves, 1 cup of water, and $\frac{1}{4}$ cup of the wine.

3. Cook, covered, over medium-low heat, shaking the pot, and adding a bit of wine every few minutes for a total of 20 minutes. Gradually add 1$\frac{3}{4}$ cup more wine and $\frac{1}{2}$ cup more water.

4. Add the mussels, clams, and parsley, continuing to mix. Cook for 5 to 7 minutes. Add salt and pepper to taste and serve in a large bowl or casserole dish. Provide diners with both a bowl and a plate so they can cut the meat.

Wine Suggestion – – – – – – – – – – – –
A Cabernet Sauvignon, such as Manso de Velasco, one of the finest from winemaker Miguel Torres.

Beef Stew

This beef stew uses three staples that originated in Latin America: potato, corn, and calabaza. Chicken Stew, or **Cazuela de Pollo,** *a popular variation on this stew, is also found daily in homes and restaurants across the country. For chicken stew, simply substitute four large chicken pieces for the beef. Further, add the potatoes immediately after the pot of chicken begins to boil (the beef needs to cook longer than the chicken in order to become tender). Then proceed in the same way.*

3 pounds beef shanks
Salt
4 small boiling potatoes (1 pound), peeled
4 whole fresh celery leaves
2 tablespoons extra-virgin olive oil
1 medium onion, cut into julienne strips
1 medium carrot, peeled and coarsely grated
1 medium green bell pepper, coarsely chopped
4 cloves garlic, finely chopped
½ teaspoon dried oregano
12 ounces *calabaza* or butternut squash, cut into 2-inch pieces
2 small ears of corn, halved
4 ounces green beans, halved lengthwise
⅓ cup uncooked rice
4 teaspoons finely chopped fresh cilantro

1. Put 8 cups (2 quarts) of cold water and the meat in a large, deep cooking pot. Add salt, cover, and bring to a boil. Remove the fat that rises to the surface and replace the lost volume with additional water.

2. Continue cooking, covered, over medium heat. After the meat becomes fairly tender inside, or after about 45 minutes to 1 hour, add the potatoes and celery leaves. Reduce the heat to medium-low and continue to cook, covered.

3. Meanwhile, heat the oil in a skillet over medium heat. When hot, add the onion, carrot, bell pepper, and garlic. Sauté for 5 minutes, stirring continuously, and remove from heat.

4. After the potatoes have cooked for about 15 minutes, add the onion mixture to the pot, along with the oregano. Reduce the heat to low and continue cooking, covered. After 10 minutes, add the *calabaza*, corn, green beans, and rice. The beef should now be quite tender. Continue cooking another 15 minutes, or until the potatoes, rice, and *calabaza* are tender. Add more water, if necessary, to ensure everything is fully submerged.

5. Add salt to taste, and serve immediately or after about 30 minutes when the flavors have mingled more thoroughly in the covered pot. Serve in a large soup bowl and sprinkle cilantro and black pepper on each person's soup.

Wine Suggestion
Armador Cabernet Sauvignon from Odfell Vineyards

Turkey and Walnut Stew

Cazuela de Pava Nogada 4 to 6 servings

This deeply satisfying dish is found in several parts of Chile, particularly in towns north of Santiago, such as San Felipe. I sniffed it out after a few San Felipe residents recommended that I make my way to La Ruca, in the nearby town of Bucalemu, about an hour and fifteen minutes north of Santiago. Upon entering the restaurant I almost bumped into an effervescent group of middle-aged gentlemen who were sitting by the fireplace, drinking, strumming the guitar, and singing classic bolero songs. They greeted me gleefully, as did a waiter, who gave me a couple of varieties of hot peppers from the region to sample, along with fresh bread and pebre. Soon I was marveling at this hearty turkey stew as the band laughed and played around me. San Felipe's specialties include walnuts, which are mixed with cream to help make a rich broth in which the turkey bones swim. You can also toast the walnuts to create a nice, smoky flavor.

Salt

4 turkey drumsticks or thighs (3 to 3½ pounds)

2 tablespoons extra-virgin olive oil

1 small onion, finely chopped

6 cloves garlic, finely chopped

1 carrot, peeled and coarsely grated

8 cups (2 quarts) hot water

5 to 6 whole fresh celery leaves

½ teaspoon dried oregano

1. Lightly sprinkle salt on both sides of the turkey pieces.

2. In a large pot, heat the oil and sauté the turkey over medium heat until golden brown on both sides. Remove the turkey from the pot.

3. Add the onion, garlic, and carrot to the pot and cook over medium heat for 2 to 3 minutes.

4. Return the turkey to the pot and add the hot water, along with the celery leaves and oregano. Cook over high heat for about 10 minutes.

12 ounces boiling potatoes, peeled and cut into 2- or 3-inch pieces
8 to 10 ounces *calabaza* or butternut squash, cut into 2- or 3-inch pieces
2 ears of corn, halved
1/2 cup cornmeal
A handful of green beans
1/4 cup shelled walnuts
1/4 cup heavy cream
1 1/2 tablespoons finely chopped fresh cilantro or parsley

5. Add the potatoes, *calabaza*, corn, and salt to taste. Cover, reduce the heat to medium, and cook for approximately 15 minutes.

6. Add the cornmeal and green beans. Reduce the heat to low and cook for 10 more minutes or until everything is tender, stirring frequently.

7. Meanwhile, prepare the walnut sauce. This is done just before the soup is ready. In a blender, briefly blend the walnuts and the cream, making a fairly chunky paste. Set aside.

8. When the soup is ready, remove from heat, and pour in individual bowls for the diners. To each bowl add a spoonful of fresh parsley or cilantro, and 1 to 2 spoonfuls of the walnut sauce. Mix thoroughly and serve.

Wine Suggestion –
Arboleda Syrah

Vegetable and Dumpling Soup

Pancutra/Pantruca   4 servings

The real name of this dish is Pancutra, but it is mistakenly called Pantruca so often in Chile that both are accepted. Some argue that there is no correct name, however, since words sometimes take on a new, fully legitimate identity in different parts of the lengthy country of Chile due to varied accents and idiosyncrasies. If possible, it is best to use fresh peas for this recipe, as they do in Chile, but if using canned peas, add them at the end of the recipe.

Instead of cutting the dough in this recipe into one-inch squares, you can take a more casual approach and cut long strips of dough, tear one-inch pieces from it, and then add it to the pot. This is what many Chileans do and it gives rise to the nickname for such dishes as: "Tira en la Olla," which means "Throw it into the pot." Be sure to cook the dough thoroughly before eating it, when it will take on a texture and taste similar to that of Chinese wontons.

Dough:
2 cups flour
3 tablespoons butter
⅓ cup water (approximately)

For the dough

1. Mix the flour and butter together with your hands, then slowly add water. Add enough water to make a dough.

2. Use your hands to knead the dough thoroughly, for about 10 to 15 minutes, until it is smooth and light. Use a rolling pin to roll the dough as thin as possible. Cut the dough into 1-inch squares.

Soup:

1 carrot, cut in julienne strips
3 cloves garlic
1/4 teaspoon ground cumin
Salt
1 1/4 pounds boiling potatoes, cut into 2-inch pieces
10 ounces lean ground beef
1 cup shelled peas
2 egg whites

For the soup

1. In a large pot, bring 8 cups (2 quarts) of water to a boil, along with the carrot, garlic, cumin, and salt to taste. Add the potatoes and reduce the heat to low, cover, and simmer.

2. Continue cooking until the potatoes begin to soften, then add the beef and the squares of dough. Remove the lid and simmer for about 15 minutes, until the dough is almost fully cooked.

3. Mix in the peas and additional salt and pepper to taste. After 5 minutes, remove the pot from the heat.

4. Mix in the egg whites and serve in individual bowls.

Wine Suggestion

Viña Tarapacá Gran Tarapacá Syrah

Saints' Meat Stew

Calapurca   8 servings

There's nothing like paying homage via a meat-and-vegetable feast. That's the case with calapurca, *a veritable stew that is northern Chile's festive take on the* cazuela. *A sure sign of its northernness is the use of giant white corn, called maíz* pelado, *rather than sweet corn. The dish incorporates three different kinds of meat, each cooked and then boned. If you're in northern Chile during the celebrations of the saints you should have no problem sampling it. Typically it is served for these festivals, in which towns give thanks to the individual saint that represents their locale. I was in the town of Huara around the time of the celebration for its saint, The Virgin of Infinite Aid (La Virgen de Perpetuo Socorro), when I jotted down the recipe basics from Digna Manuela Espinoza.*

1½ cups giant white corn (available at some grocery stores; Goya is a common brand)
2½ pounds boiling potatoes
2 tablespoons extra-virgin olive oil
1 large onion, finely chopped
½ teaspoon ground cumin
1 to 1½ teaspoons paprika
1½ pounds lamb, such as shank, in several pieces
1½ pounds beef, such as shank, in several pieces
2 carrots, cut into six stubby pieces
1½ pounds chicken, cut in several pieces
3 cloves garlic, halved
4 celery leaves
1 beef or chicken bouillon cube
Salt and freshly ground black pepper
Finely chopped fresh parsley

1. Follow instructions on the corn package, which may include soaking it in a pot of water overnight. If it is presoaked, it may only need to be cooked briefly.

2. Boil the potatoes. When they are tender, remove them, peel and thinly slice them.

3. Heat the oil in a skillet over medium heat. When the oil is hot but not smoking, add the onion, cumin, and 1 teaspoon of paprika. Stir continuously until the onion is translucent.

4. Meanwhile, put the lamb, beef, and carrots in a very large pot, along with 14 cups (3½ quarts) salted water. Cover and bring to a boil, removing any fat that rises to the surface. After 15 minutes, add the chicken, garlic, celery leaves, bouillon cube, and black pepper to taste. Reduce the heat to medium and continue cooking, covered, until all of the meats are cooked and tender, or about 30 to 45 minutes after adding the chicken. Add more water as you cook, if necessary, to maintain the level of liquid.

5. Remove the cooked meats and stir the onion mixture into the pot. Cover the pot and remove it from the heat. When the meats have cooled enough to handle them, shred the meat into pieces. Discard the bones.

6. Bring the stew back to a boil, then add the meats, potatoes, giant white corn (unless otherwise instructed), and additional salt, pepper, and paprika to taste. Stir for a couple of minutes, then remove the pot from the stove. Sprinkle with parsley before serving.

Wine Suggestion –

Luis Felipe Edwards Doña Bernarda Cabernet Sauvignon

Hot Pepper and Beef Soup

Ajiaco   4 servings

For Isabel Mansilla, food has always been serious business. For about thirty years she worked as a fishmonger on the streets of chilly Puerto Varas, shouting to passersby about the splendors of salmon, conger eel, hake, and more. In 1984 she decided to take her fish fancy into a warm kitchen, so she started her own restaurant in Puerto Varas called El Mercado Chamaca Inn, where I met her in 2001. Isabel's eyes light up and she smiles deeply when it comes to talking cuisine. And she has unquestionably used her culinary skills to intoxicating effect: She related that her cooking prowess is what lured a Czech Navy man into her arms, whom she then married. Her version of ajiaco is spicy, which is a tribute to its name, that comes from the word aji, Chile's hot pepper. The soup that I ate was the perfect tonic to a frigid winter day in the Chilean south. Adjust the level of hot pepper according to how spicy you like your soup. And, depending on the spiciness of your hot peppers, you may want to remove them or advise guests to eat around them, since some may find them unpleasantly hot.

1. Heat 2 tablespoons of the olive oil in a deep pot over medium heat. When the oil is hot, add the onion, garlic, and bell pepper and cook for 5 to 7 minutes or until the onion is translucent.

2. Remove the vegetables from the skillet, add the remaining tablespoon of oil, and add the beef. Add salt and briefly cook the beef over medium-high heat, browning on all sides.

3 tablespoons olive oil
1 medium onion, cut in
  julienne strips
4 cloves garlic, finely
  chopped
1 small red bell pepper,
  cut in julienne strips
1 pound boneless stew beef,
  cut in 2 x 1-inch
  rectangular pieces
Salt
1¼ pounds boiling potatoes,
  cut in the shape of fat
  French fries (about 1 x 5
  inches)
1 teaspoon oregano
1 medium dried, hot pepper,
  cut in thin rings; or ¼ teaspoon hot red pepper flakes,
  plus additional hot pepper
  to taste
1 beef bouillon cube
2 eggs
Fresh chopped parsley

3. Return the vegetables to the pot, along with 8 cups of water, potatoes, oregano, hot pepper, and beef bouillon cube. Cover and bring to a boil over high heat.

4. When it is boiling, reduce the heat and simmer, covered, for about 25 minutes, or until the potatoes are tender. Adjust the flavor by adding additional salt and hot pepper.

5. Just before removing the soup from the heat, add the eggs and mix thoroughly. Sprinkle the parsley over the soup and serve.

Chicken Soup

From the French word consommé, *this is the lightest of the Chilean soups, and is what the doctor orders in Chile when you come down with a cold. I generally use a few bones that I have frozen, to make the broth. It's also delicious with croutons, made by coarsely cutting up fresh bread and frying it in just a touch of oil.*

1 pound chicken parts, with bones
½ small onion, sliced in thin strips
¼ red bell pepper, sliced in thin strips
2 cloves garlic, chopped finely
Salt
2 tablespoons cornstarch
¼ cup milk
Freshly ground black pepper
2 eggs, lightly beaten
1 tablespoon finely chopped fresh cilantro or parsley

1. In a large pot, heat 8 cups (2 quarts) of water and the chicken parts over high heat, and bring to a boil. Skim fat from the surface.

2. When the water boils, add the onion, bell pepper, garlic, and a bit of salt to the pot and reduce the heat to low. Cover and simmer for another 30 to 35 minutes.

3. Meanwhile, in a bowl, use a fork to dissolve the cornstarch in the milk. Set aside.

4. Remove the cooked chicken from the pot, and strip the meat from the bones. Discard the bones and fat. Chop the chicken very coarsely (into 1-inch pieces) and return it to the pot. Add just 1 cup of chopped chicken to the pot, as this is not a hearty chicken soup. Mix in the cornstarch mixture, black pepper, and additional salt to taste. Cook, uncovered, on low heat for 3 to 4 minutes.

5. Remove the pot from the heat, mix in the eggs and cilantro, and serve.

Cream of Chard

As Americans may crave cream of spinach, many Chileans crave cream of chard. Acelga is easy to spot in the stalls of markets and Chileans put it to good use in casseroles, pies, and soups as described here. Other typical cremas include cream of asparagus, tomato, chicken, and mixed vegetables.

9 ounces fresh chard, coarsely chopped
2 cups whole milk
1½ tablespoons cornstarch
1 tablespoon extra-virgin olive oil
Salt
½ red bell pepper, finely chopped
¼ cup finely chopped green onion
2 hard-boiled eggs, finely chopped

1. Put the chard and 1 cup of cold water in a small pot. Cover and cook over a low flame until cooked, about 10 minutes.

2. Let the chard cool a bit, drain it, then put it in a blender with the milk. Blend until well-pureed.

3. Dissolve the cornstarch in about ¼ cup water.

4. Cook the chard mixture over low heat, covered, for 10 minutes.

5. Mix in the cornstarch mixture, oil and salt to taste. Continue simmering for 5 minutes, stirring occasionally. Remove the pot from the heat.

6. Place the bell pepper, green onion, and eggs on a plate and set on the table for people to add at will to their soup.

Seaweed Soup

Cazuela Chilote   4 to 6 servings

Also called Sopa de Cochayuyo, *this dish originated in* Chiloé *(a Chilote is a native of Chiloé). I had always hoped to find a recipe that incorporated the* cochayuyo, *because of this alga's odd shape and texture. It is a series of thick brown strings that are folded upon one another, so it hardly looks edible at first. And its bouquet is hardly on the level of Chile's wines. Yet, after soaking in water overnight it becomes quite soft and fragrant and is then recognizable as seaweed.*

2 ounces kelp seaweed (available in many Asian stores)
2 tablespoons vegetable oil
7 cloves garlic, finely chopped
9 ounces calabaza or butternut squash, chopped in 1-inch cubes
Kernels from 1 large ear of corn (about 1 cup)
1 large carrot, peeled and grated
1 teaspoon paprika
½ cup milk
3 boiling potatoes (1¼ pounds), each cut in three pieces
½ cup uncooked rice
½ teaspoon dried oregano
Salt
2 tablespoons finely chopped fresh cilantro

1. Soak the seaweed in a large pot of water to moisten for the time prescribed on the package.

2. Remove the seaweed, drain it, and cut it into ¾-inch strips.

3. Heat the vegetable oil in a large pot over a medium flame. When hot, add the garlic. When the garlic is golden, add the moistened seaweed, and the *calabaza*, corn, carrot, and paprika. Stir for three minutes over medium heat.

4. Add 8 cups of water, the milk, and the potatoes, cover, and bring to a boil. When boiling, reduce the heat to low and continue cooking, covered, for approximately 20 minutes. The potatoes should be somewhat tender.

5. Add the rice, oregano, and salt to taste. Continue cooking, covered, over low heat until the rice is cooked, 13 to 15 minutes. As the rice is cooking, add more water or salt, as needed.

6. Remove the soup and serve it in individual bowls. Sprinkle 1 teaspoon of cilantro on each person's soup.

Offal Stew

— — — — — Offal is often overlooked in popular cuisine, but forms the essence of such long-treasured dishes as this one. The recipe came from Rosa Herrera, in the northern town of La Pampa. While Rosa uses lamb, beef is easier to find and is also tasty.

3 tablespoons extra-virgin olive oil

1¼ pounds cow or lamb offal, preferably a mix of heart and liver, all cut into 1½-inch pieces

Salt and freshly ground black pepper

1¼ pounds boiling potatoes, chopped into 1-inch cubes

1 medium onion, finely chopped

3 cloves garlic, finely chopped

8 ounces *calabaza* or butternut squash, chopped in small cubes

1 teaspoon *Aliño Completo* (see recipe, page 28), or ½ teaspoon paprika and ½ teaspoon oregano

Finely chopped fresh cilantro

1. Heat the oil in a large pot over a medium flame. When the oil is hot but not smoking, add the offal and season with salt and pepper to taste. Fry until browned on all sides and remove from the pan.

2. Turn the heat up to medium-high and add the potatoes, onion, garlic, and salt to taste. Continue cooking for 5 minutes, stirring frequently.

3. Return the offal to the skillet, along with the *calabaza*, *aliño completo*, and 1 cup of water. Reduce the heat to low and cover.

4. Cook until everything is tender, about 15 minutes. Sprinkle with cilantro and serve hot.

Wine Suggestion — — — — — — — — — — — —
Siegel El Crucero Cabernet Sauvignon Varietal

Beef and Vegetable Soup

Carbonada   4 servings

Some claim that carbonada *originated across the Chilean border in Mendoza, Argentina. Yet, Chile once controlled Mendoza, further muddling who deserves credit for its creation. Similar to other popular dishes such as* El Valdiviano, carbonada *calls upon seasonal vegetables complement a hearty portion of beef. This recipe includes a couple of celery leaves to add a hint of celery flavor. If you don't plan to make much use of the celery stalks after this recipe, try asking your greengrocer for a few celery leaves (preferably Chinese celery) for free instead of purchasing an entire stalk. In Chile, vendors almost always provide a few complimentary leaves.*

2 tablespoons extra-virgin olive oil
3 cloves garlic, finely chopped
1 pound boneless beef, cut into 1-inch cubes
1¾ pounds boiling potatoes, cut into 1½-inch cubes
½ onion, finely chopped
1 medium carrot, peeled and grated
1 small red bell pepper, finely chopped
2 fresh celery leaves or several fresh parsley leaves
½ teaspoon ground cumin
8 cups (2 quarts) hot water
⅓ cup uncooked rice
1 tablespoon salt
¼ cup finely chopped fresh cilantro

1. Heat the oil in a large pot over medium heat. When it is hot but not smoking, add the garlic and reduce the heat to low. Cook the garlic until golden brown, about 2 to 3 minutes.

2. Increase the heat to medium and add the meat. Cook the meat, stirring frequently, until it is thoroughly browned, about 5 to 7 minutes.

3. Add the potatoes, onions, carrot, bell pepper, celery leaves, and cumin. Continue frying for an additional 5 to 7 minutes over medium heat. Add the hot water, the rice, and salt.

4. Bring to a boil, then cover, reduce heat to low, and continue cooking until the rice and potatoes are cooked, or about 15 minutes. The total cooking time for the dish is about 35 minutes.

5. Mix in additional salt to taste and remove the pot from the heat. After several minutes, serve the soup with a bit of fresh cilantro in each bowl.

Wine Suggestion -
Pueblo Antiguo Merlot

Tomato and Beef Stew

As in many of Chile's dishes, tomatoes are predominant in this one, tomaticán. Indeed, the tomato takes center stage here in just one of the many homemade dishes that Yenny Montecinos makes from the abundant vegetables she buys from a couple of terrific farmers markets in Valparaíso. Yenny, who buys all of her fruits and vegetables in the market, likes to make tomaticán in the summer when corn, tomatoes, and basil are at their finest.

1 pound boiling potatoes, peeled
1 cup corn kernels (cut from about 2 ears)
2 tablespoons extra-virgin olive oil
1 medium onion, finely chopped
2 cloves garlic, finely chopped
1 medium carrot, peeled and grated
7 to 8 fresh basil leaves, finely chopped
Salt
1 pound boneless beef, cut into 2-inch-long pieces
3¼ pounds tomatoes, peeled and finely chopped
Freshly ground black pepper

1. Boil the potatoes. When they are tender, remove them from the water, drain, and set them aside.

2. Meanwhile, boil the corn. When it is cooked, strip off the kernels and set them aside.

3. Heat the oil in a skillet. When hot, add the onions, garlic, carrot, and basil. When the onions are translucent, remove the vegetables. Salt the beef slices and briefly fry them over medium heat in the skillet until they are cooked.

4. Put the tomatoes in a medium-sized pot and cook them over medium heat, for 10 to 15 minutes.

5. Mix everything with the tomatoes except the potatoes. Cook over medium heat for a few minutes to blend flavors. Add a bit of water (½ to 1 cup), if the soup is too thick. It shouldn't be too heavy. Add salt and pepper to taste. Remove from heat. (Total cooking time for entire dish is about 30 minutes.)

6. Serve in individual bowls, adding a whole potato to each bowl.

Wine Suggestion -
Casas del Bosque Merlot Reserve

Pasteles y Chupes

Chile has a tantalizing array of *pasteles*, or casseroles. Among the favorites are *Pastel de Jaibas* (crab) and *Pastel de Choclo* (sweet corn), one of the nation's most prized dishes. However, there is also *Pastel de Acelga* (chard), *Pastel de Papas* (potatoes), and many others. There's even a casserole called *Pastel de Ortiga* made with *ortiga* (a nettle plant), which I found in the town of Olmué in central Chile.

Their glory is largely in their creaminess, which seems to leave a warm and fuzzy feeling inside. And when eating them I almost always feel as though I am transported back to an earlier time or another place. That is because they are usually cooked in individual-sized mud bowls called *gredas*, and just when I'm disappointed to see that I've finished everything, there appears a little more stuck to a nook or cranny in one of the bowl's sides. Those are often the best parts.

Potato and Beef Casserole

Pastel de Papas   6 servings

- - - - - - *Pastel de Papas* *is Chile's equivalent to Britain's shepherd's pie. Like* **Pastel de Choclo**, *it is a very hearty dish and can be eaten alone as a full meal along with a simple salad of fresh tomatoes, cilantro, olive oil, and salt. The dish can be cooked in the oven in a large, rectangular glass pan or in individual oven-proof bowls. You can substitute ground beef for sliced beef.*

2¼ to 2½ pounds baking potatoes, such as russets, peeled
1 cup milk
3 tablespoons butter
Salt
¼ cup extra-virgin olive oil
1½ pounds onions, finely chopped
2 pounds boneless beef, sliced into ½-inch cubes
2 teaspoons ground cumin
2 teaspoons paprika
20 large raisins
15 black olives
3 hard-boiled eggs, very coarsely chopped
3 egg yolks, lightly beaten

1. Boil the potatoes until tender. Remove, strain and mash into a puree. Use a spoon to gradually mix in the milk and butter in order to make creamy mashed potatoes. Stir in a bit of salt to taste.

2. Preheat the oven to 400° F.

3. Heat 2 tablespoons of the olive oil in a large skillet over medium-high heat. When hot, add the onions. Cook until translucent and remove from the skillet.

4. In the same skillet, add the remaining oil. Fry the beef briefly, until just cooked. Add the onions and mix in the cumin, paprika and salt to taste. Continue cooking over medium-low heat, stirring frequently, for another three minutes. Remove from heat.

5. Use a large baking pan (approximately 9 x 13) or individual oven-proof bowls (*gredas*). First put the beef mixture on the base of the pan or bowls. Include the meat juices so that the casserole will not be dry. Top with the raisins, olives, and chopped egg. Cover with the mashed potatoes. Smooth with a spoon. Brush with the egg yolks.

6. Put into the oven and cook until the surface is golden brown, 15 to 20 minutes.

Wine Suggestion -
Viña Tarapaca La Cuesta Cabernet Sauvignon/Syrah blend

Sweet Corn and Meat Casserole

Pastel de Choclo   4 servings

Chileans love the combination of basil and corn, which become blissful bedfellows in humitas and in Pastel de Choclo. *Together, they create a hearty, fragrant meal. Invariably found in Chilean marketplace restaurants when basil and corn are in season,* Pastel de Choclo *requires planning and is best prepared in stages. Restaurants prepare it ahead of time and then reheat it, when its flavor has reached its peak. Eat the casserole with a fork and spoon, along with a side dish of fresh, chopped tomatoes. You may also want to sprinkle some sugar on it, as Chileans often do, though I find that U.S. sweet corn makes the dish pleasantly sweet enough.*

The chicken mixture
Salt
4 chicken pieces, such as 2 thighs and 2 legs, skins removed (1¾ pounds)
2 tablespoons extra-virgin olive oil
2 cloves garlic, coarsely chopped

The beef mixture
3 tablespoons extra-virgin olive oil
3 cloves garlic, finely chopped
1 pound ground beef
1 medium onion, finely chopped
½ teaspoon ground cumin
¾ teaspoon paprika
Salt to taste

For the chicken mixture

1. Lightly salt the chicken on both sides. In a skillet, heat the oil over medium heat. When hot add the chicken and garlic. Cook 15 to 20 minutes, turning once. Do not let the garlic burn, and remove any pieces that blacken.

2. Remove the chicken from the skillet just before it is fully cooked. Discard the fat and garlic.

For the beef mixture

1. In a skillet, heat the oil over medium heat. When hot, add the garlic and cook until golden. Add the ground beef. Continue cooking for 2 minutes, stirring often. Add the onions, cumin, and paprika and continue cooking for five more minutes. Add salt to taste and set aside.

The corn mixture

6 cups corn kernels, cut from about 6 ears
15 fresh basil leaves
2 cups milk
1 teaspoon salt
Cornstarch

Additions

8 large black, whole olives (about ¼ cup)
⅛ cup golden raisins
3 hard-boiled eggs, quartered
1 to 2 egg yolks, lightly beaten

For the corn mixture - - - - - - - - - - -

1. Grind the corn and basil into a paste. I make a creamy paste by using a food processor or a juicer. Slowly add the milk as you grind the corn and basil.

2. Put the mixture in a large pot and cook on medium-low heat, stirring constantly so that it does not stick to the bottom of the pot. As it cooks, add the salt.

3. Dissolve a few tablespoons of cornstarch in ½ cup water and gradually stir it into the mixture, until it is thick and creamy. Cook for about 30 minutes, or until the corn no longer has a raw taste. Set aside.

For the casserole -

1. Preheat oven to 400° F

2. Place a piece of chicken in each of four earthenware bowls or in a large baking pan (approximately 9 x 13). Spread the beef mixture over the chicken. Evenly distribute the egg, raisins, and olives, burrowing them slightly into the beef mixture. Cover with equal amounts of the corn mixture. Smooth the surface so it is completely even. Brush the egg yolk over the casserole.

3. Put the dish into the oven. Bake for 20 minutes, or until golden.

Wine Suggestion -

Santa Carolina Reserva de Familia Cabernet Sauvignon

Crab Casserole

4 servings

Guests always like to see elaborate recipes served in seashells. This dish gives you the ideal chance to charm them. If you have shells from the crabmeat, bake the Pastel de Jaibas in the shells. When cooked, remove from the oven and serve in the shells on a bed of lettuce with a slice of lemon. For variations of this pastel, chefs can substitute a variety of shellfish or shrimp for the crab. You can also make this dish using king crab, which is how they do it in Patagonia.

6 thin slices commercial white bread, coarsely chopped or torn into bits
1½ cups whole milk
¼ cup extra-virgin olive oil
½ cup finely chopped onion (about ½ small onion)
3 cloves garlic, finely chopped
½ teaspoon paprika
¼ teaspoon dried oregano
¼ teaspoon ground cumin
⅓ cup white wine
¼ cup heavy cream
¾ cups Fish Stock (see recipe, page 132)
1 pound crabmeat (from about 6 large crabs)
⅓ cup Parmesan cheese, plus 1 tablespoon
2 eggs, lightly beaten
Salt and freshly ground black pepper
Lemon wedges (optional)

1. Preheat the oven to 400° F.

2. Place the bread in a bowl. Add the milk, and let the bread absorb it for about 10 minutes. Squeeze the milk from the bread and discard all remaining milk.

3. Place the olive oil in a skillet over medium heat. When hot, add the onion and garlic and fry for about five minutes. Mix in the paprika, oregano, and cumin. Reduce the heat to low, add the wine, and boil gently for five minutes. Add the moistened bread and mix thoroughly. Increase heat to medium-low and add the cream.

4. Continue mixing and after 3 minutes, add the fish stock and stir. Then add the crabmeat and stir in thoroughly. After 1 to 2 minutes add ⅓ cup of the Parmesan cheese and the egg, and mix thoroughly. Add salt and a bit of pepper to taste and remove from heat.

5. Divide the mixture between three or four individual oven-proof bowls (*gredas*) or a square pan (approximately 9 x 9). Sprinkle with the remaining Parmesan cheese.

6. Put in the oven and bake until browned, about 10 minutes. Serve with freshly ground pepper and additional Parmesan cheese. Also, diners can sprinkle on the juice from lemon wedges.

Wine Suggestion –
Concha y Toro Terrunyo Chardonnay

Creamy Shellfish Casserole

Coastal Chile is pulsing with activity during the summer months (from December through March). And the most popular region is near the cities of Viña del Mar and Valparaíso. Such towns as Concón have restaurants lining the sea with beautiful views and wonderful seafood. Inspiration for this recipe comes from Italo Bravo of the restaurant, La Perla del Pacífico, which is translated as "The Pearl of the Pacific." This name is also the moniker for Valparaíso, the province in which Concón and its black sands lie. If by necessity or preference you buy shellfish in their shells, you will need to buy three or four times the amount listed below. In that case, boil the shellfish in water until cooked, remove them from their shells, and chop them coarsely. Save the broth, which can serve as shellfish stock.

7 ounces white bread (7 to 8 slices commercial bread)
2 cups milk
2 tablespoons extra-virgin olive oil or butter
5 cloves garlic
1/2 teaspoon dried oregano
1/2 cup white wine
1 to 1 1/2 cups shellfish stock (or see recipe for Fish Stock on page 132)
1 3/4 pounds cooked mussels, clams, shrimp and oysters, all coarsely chopped
1/3 cup heavy cream
2 tablespoons chopped fresh parsley
Salt and freshly ground black pepper
5 to 6 ounces mozzarella cheese, cut in 4 to 6 slices

1. Preheat the oven to 400° F.

2. Put the bread in a bowl and moisten by covering with the milk. Let the bread absorb the milk for at least 10 minutes.

3. Heat the oil into a large skillet over a medium flame. When hot, add the garlic and cook until golden. Add the moistened bread and the oregano. Continue cooking, stirring sufficiently to remove lumps.

4. After about 3 minutes, add the white wine and 2/3 cup of shellfish stock. Reduce heat to medium-low and continue stirring for 2 to 3 minutes.

5. Mix in the chopped shellfish and stir thoroughly. Mix in the cream, parsley, and salt, and a touch of black pepper to taste. If necessary, add more shellfish broth to have a creamy (but not dense) mixture.

6. Place the mixture in 4 individual oven-proof earthenware bowls or a square pan (approximately 9 x 9). Cover the mixture with the cheese.

7. Put the baking pan into the oven and cook until the cheese melts, about 6 to 8 minutes. Remove and serve hot.

Wine Suggestion —
Torreón de Paredes Chardonnay Colección Privada

Zucchini Casserole

Digna Uribe Ceballos introduced me to this casserole, which she learned from an Italian named Atilio Zunino. Atilio arrived in Chile in 1948 eager to share his native cuisine with those he met, such as Digna's mother. Other Italians appear to have done much the same, since for decades Chileans have been preparing a similar dish. Atilio passed this recipe to Digna's mother, who passed it on to me. It seems only fitting since zucchini—which is the Italian plural for summer squash—are believed to have originated in Italy, and Chileans call them zapallo italiano (literally "Italian squash"). This dish could please many a vegetarian since it is full of flavor and can be eaten alone, but Digna also enjoys it with a pork chop, typically sautéed in Chile with minced garlic.

6 medium zucchini (2½ to 3 pounds), peeled and coarsely chopped in 1- to 2-inch pieces
6 thin slices (7 ounces) commercial white bread
1 cup milk
3 tablespoons extra-virgin olive oil
1 medium onion, finely chopped
2 large carrots, peeled and grated
1 medium red bell pepper, coarsely chopped
8 cloves garlic, pureed or coarsely chopped
4 eggs, lightly beaten
⅓ cup grated Parmesan cheese, plus additional for topping
Butter or vegetable oil for greasing the pan
Salt and freshly ground black pepper

1. Preheat the oven to 400° F.

2. Boil the zucchini in a large pot of water, covered, until tender, about 10 to 15 minutes. Remove, drain and smash, making a puree. Drain.

3. Place the bread in a bowl and moisten with the milk. Let sit for 10 minutes. Then, using your hands, mix together, making a dough.

4. Heat the oil and sautée the onion, carrots, bell pepper, and garlic in the oil. When the onion is translucent add the softened bread. Cook for about three more minutes, stirring frequently so that the bread mixes with the vegetables. Remove from heat.

5. Drain the zucchini again, if necessary. Stir the drained zucchini and the eggs into the vegetable mixture. Add salt and pepper to taste.

6. Grease a rectangular baking pan (approximately 9 x 13) or individual, oven-proof bowls (*gredas*). Place the zucchini mixture in the pan and sprinkle with grated cheese.

7. Place in the oven and cook until the surface is golden brown, 10 to 15 minutes. Serve the dish with freshly ground black pepper and additional Parmesan cheese.

Serving Suggestion –
Serve with pork chops, sautéed in garlic as is typical in Chile, with a Merlot.

Beef and Cabbage Casserole

Guiso Fausto   4 to 6 servings

Don Fausto was the name of a comic strip popular in Chile in decades past. The main character was named Don Fausto, and he always seemed to have at it with his wife. They were like the Archie and Edith Bunker of the Chilean comic pages, and they developed quite a following. People would race their fingers through El Mercurio—*the well-respected newspaper whose size was nearly that of an encyclopedia in those days—to see what the Faustos were up to. Despite the couple's bickering, there was one thing that always calmed nerves and made Don Fausto happy: a cabbage casserole. Because of that many people now call* guiso de repollo *by the name* **Guiso Fausto** *(Fausto Casserole). If you have a food processor handy this recipe is a snap, since the bulk of the work is the chopping.*

10 cups finely chopped green cabbage (2¼ pounds)
2½ to 3 ounces white bread (3 slices commercial bread)
½ cup milk
2 tablespoons olive oil
13 ounces boneless stew beef, cut into 1-inch cubes
1 onion, finely chopped
5 cloves garlic, finely chopped
1 teaspoon dried oregano
Salt to taste
3 eggs
Freshly ground black pepper
6 ounces mild cheese, such as Muenster

1. Preheat the oven to 400° F.

2. Put the cabbage in a pot and cover with cold water. Boil, covered, until soft, about 12 minutes. Drain thoroughly.

3. Place the bread in a bowl and moisten with the milk. Let it soak until very soft (5 to 7 minutes). The bread will absorb the milk. Squeeze the bread with your fingers to remove any large lumps.

4. Heat 1 tablespoon of the oil in a skillet over medium-high heat. Add the meat and brown on both sides. Remove the meat and add the onions, garlic, and oregano to the skillet. Continue cooking for a few minutes, stirring frequently. Return the meat to the skillet and mix thoroughly, along with about 1 teaspoon of salt. Remove from heat.

5. Place the rest of the oil in a skillet over medium heat. When hot, add the softened bread and cook until lightly golden, stirring frequently (about 2 minutes). Mix in the cabbage. Add the eggs and a touch of salt and pepper and mix thoroughly, continuing to cook for about 2 minutes. Remove from heat.

6. Thoroughly combine the meat mixture with the cabbage mixture (including all the pan juices). Taste the mixture, adding additional salt if necessary.

7. Place the mixture in a baking pan (approximately 9 x 13). Cover with thin slices of cheese.

8. Put into the oven and cook until the cheese melts and turns golden brown, about 15 minutes.

Wine Suggestion
De Martino Cabernet Franc from the Single Vineyard line

Creamy Tripe Casserole

Food squeamishness is low in Chile, and tripe is enjoyed with abandon. For those who don't like to eat it in a summer salad, this dish is ideal, because the guatitas (tripe) are neither overpowering, nor do they disappear from center stage

1½ pounds beef tripe
2 bay leaves
3½ ounces white bread (4 slices commercial bread)
2 tablespoons extra-virgin olive oil, plus extra
1 onion (7 ounces), finely chopped
3 cloves garlic, finely chopped
1 teaspoon paprika, plus extra
1 teaspoon salt
¼ teaspoon *Aliño Completo* (see recipe, page 28)
Freshly ground black pepper
½ cup Parmesan cheese
2 eggs, whisked
½ small red bell pepper, cut in julienne
2 tablespoons finely chopped fresh parsley

1. Bring a large pot of lightly salted water to a boil. Fully submerge the tripe and bay leaves, cover, and simmer. Turn the tripe occasionally to cook it evenly. The tripe is cooked when it is soft and a sharp knife pierces it easily, about 2 hours. When the tripe is cooked, remove it from the heat. Reserve 1 cup of the broth, discarding the rest. Let the tripe cool, then remove any excess fat and discard. Cut the tripe into 1-inch squares.

2. Soak the bread in a small bowl of water. When the bread is fully moistened, or after at least 10 minutes, drain it. Using your fingers, squeeze and mash the bread, making it into a soft dough. Remove any large lumps.

3. Heat the oil in a large pot over medium heat. When the oil is hot, add the onion and garlic. Cook the onion until it is translucent, add the paprika, salt, and 2 cups of water, and mix thoroughly. After 1 minute, add the bread. Reduce the heat to low, cover, and cook, stirring occasionally. After 5 minutes, stir in the reserved broth, the *aliño completo* and the black pepper, and cook for another 5 minutes.

4. Add the tripe and 1 cup of water to the pot. Increase the heat to medium-low and cook for 5 minutes, stirring frequently. Add the cheese and eggs and continue cooking for 3 minutes, stirring frequently. The dish should be light and creamy, so add a bit more water if it is too heavy. Stir in the bell pepper and parsley to add additional color and flavor to the dish, and salt to taste. Cook for 3 to 4 more minutes and serve hot.

Wine Suggestion

Piduco Creek Merlot

Porotos, Legumbres, y Verduras

"That fellow is more Chilean than even beans are." Such is the popular adage that Chileans use to refer to their countrymen, and it's no surprise why: for the average Chilean cook, beans are indispensable. They were a major source of the indigenous diet in the early days of Chile's history and they remain crucial today. There are a dazzling number of varieties here, expanding far past the basic green, lima, and garbanzo bean. Just one bean salesmen in the market in Chillán had the following types: magnum, garbonzo, señorita, coliguado, blanco español, blanco, arroz, cachipora, frutilla, pajarito, guinia, tortolita, gramber, gringo, and boloto.

Porotos Granados and the equally popular *Porotos Mazamorra* deftly combine two basics, corn and beans, to leave many complementary textures and flavors on the tongue. These two dishes are the same except that the corn is not ground in the former. Instead, it is simply stripped whole from the cob and added to the pot of beans. In Chile, this stripped corn is called *choclo picado* or *pilco*, while ground corn is *choclo molido* or *mazamorra*.

While Chilean bean dishes vary considerably, they do have a couple of things in common. To begin with, they are inexpensive, which has helped keep them ubiquitous in this developing country. Also, they tend to taste even better if they sit for a while before being consumed. Letting the flavors soak in for an hour or two after cooking, or even saving the dish for the next day, rewards the chef immensely. Lastly, in Chile they are typically served with the pickled onion dish known as *Escabeche* (see recipe, page 40).

The key to making an excellent Chilean bean dish is to have a bit of patience and to meticulously balance the appropriate amounts of salt, water and herbs. The beans must be cooked until tender and, as they absorb water, additional water must be added to the pot. To create a richer, thicker sauce, simply add less water as you cook.

When cooking beans, you need to plan ahead. They are almost invariably soaked for twelve to twenty-four hours to make them more tender. During that time they can double in size.

Cannellini Beans
and Pasta

- - - - - *It is speculated that this dish is one of the few in Chile that came from Italian immigrants, as it may be related to the Italian soup,* **pasta e fagiole.** *In this dish, the spaghetti are "riendas" or "reins," perhaps because of their long and thin appearance.*

2 cups dried cannellini beans, soaked in a pot of water for 12 to 24 hours

2 tablespoons extra-virgin olive oil

1 small onion, finely chopped

3 cloves garlic, finely chopped

¼ green bell pepper, coarsely chopped

1 teaspoon *Aliño Completo* (see recipe, page 28), or use ½ teaspoon ground cumin and ¼ teaspoon each of paprika and dried oregano

12 ounces *calabaza*, cut into 1½-inch pieces

7 ounces spaghetti

Salt and freshly ground black pepper

1. Drain the beans and put them in a large pot, along with 10 cups (2½ quarts) of water. Bring to a boil. When the water is boiling, cover, and reduce the heat to medium.

2. Heat the oil in a skillet over a medium flame. Add the onion, garlic, and bell pepper. Cook until the onions are translucent and then mix in the *aliño completo*. Immediately add this mixture to the pot of beans that are cooking. Cover and continue cooking the beans over medium heat until they are tender, about 1 hour. Stir occasionally.

3. When the beans are tender add the *calabaza*. Continue cooking, covered. When the *calabaza* is almost tender, add the spaghetti. If the spaghetti is not fully submerged in liquid, add more water. Mix in a generous amount of salt and pepper. When the pasta is al dente, remove the pot from the heat and set aside, covered, for 10 to 15 minutes, to absorb flavors. Upon standing, the broth will thicken considerably so stir in more water, as necessary, before serving. Serve hot with *Escabeche* (see recipe, page 40).

Spareribs Bathed in Cranberry Beans and Pureed Corn

You may have seen a cowboy from Texas, but you probably haven't had the privilege of meeting the huasos *of Curacaví. These cowboy hat-toting* campesinos *cultivate vegetables or raise livestock in rural areas like Curacaví, and they are very finicky about their food. Beans and ribs, staples for* huasos, *are coupled to make the dish below, in which the bean broth bathes the ribs to make them wonderfully moist and tasty. I tried this dish at Los Hornitos, a restaurant founded in the mid-1970s to bring the feel of the countryside to those traveling to and from the major cities of Valparaíso and Santiago. At Los Hornitos, the waiters dress like* huasos, *the floors are gravel and sand, the lamps are made of ceramic, the ceilings are thatched with bamboo sticks, and the chairs and tables are constructed from old-fashioned wood. I dined there in the winter, when coals burned in open cauldrons throughout the restaurant. The restaurant's menu proclaimed that Los Hornitos was established "to unite the characteristics of our* campesino *(country) taste. In this way our kitchen is characterized by dishes that keep the tastes of our grandparents alive." Try the recipe below to see for yourself!*

2 cups shelled fresh cranberry beans or 1 pound, unshelled
10 ounces *calabaza* or butternut squash, cut in 1-inch cubes
1⅓ cups corn kernels (from 2 to 3 ears of corn), ground in a food processor or juicer
5 tablespoons extra-virgin olive oil
1 small onion, finely chopped
3 cloves garlic, finely chopped
6 basil leaves, finely chopped
⅔ teaspoon paprika
Salt
3 to 3½ pounds pork spareribs
Freshly ground black pepper

1. Place the shelled beans in a pot with 4 cups of water. Cover and cook over a high flame. When boiling, tilt the lid to give the beans some air and reduce the heat to medium. After 25 minutes, add 3 cups more water, the *calabaza*, and the corn. Continue cooking over medium heat, partly covered, stirring frequently with a wooden spoon for approximately 20 minutes. As it cooks, the water will dissipate and the bean mixture will begin to stick to the base of the pot, so stir frequently. Add ½ to 1 cup more water, if necessary, to maintain the consistency of a thick soup.

2. Meanwhile, add 2 tablespoons of the oil to a skillet over medium heat. When hot, add the onions and garlic. Sauté until the onions are translucent, mix in the basil and paprika, and set aside.

3. The beans and *calabaza* are cooked when they are tender, after about 45 minutes total cooking time for the beans. At this point, add the onion mixture and salt to taste, and stir thoroughly. You can time the recipe so that the ribs and beans are ready at the same time, but the dish is enhanced if you set the cooked beans aside, covered, for 30 minutes to an hour to let flavors mingle.

4. Preheat the oven to 400° F.

5. Lightly sprinkle salt on the ribs. Top with 3 tablespoons of the oil.

6. Put the ribs in a baking pan and place it in the oven. While the ribs cook, baste them often with their juices or, if they are dry, a bit more oil.

7. Remove the ribs when well cooked, after about 40 minutes. Cut the ribs into four pieces. Divide the soup mixture between four large soup bowls. Add a portion of ribs to each bowl. Serve diners a side plate on which they can cut the ribs in smaller pieces, and have a peppermill handy.

Wine Suggestion

Viñedo Chadwick Cabernet Sauvignon

White Beans with Pigskin

Porotos con Cuero de Chancho 4 servings

Below is one of the classic bean recipes that involves pigskin, which is rather common in Chilean meat markets. When cooked, it becomes very tender and tasty. If you can't obtain pigskin, substitute a similar amount of bacon, fry it separately, and then add it to the cooked bean and vegetable mixture.

1½ cups dried white beans, soaked in a pot of water for 12 to 24 hours
9 ounces pigskin, cut in two-inch pieces
⅓ cup fresh celery leaves
1 tablespoon extra-virgin olive oil
1 medium onion, finely chopped
1 pound *calabaza* or butternut squash, chopped into 1-inch pieces
½ red bell pepper, coarsely chopped
1 carrot, peeled and coarsely chopped
3 large cloves garlic, finely chopped
⅓ cup finely chopped fresh parsley
1 teaspoon paprika
Salt and freshly ground black pepper

1. Discard the water from the pot of beans. Put approximately 8 cups (2 quarts) of cold water, the beans, and the chopped pigskin in a large pot. Cover and bring to a boil over high heat. Reduce the heat to medium and add half of the celery leaves. Continue cooking, covered, for approximately 1 hour, adding water if necessary to keep the dish soupy.

2. Meanwhile, heat the oil in a skillet. When hot, add the onions and cook over medium heat. When translucent, add the *calabaza*, bell pepper, carrots, and garlic. Add ½ cup water and cook, stirring frequently. Cook for about 8 to 10 minutes, or until the carrots and *calabaza* become somewhat tender. Remove from the heat.

3. When the shells begin to fall off the beans, after approximately an hour, add the *calabaza* mixture, parsley, remaining celery leaves, and paprika. Cook until the *calabaza* and carrots are tender, about another 10 minutes, adding more water if necessary and stirring frequently. Add salt and pepper to taste.

4. Serve immediately or refrigerate the dish for a day to allow the flavors to mingle.

Serving Suggestion

Serve with *Escabeche* (see page 40).

Green Beans in Hot Calabaza Sauce

Porotos Quebrados

When you cook calabaza long enough it becomes nice and creamy. It showers the foods around it with its terrific aroma and color, and there's no turning back. In this recipe, green beans and fresh corn soak in its rich juices. While one of the Spanish names for this dish is Ensalada de Porotos Calientes *(Warm Bean Salad), it isn't a salad, as the name would suggest. More accurately, it is also called* Porotos Quebrados, *or "Broken Beans."*

2 tablespoons extra-virgin olive oil

1 small onion, finely chopped

1 large clove garlic, finely chopped

6 to 7 ounces boneless beef (optional, see "Serving Suggestion" below)

10 ounces *calabaza* or butter-nut squash, cut in thin slices

1 teaspoon paprika

2 cups corn kernels (from 2 to 3 ears of corn)

1¼ pounds green beans, cut into 1-inch pieces

½ teaspoon *Aliño Completo* (see recipe, page 28)

Salt and freshly ground black pepper

1. Heat the oil in a medium pot over medium heat. When hot, add the onion, garlic, and beef.

2. When the onions are translucent, add the *calabaza* and the paprika. Stir briefly and then add 2 cups of water. Increase the heat to high. When the water boils, reduce the heat to medium and continue cooking for about 15 minutes, stirring continuously, until the *calabaza* is soft.

3. Add the corn and beans, the *aliño completo*, salt, and pepper. Add an additional ¼ cup of cold water, increase the heat to high, and bring to a boil. Then, reduce the heat to medium and cook, stirring frequently, until the beans and corn are cooked, about 15 minutes. While cooking, either add a bit of water or reduce the water until you have a rich *calabaza* sauce (it should not be soupy). Serve hot.

Serving Suggestion

Serve this as a side dish or make it a main course. In that case, include the sliced beef, as indicated above, and accompany it with white rice, mashed potatoes, or French fries.

Split Pea and Sausage Stew

Arvejas Partidas con Longanizas   4 servings

I ducked into a little shop on a cold winter day in Puerto Varas to warm up a bit and started talking detachedly with the owner about her wares—hats, sweaters, rugs, and the usual warm-weather gear and souvenirs. When I turned the conversation to food, though, the elderly, round-faced woman named Orfeli Vidal became animated and then counted and recounted with relish how to make this dish. I tried it at home, trying to get the proportions right, and instantly took a liking to it.

3 cups (1 pound) green split peas, soaked in a pot of water for 12 to 24 hours
1/4 cup uncooked rice
2 whole fresh celery leaves
1/2 pound sweet sausage
1/2 pound spicy sausage
2 tablespoons extra-virgin olive oil
1/2 small onion, finely chopped
1/4 red bell pepper, cut into julienne strips
5 cloves garlic, finely chopped
3/4 teaspoon paprika
10 ounces calabaza or butternut squash, cut in one-inch cubes
Salt and freshly ground black pepper

1. Drain the peas and put them in a large pot with 8 cups (2 quarts) of water. Bring to a boil, and then reduce the heat and simmer. Add a cup of water when necessary so that the peas do not dry out and the bottom of the pot does not burn. The cooking time ranges greatly, depending on the hardness of the peas. It can be from 1 hour up to 3 hours. The peas are almost cooked when they start giving off their shells and become soft or dissolve, and the broth becomes creamy.

2. Add the rice and celery leaves. Continue cooking for 10 minutes, adding water if necessary to maintain a creamy consistency.

3. While the peas are cooking, cover the bottom of a skillet with water and cook the sausages over medium heat until golden brown and cooked inside, 8 to 10 minutes. Remove from the skillet and cut into 1-inch pieces.

4. Add 2 tablespoons of oil to the skillet or use 2 tablespoons of the sausage grease, and heat over a medium-low flame. When hot, add the onion. After the onion is translucent, add the bell pepper, garlic, and paprika. Mix briefly and add the *calabaza*. Continue cooking for about five minutes, or until the *calabaza* is slightly tender, but not fully cooked, stirring regularly.

5. Add the sausages, *calabaza* mixture, and salt (about $1\frac{1}{2}$ teaspoons) and pepper to taste to the peas. Cook until the rice is tender, stirring frequently.

6. Remove from the heat and serve, topping with more freshly ground pepper. When reheating, add $\frac{1}{2}$ to 1 cup additional water so that the peas do not stick to the bottom of the pot and the dish remains sufficiently light.

Wine Suggestion —
Vistamar Cabernet Sauvignon

Stewed Lentils with Bacon

— — — — — — —*In Chile, they say you're* lenteja *(or lentil-like) if you're slow or dim-witted. The term may owe itself to the fact that Chileans cook lentils very slowly. However, faster-cooking lentils are now available, cutting cooking time from a few hours to just 30 minutes. Read the instructions on your lentil package to figure out the appropriate cooking time.*

1½ cups uncooked brown
   lentils, soaked in a pot of
   water for 12 to 24 hours
5 slices commercial bread
   (4 to 5 ounces)
1 cup milk
5 ounces bacon
1 small onion, finely chopped
1 carrot, peeled and coarsely
   chopped
3 cloves garlic, finely
   chopped
2 to 3 tablespoons Parmesan
   cheese, plus additional for
   serving
Salt and freshly ground black
   pepper

1. Drain and rinse lentils. Place the lentils in a large pot with 9 cups (2¼ quarts) of lightly salted water and cook, partially covered, over high heat. Stir occasionally. Cook until the lentils begin to split open, approximately 30 minutes.

2. Meanwhile, submerge the bread in the milk and soak. After approximately 10 minutes, remove the bread, squeeze it to remove excess milk, and discard the milk. Mash the bread with your hands and remove any major lumps.

3. Fry the bacon in a skillet over medium heat. Remove and finely chop. Discard all but 2 tablespoons of fat from the skillet.

4. Add the onion, carrot, and garlic to the skillet and sauté in the bacon grease over medium heat for approximately 5 minutes (or until the onion is translucent).

5. When the lentils are cooked, reduce the heat to medium and add the bacon mixture to the pot. Cook for a few minutes, stirring frequently with a wooden spoon. Add the moistened bread and the Parmesan cheese and, cooking for another 2 to 3 minutes. Add more water if the dish is too thick

6. Add salt and pepper to taste, and remove from heat. Serve immediately with ground pepper and/or additional grated Parmesan cheese.

Wine Suggestion— —
Try one of the outstanding malbecs from Viu Manent, such as its Special Selection Malbec.

Shelled Wheat and Potatoes with Sliced Beef

Papas con Mote   4 servings

― ― ― ― ― *Trigo mote isn't just for Chile's national juice,* **Mote con Huesillo.** *Shelled wheat is also used in hot main courses, such as stews and bean dishes. Teresa Jeldes, who runs a small store in Valparaíso, told me about this recipe that she learned from her mother. Like many dishes, she says its origin rests in Chiloé.*

The beef and shelled wheat

½ cup shelled wheat
2 tablespoons extra-virgin olive oil
1 medium onion, finely chopped
3 cloves garlic, finely chopped
¼ teaspoon ground cumin
⅓ teaspoon dried oregano
1 to 1¼ pound boneless beef, cut in small slices
1 beef bouillon cube
1½ pounds baking potatoes, such as russets, peeled and thinly sliced (2 inches wide, ¼-inch thick)
Salt

The paprika sauce

1 teaspoon extra-virgin olive oil
1 teaspoon paprika

1. Boil the wheat in a pot of water for about 40 minutes, or until soft. Drain and set aside.

2. Heat the oil in a medium-size pot over a medium flame. When hot, add the onion, garlic, cumin, and oregano. When the onion is translucent, add the beef.

3. When the beef has browned, add one cup of water, the beef bouillon cube, potatoes, and salt, and cover. Reduce the heat to medium-low and stir occasionally.

4. When the potatoes are almost tender, add the wheat. Reduce the heat to low and cook for 5 more minutes, until the flavors have mingled and the potatoes are fully cooked. Add additional water (about ½ to 1 cup) if the mixture becomes dry.

5. **For the paprika sauce** ― ― ― ― ― ― ― ―
Heat ¼ cup water, the oil, and paprika in a saucepan over a medium flame. When it bubbles, ladle it into the pot of cooked wheat. Serve hot.

Stuffed Cabbage Leaves

Niños Envueltos

5 to 6 stuffed cabbage leaves
(enough for four to six people as an appetizer,
or two to three people as a main course)

When translated from the Spanish, the name for these stuffed cabbages means "babies rolled up" or "babies wrapped in diapers." The babies refer to the concoction of rice, beef, and vegetables that is folded snugly into each cabbage leaf. It is recommended that you use a green cabbage with soft, flexible leaves. Softer cabbage better resembles a soft blanket in which you will wrap these babies, and also allows for quicker cooking. You will need to briefly cook the cabbage leaves in water to make them pliant for folding; otherwise, when you roll the cabbage leaves they will be too rigid and will split.

When making **Niños Envueltos,** *some Chileans forgo cabbage altogether and simply roll a piece of meat around vegetables and seal them shut. Those wraps, however, are now generally referred to as* **arrollados,** *such as* **Arrollado Huaso** *(see recipe, page 175), or as* **malayas** *(see recipes page 170 and page 172). In the old days of this grape-rich nation, Chileans used grape leaves rather than cabbage leaves for* **Niños Envueltos.** *However, cabbage leaves are larger, are easy to work with, and make for a tasty "blanket." As luck would have it, I literally heard this recipe through the grapevine: Elcira Parra (whose surname means "grapevine") passed it along to me.*

1. Bring a medium-size pot of water to a boil, then add a cabbage leaf to the pot. You may need to fold it in order to fully submerge it. Use a spatula to remove the cabbage leaf when it's soft and pliant. This should take about 15 seconds if the cabbage leaves are fairly flexible, but can take over a minute if they are stiff. (Turn them over in the water to ensure they cook evenly.) Repeat with remaining leaves. (You can also boil more than one leaf at a time). Allow the cabbage leaves to cool.

2. Heat the oil in a skillet over medium heat. When hot, add the beef. Stir frequently and add hot pepper flakes to taste. When the beef has browned, add the garlic and rice. After a few minutes, add the carrot, bell pepper and salt (about ½ teaspoon). Stir frequently.

The stuffed cabbage leaves

5 to 6 large leaves from one small green cabbage, thoroughly washed and carefully removed from the head (without breaking)

1 tablespoon extra-virgin olive oil

6 ounces boneless beef, cut in ½-inch squares

Hot red pepper flakes

3 large cloves garlic, finely chopped

¼ cup uncooked rice

1 small carrot, diced into ¼-inch cubes

¼ red bell pepper, chopped in small pieces

Salt

2 tablespoons finely chopped fresh parsley

The sauce

3 tomatoes (12 ounces), peeled and thinly sliced (from top to bottom)

1 small onion, thinly sliced (from top to bottom)

1 clove garlic, finely chopped

Salt and freshly ground black pepper

3. After three minutes, add 1 cup water and the parsley. Cover and reduce the heat to low.

4. When the water is fully absorbed, after about 10 to 15 minutes, remove the skillet from the heat. Add more water while cooking if the rice is still hard.

5. Remove the core from the cabbage leaves and discard because the cabbage leaves need to be flexible for rolling.

6. Place a cabbage leaf on a board. Place ¼ to ⅓ cup of the meat mixture on the part of the leaf nearest you. First fold the two sides over the mixture and then roll the leaf away from you, so the mixture is snugly inside the leaf and will not fall out. Secure the stuffed cabbage leaf with a toothpick by wedging it into the leaf as you would wedge a safety pin into a folded diaper. Repeat for each leaf. If you find that folding the leaves is simple, you can fold the same amount of meat mixture in only a half, rather than a whole, leaf. Or you can double the amount of stuffed leaves by wrapping just 1½ tablespoons of meat mixture in a half leaf.

7. Put the tomatoes, onion, garlic, salt and pepper, and ½ cup of water in a pot. Place the stuffed cabbage leaves on top. Do not overlap. (Cook in two batches if the pot is not wide enough.) Cook, covered, over high heat. When mixture boils, reduce the heat to low and cook 10 more minutes so that the rice inside the cabbage leaves is fully cooked. Remove the toothpicks before serving. Serve hot, with a side dish of *Salsa de Ají Verde* (see recipe, page 25).

Wine Suggestion -
Valdivieso Pinot Noir Reserva

Stuffed Zucchini Layered with Melted Cheese

Zapallo Italiano Relleno   4 servings

Chilean cuisine is littered with Arabic words, attesting to the Moorish influence on Chile's own colonizers, the Spanish. While the flavors of the Middle East are most salient in Chile's desserts, this dish illustrates how the Arab's predilection for stuffed vegetables also found its ways into the Chilean diet. Stuffed bell peppers, hot peppers, tomatoes, and zucchini all festoon the Chilean dinner table. The recipe below appears to be a hybrid of the legacy left on Chile by both the Arabs and Italians, with zucchini and cheese serving as the base and topping of this pleasantly smoky dish.

4 large zucchini (3½ pounds)
6 tablespoons olive oil
2 small onions, finely chopped
1 carrot, peeled and grated
4 cloves garlic, finely chopped
14 ounces ground beef
⅓ teaspoon ground cumin
Salt
8 long strips of cheddar cheese (6 ounces)

1. Preheat the oven to 400° F

2. Boil the zucchini whole until tender. Remove and let cool. Peel if the skin is scarred or undesirable.

3. When the zucchini are cool, cut each in half lengthwise, and remove the seeds and a bit of the zucchini flesh to create a hole, discard. Lightly sprinkle salt on the zucchini halves.

4. Put 2 tablespoons of olive oil in a skillet over medium heat. When hot, add the onion, carrot, and garlic. When the onion is translucent, add the ground beef. Stir frequently until the beef is just cooked, then remove from heat. Mix in cumin and salt to taste.

5. Evenly divide the beef mixture between the zucchini halves by placing 3 to 4 tablespoons into each. Sprinkle the remaining olive oil over the zucchini. Cover with slices of cheese.

6. Place the stuffed zucchini on a baking pan.

7. Place the pan in the oven and remove the dish when the cheese has melted thoroughly, about 5 to 7 minutes.

Wine Suggestion
Gracia Merlot Shiraz Leyenda

Pescado y Mariscos

C hile has won the reputation of being home to wonderful fish for more than a few reasons. The sea bass, also known as Patagonian toothfish, or in Chile as *bacalao de profundidad*, has been all of the rage at posh restaurants in the U.S. over the past few years. And Chile has been battling with Norway to be the leader in salmon exports worldwide. Fish seems to take on a romantic quality in Chile, with two of its prized writers, Pablo Neruda and Isabel Allende, singing praises to its intoxicating effects. For Allende, it is the sea urchin that holds a powerful allure, bringing her back to her youth and stoking her passions, while Neruda has spawned a legion of recipes for conger eel soup, with people trying to recreate the soup that he so treasured before his death.

It is almost impossible to make a sustained trip to Chile without bearing witness to the vivacity bubbling out of the fish markets that dot the country's lanky coast and to experiment some of those fish not seen elsewhere. While it is true that Chile has much more than fish, it is also true that if you arrive with your belly hyperfocused on sea creatures, you will not go home disappointed. Chile has streams and streams of different fish, and a dictionary on page 257 indicates those that you will most likely find in Chile and what they are, or approximate, in the U.S.

Fish and Seafood

Creamy Flounder

Reineta a la Alusafoy   2 servings

This fish dish makes up a part of what Claudia Charlin considers the ideal meal in beautiful La Serena. This is a sunny beach resort neighboring the mountainous and fruit-rich Elqui Valley (Valle del Elqui). The meal calls upon numerous specialties of the region, beginning with a **Serena Libre** cocktail (see recipe, page 222), then follows with an appetizer of **Empanadas con Ostiones y Queso** or other shellfish turnover (see recipe, page 62). Below is a recipe for the main course, which goes well with boiled potatoes or **Arroz Chileno** (see recipe, page 46). The meal is topped off with **Papayas con Crema** (see recipe, page 210).

Salt
1 medium flounder
(1¼ pounds), cut in half
down the side
1 tablespoon softened butter
2 cloves garlic, pureed with a
mortar and pestle
1 teaspoon dried oregano
3 tablespoons extra-virgin
olive oil
4 thin strips (about 3 ounces)
Swiss cheese
1 tablespoon heavy cream

1. Preheat the oven to 350 degrees F.

2. Sprinkle salt generously on both sides of the fish.

3. Brush butter on a sheet of aluminum foil long enough to enclose the fish.

4. Mix the garlic, oregano and olive oil in a bowl. Brush both sides of fish with the mixture. Place in the center of the aluminum foil. Top with thin slices of cheese and brush lightly with the cream. Fold the aluminum foil over the fish. Do not cover tightly as the cheese will melt onto the aluminum foil. Place the wrapped fish in a baking pan if you're concerned that the fish juice will spill out of the aluminum foil into the oven.

5. Cook in the oven for 10 to 15 minutes, or until the fish becomes opaque. Poke a knife into the center to ensure that the middle is just-cooked, white and moist. Remove the fish from the pan and pour the juices over the fish. Serve with rice, potato salad, or boiled potatoes.

Wine Suggestion
Montes Chardonnay

Sole Layered with Olives and Zucchini

Lenguado a la Aceituna   2 servings

One of the keys to this dish is a rich, tasty fish broth, since when serving you add several spoonfuls of broth to provide added moistness and flavor. Most of the work in this recipe is in the slicing of the potatoes, zucchini and olives. I recommend you have everything sliced, all three skillets ready (with oil or broth), and plates ready on the table before you start cooking. That is because you will be cooking with three skillets and each of the dishes requires no more than five to seven minutes of cooking time.

The fish

3/4 cup Fish Stock (see recipe, page 132)
1 sole fillet (14 ounces), cut into 3-inch pieces
1 zucchini (6 ounces)
1/2 cup pitted olives, half green and half black
1 tablespoon extra-virgin olive oil
Salt and freshly ground black pepper
10 to 12 ounces baking potatoes, such as russets, cut into shoestring French fries
2 cups vegetable oil for deep-frying
Salt

1. Heat the fish stock in a skillet over medium heat. When hot, add the fish. Cook for five to seven minutes, turning once. Remove when the fish has become opaque. Poke a knife in the center to ensure that the middle is just-cooked, white and moist.

2. Cut the zucchini lengthwise into 1/2-inch-thick slices. Cut the olives lengthwise into about five pieces. Heat the olive oil in a skillet over medium heat. When hot, add the zucchini and olives, salt and ground black pepper. Sauté for three minutes.

3. Heat the oil in a skillet on high heat. When the skillet is hot, submerge the potatoes in the vegetable oil, lightly salt and deep-fry until the potatoes are golden brown. Remove.

4. Synchronizing all of the dishes to be hot and ready at the same time, remove the sole, leaving the fish broth in the skillet. Place the sole on a hot plate, and cover it with the zucchini mixture. Place shoestring fries around the fish. Ladle about 1/4 cup of fish broth onto each dish.

Wine Suggestion

Misiones de Rengo Reserva Chardonnay

Fried Hake

Merluza Frita

One of the luxuries of being in Chile is the ability to enjoy fresh, fried fish at restaurants all over the country for just a few dollars. Or, for those Chileans who cook at home, a few fish can be bought on the street for just a dollar or two. Consequently, there is no dearth of ways that Chileans fry fish. Below are two of my favorite ways. The first method produces a rich, fried fish with a thick shell. It calls upon hake, the most common and inexpensive fish in Chile that is alternatively called **merluza** *and* **pescada***. Home chefs often fry the hake eggs as well, either alone with a bit of salt or first coating it in toasted flour. The second recipe creates a lighter and spicier way to enjoying fresh fish.*

The fish
2 medium hake or conger eel
  (2 pounds, without head)
Salt
3 teaspoons dried oregano

The batter
1¼ cup flour
½ cup beer, straight from the
  can or bottle
2 eggs
¼ cup finely grated carrot
  (about 1 small carrot)

2 cups vegetable oil for
  deep-frying

1. Wash the fish and cut it into four pieces. Sprinkle both sides with the salt and oregano.

2. Put the flour, beer, and ⅓ cup of water in a bowl. Mix lightly. Add the eggs and the grated carrot and mix thoroughly, removing any lumps. Add a bit more water, if necessary, to ensure that the mixture is neither very dense nor very light.

3. Coat the fish thoroughly in the batter.

4. Heat the oil in a skillet over medium heat. Add enough oil to fully submerge the fish pieces. When the oil is hot but not smoking, carefully add the fish, being sure not to lose much of the batter when putting it in the skillet. Do not crowd the fish in the skillet. You will probably have to cook the fish in batches or in two skillets simultaneously.

5. Reduce the heat to medium-low. Fry the fish until golden brown on both sides and cooked inside, about 8 to 10 minutes (the precise time will vary according to the fish's thickness). Remove the fish from the skillet and place on paper towels to absorb excess oil.

Wine Suggestion - - - - - - - - - - - - Or - - - - - - - - - - -
Valdivieso Chardonnay

Spicy Fried Smelt

*In Chile, smelt is typically doused in batter and fried. This has given rise to a range of simple "imitation" vegetable dishes. Called **Pejeyrrey Falso** (False Smelt), a vegetable such as green beans, eggplant, or chard is salted and then battered. They are then fried and served hot. This recipe was brainstormed by Hortensia Mora in Lota.*

The fish

2 pounds smelt
Salt
1/2 teaspoon hot red pepper
  flakes
1/2 teaspoon ground cumin

The batter

1 cup flour
1/4 cup finely grated carrot
  (about 1 small carrot)
1 teaspoon baking powder

2 cups vegetable oil for
  deep-frying

1. Halve each fish lengthwise and wash thoroughly. Sprinkle the salt, hot pepper flakes, and cumin on one side of each piece of fish.

2. Mix the flour, water, grated carrot, and baking powder together in a bowl to make the batter.

3. Coat the fish thoroughly in the batter.

4. Heat the oil in a skillet over medium heat. Add enough oil to fully submerge the fish pieces. When the oil is hot but not smoking, add the fish. Do not crowd the fish in the skillet. You will probably have to cook the fish in batches or in two skillets simultaneously.

5. Reduce the heat to medium-low. Fry the fish until golden brown on both sides, about 5 to 7 minutes (the precise time will vary according to the fish's thickness). The fish will become opaque when cooked. Poke a knife in the center to ensure that the middle is just-cooked, white and moist. Remove the fish from the skillet and place on paper towels to absorb excess oil.

Wine Suggestion

Veramonte Sauvignon Blanc

Chilean Sea Bass in White Wine Sauce

Pescado al Horno   4 servings

Found all over Chile, this dish is a tasty combination of layers of potatoes, onions, and tomatoes, with a fish nestled within. Everything cooks slowly in white wine. Make sure that the potatoes and onions are finely sliced, so that the fish and potatoes are both cooked within thirty minutes or so. I love how the tomatoes and white wine combine to create a delicious, moist sauce for the fish. Tomatoes, onions, and potatoes are all cut in julienne strips. The potatoes are placed on top in order to cook fully. Since there aren't that many potatoes, and there is a rich sauce, you can also serve diners white rice as a side dish.

1½ to 2 pounds Chilean sea bass (with skin and bones)
Salt
4 cloves garlic, finely chopped
1½ teaspoons dried oregano
1½ teaspoons butter
1 small onion, thinly sliced
2 medium tomatoes (10 ounces), peeled and thinly sliced widthwise
½ pound baking potatoes, such as russets, thinly sliced widthwise
½ cup dry white wine
2 to 3 tablespoons extra-virgin olive oil

1. Preheat the oven to 400° F. Grease the bottom of a baking pan (approximately 9 x 13).

2. Wash the fish and cut it into 4-inch pieces. Season lightly on both sides with salt, garlic, and oregano.

3. Add half of the onion, then half of the tomatoes to the prepared pan. Place the fish on top. Cover the fish with the rest of the onion, then the tomatoes, and then the potatoes. Pour the white wine over the entire dish. Sprinkle with salt and the olive oil.

4. Put the pan into the oven and bake the fish for about 20 to 25 minutes, removing when the potatoes are golden and tender. While cooking ensure the potatoes stay moist by occasionally basting with the pan juices. The fish will become opaque when cooked. Poke a knife in the center to ensure that the middle is just-cooked, white and moist.

Wine Suggestion

Undurraga Sauvignon Blanc

Rockfish and Shrimp with Melted Cheese

Pescado al Jugo 4 servings

One of the traditional ways of cooking fish in Chile is in the oven, layered with onions, tomatoes, and cheese. Many mothers amble to the fishmonger on the corner of their street, in their port, or at their local outdoors market to get the fresh catch of the day. As with many Chilean fish recipes, home chefs stick to one technique of preparation but vary the fish they use, which is ultimately dictated by the whims or wishes of the fishermen, or the day's winds.

Salt
1½ teaspoons dried oregano
1¾ pounds rockfish fillet, cut into four pieces
1½ tablespoons softened butter or extra-virgin olive oil
1 onion (5 ounces), cut into thin rings
2 tomatoes (10 ounces), peeled and cut into rings
¼ cup white wine
3 to 4 ounces mild cheese such as thin mozzarella strips
2 tablespoons Parmesan cheese
½ cup (3½ ounces) shrimp

1. Preheat the oven to 350° F.

2. Sprinkle salt and oregano on both sides of the fish and place the fish in a large baking pan (approximately 9 x 13 inches). Spread the butter on the top of the fish, and place the onion and tomatoes evenly on top.

3. Put the baking pan into the oven. After about 3 minutes, when the butter has melted, pour ¼ cup white wine over the fish.

4. Bake the fish another 15 minutes. About 3 minutes before the fish is done, add the shrimp, then cover it with the mild and Parmesan cheeses. Remove the fish from the oven when the cheese has melted and the fish has become opaque. Poke a knife in the center to ensure that the middle is just-cooked, white and moist.

Wine Suggestion

MontGras Estate Chardonnay

Croaker in Ham, Bacon, and Mushroom Sauce

Corvina Papillón   4 servings

- - - - - - *This dish's name refers to fish cooked in aluminum foil. Such a technique is popular in southern Chile, as it is elsewhere in the country. If you are in Chile and are looking for fish dishes like these, check for the words* **papillote or alusafoy** *on the menu as well. They are almost always moist and delicious.*

2¼ pounds filleted croaker or conger eel, halved lengthwise
Salt
1½ ounces ham, coarsely chopped
1½ ounces bacon, finely chopped
4½ ounces mushrooms, coarsely chopped
½ medium onion, finely chopped
3 tablespoons olive oil
½ cup white wine
10 mussels, cleaned and scrubbed

1. Preheat the oven to 350° F.

2. Bring a medium-size pot of water to a boil.

3. Put the fish in a large baking pan (approximately 9 x 13) and sprinkle with salt. Add the ham, bacon, mushrooms, and onion. Pour the olive oil and white wine over the fish. Cover with aluminum foil.

4. Put the fish in the oven and cook for 15 to 20 minutes.

5. About 6 to 8 minutes before the fish is cooked, add the mussels to the boiling water. Cook them until they open, about 5 minutes. Remove the mussels from their shells and halve them.

6. When the fish is cooked, the flesh will become opaque. Remove it from the oven. Poke a knife in the center to ensure that the middle is just-cooked, white, and moist. Sprinkle the mussels over the fish. Ladle the pan juices over the fish.

Wine Suggestion -
Siegel El Crucero Chardonnay Reserve

Stuffed Salmon

Cancato 4 servings

Chiloé is a lovely archipelago on the Pacific Ocean filled with its own lore and recipes. One arrives at the island via ferry from the mainland and it is immediately clear that this is not a place consumed by supersonic economic and technological change, but rather a place that cherishes simple honest-to-goodness cooking and living. Soledad Vera López and her husband Jorge treated me like a special guest in their home. In actuality I was in their restaurant in the town of Ancud, in Chiloé, which offered the salmon dish below.

3 tablespoons extra-virgin olive oil

1 small onion (5 ounces), cut in julienne strips

2 tomatoes (10 ounces), peeled and coarsely chopped

5 ounces mild sausage, cooked and coarsely chopped

2 salmon fillets (1½ pounds), each halved lengthwise

3 ounces mozzarella cheese, thinly sliced

1 teaspoon dried oregano

Salt and freshly ground black pepper

lemon wedges for serving (optional)

1. Heat 1 tablespoon of the oil in a skillet over medium heat. When the oil is hot, add the onions and tomatoes and cook for 3 minutes, stirring frequently. The onions will be translucent and the tomatoes somewhat saucy. Add the sausage and cook for an additional minute. Keep warm.

2. Lightly salt and pepper both sides of the salmon. Divide the remaining oil between two skillets and heat over a low flame. When the oil in the two skillets is hot but not smoking, add the fillets. Flip each of the fillets when golden brown, or after about 3½ minutes.

3. Place the cheese on two of the fillets and sprinkle with the oregano. Cover the skillet, and continue cooking for about 3 minutes, until the salmon is cooked and the cheese has melted. Like steak, salmon can be eaten rare. If you prefer it well-done, do not overdo it or the flesh will toughen and become dry. In the other skillet, continue cooking the two fillets without cheese, uncovered, until they are cooked to your desired taste.

4. Place the salmon without the cheese on a plate. Layer the sausage mixture over them, then top with one of the remaining fillets. Cut each in half and serve on four plates with lemon.

Wine Suggestion

San Esteban Cabernet Sauvignon

Sautéed Salmon with Shrimp and Mushrooms

Salmón con Salsa Mar y Tierra   4 servings

Chile is one of the world's leading providers of salmon, with almost half of the world's top salmon producers. Not surprisingly, recipes for salmon abound. This one comes from Bellamar Restaurant in Concón, a restaurant offering a wonderful seaside view of the Pacific Ocean. Santiago Herrera and Georgina Pardo, from the restaurant, substitute cognac or whiskey for sherry on occasion.

2 tablespoons extra-virgin
  olive oil
2¼ pounds fresh salmon
  fillets
8 cloves garlic, finely
  chopped
7 ounces mushrooms, cut in
  julienne strips
10 ounces shelled shrimp
¾ cup dry sherry
¼ cup finely chopped fresh
  parsley
Salt and freshly ground black
  pepper

1. Heat 1 tablespoon of the oil in a skillet over medium heat. When the skillet is hot add the salmon. Cook until it is golden brown on both sides, about 7 minutes. Like steak, salmon can be eaten rare. If you prefer it well-done, do not overdo it or the flesh will toughen and become dry.

2. Meanwhile, put the remaining oil in a saucepan or skillet over medium heat. When the saucepan is hot, add the garlic. After 2 minutes, add the mushrooms and cook for two more minutes, stirring frequently. Add the shrimp and cook about 2 to 3 minutes, stirring frequently.

3. Increase the heat to high, add the sherry, and ignite it for a few seconds. Shake the saucepan and continue cooking until the sherry boils down to make a sauce, about 45 seconds.

4. Remove the saucepan from the heat and sprinkle with chopped parsley and salt and pepper to taste.

5. Ladle the sauce over the salmon. Serve with white rice or *Papas Duquesas* (see recipe, page 49).

Wine Suggestion - - - - - - - - - - - - - - - - - -
Calina Chardonnay Reserve

Croaker Salad

Ceviche de Corvina   4 servings

Ceviche is found all across Chile. There are numerous variations, but it almost always includes raw fish, onions, garlic, cilantro, and ample lemon juice. While in neighboring Peru lime juice is common, in Chile lemon juice is generally used, except in northern Chile where lime is plentiful. In the north the dish is also often hotter, with the addition of the rocoto *pepper. Lemon or lime juice is what "cooks" the* ceviche, *so be generous with it.*

1 filleted croaker (1¼ pounds), or if you are filleting yourself, buy a 2 pound croaker
⅔ cup freshly squeezed lemon juice
⅓ cup finely chopped onions or scallions (about ½ small onion)
1 clove garlic, finely chopped
4 tablespoons finely chopped cilantro
1 teaspoon vegetable oil
1 teaspoon salt
Freshly ground black pepper

1. Wash the fish thoroughly.

2. Mix the lemon juice, onions, garlic, cilantro, vegetable oil, and salt in a bowl. Cut the fish into ½-inch cubes and place in the bowl. Cover and place in the refrigerator. Stir occasionally.

3. Allow the fish to marinate at least 2 to 3 hours, until the fish turns from red to white or gray (i.e., when it is fully "cooked" by the lemon). If you marinate the fish for the entire day, the *ceviche* is even tastier. You can refrigerate *ceviche* for up to 5 days.

4. Before serving, mix again, and add salt and ground pepper to taste.

Wine Suggestion
Gracia de Chile Chardonnay

Mussel and Clam Salad

Mariscal Frio   4 servings, as an appetizer

With shellfish so fresh in Chile, many people have no fear of eating it raw. That is how mariscal frio *is often prepared, with a good dose of lemon dousing out anyone's concerns about eating raw such shellfish such as* choritos *(mussels),* almejas *(little neck clams),* machas *(razor clams), or* ulte *and* piure, *two native specimens (the former a soft, long, brown fish, the latter a fish that looks like a marinated red bell pepper and is quite pungent). However, many also prepare* mariscal frio *by steaming the shellfish (cooking "al vapor"), as the recipe below has you do. A second dish,* mariscal caliente, *is also quite common in Chile, and serves as the hot, richer version. The recipe below can easily be doubled to serve as a meal in itself.*

6½ pounds shellfish, such as mussels and clams, cleaned and scrubbed
3 tablespoons freshly squeezed lemon juice
1 tablespoon vegetable oil
2 tablespoons finely chopped onion
1 tablespoon finely chopped fresh cilantro
1 tablespoon finely chopped fresh chives
1 tablespoon finely chopped red bell pepper
Salt
A few drops hot pepper sauce

1. Steam the shellfish by placing it in a large pot with about 2 inches of water. You may have to do this in batches. Cover and cook over medium heat. When the shells have completely opened, remove the meat.

2. Mix the lemon juice, vegetable oil, onion, cilantro, chives, and bell pepper in a medium bowl. When the shellfish have cooled, remove the meat, and place in the bowl. Add salt to taste and two or three drops of hot pepper, mix again, and serve.

Wine Suggestion

Santa Emiliana Sauvignon Blanc

Fish Stock

This is a stock that can be used for many Chilean dishes and fish recipes, in general. Subtle, it is essential for dishes like **Paila Marina** *and* **Caldillo de Congrio**.

1½ pounds fish parts (such as conger eel)
1 large red bell pepper, coarsely chopped
1 large onion, coarsely chopped
6 to 8 whole peppercorns

1. Put the fish, bell pepper, onion, and peppercorns in a large pot with 12 cups (3 quarts) of water. Cover and bring to a boil.

2. When the water boils, remove the lid, reduce the heat to medium-low and simmer. Skim frequently to remove any fat that rises to the surface. Simmer 1½ hours, leaving about 7 cups of stock. To make a stronger stock, you can continue cooking until 3½ to 4 cups of liquid remain.

3. Strain and discard the fish and vegetables.

Conger Eel Chowder

Caldillo de Congrio   4 servings

The conger eel holds a special place in the heart of many Chileans. That is because the famed national poet Pablo Neruda—an inspiration to countless people in the country—paid special homage to the conger eel in a poem that captured the writer's sensuality and the fish's essence. That poem is found following this recipe, which also faithfully honors the way that the chowder to this day is prepared with love and that exquisite sea creature. Tasty, and long and lean in form, the poem is much like the nation of Chile.

7 cups Fish Stock (see recipe, page 132)
1 tablespoon extra-virgin olive oil
1 onion, finely chopped
1 medium carrot, coarsely grated
3 cloves garlic, finely chopped
½ small red bell pepper, finely chopped
1 large tomato (7 ounces), peeled and coarsely chopped
⅔ teaspoon paprika
½ teaspoon dried oregano
2 large boiling potatoes (1 pound), peeled and halved
¾ cup dry white wine
1 tablespoon freshly squeezed lemon juice
¼ teaspoon Pure Hot Pepper Sauce (see recipe, page 25)
Salt and freshly ground black pepper to taste
1 conger eel (2½ pounds), cut in four parts, about 4 or 5 x 2-inches each
1 tablespoon heavy cream
Lemon wedges

1. Heat the fish stock in a large pot.

2. Meanwhile, heat the oil in a skillet over medium heat. When it is hot but not smoking, add the onion, carrot, garlic, and bell pepper. Stir frequently, and after 3 minutes add the tomato, paprika, and oregano.

3. Cook the tomato mixture for 3 minutes and then add it to the fish stock. Add the potatoes, wine, lemon juice, hot sauce, and salt and pepper to taste. Cover and bring to a boil. Then reduce the heat, and simmer until the potatoes are slightly tender, about 15 minutes.

4. Add the fish. Continue simmering, until the fish begins to fall off the bone, about 15 minutes. Typically the bones are not discarded before serving. Skim off any excess oil that rises to the surface of the pot. Mix in the cream and additional salt to taste and remove the pot from the heat. Serve in individual earthenware bowls with lemon wedges.

Wine Suggestion

Casa Lapostolle Cuvée Alexandre Chardonnay

Ode to Conger Chowder

by Pablo Neruda

IN THE tempestuous
sea
of Chile
there lives the rosy conger,
a gigantic eel
of snow-white flesh.
And in Chilean
stewpots,
along the coast,
the chowder was born
rich and succulent,
a boon.
Bring to the kitchen
the stripped conger,
its spotty skin yielding
like a glove
and then revealed
is
the cluster from the sea,
the tender conger
sparkles
now nude,
prepared
for our appetite.
Now
you gather
garlic,
caressing first
that precious
ivory,
smelling
its ireful fragrance,
then
allow the minced garlic
to plunge in with the onion
and the tomato
until the onion

Oda al Caldillo de Congrio

EN EL mar
tormentoso
de Chile
vive el rosado congrio,
gigante anguila
de nevada carne.
Y en las ollas
chilenas,
en la costa,
nació el caldillo
grávido y suculento,
provechoso.
Lleven a la cocina
el congrio desollado,
su piel machada cede
como un guante
y al descubierto queda
entonces
el racimo del mar,
el congrio tierno
reluce
ya desnudo,
preparado
para nuestro apetito.
Ahora
recoges
ajos,
acaricia primero
ese marfil
precioso
huele
su fragancia iracunda,
entonces
deja el ajo picado
caer con la cebolla
y el tomate
hasta que la cebolla

takes on the color of gold.	*tenga color de oro.*
Meanwhile	*Mientras tanto*
cook	*se cuecen*
in the steam	*con el vapor*
the regal	*los regios*
marine shrimp	*camarones marinos*
and when they have reached	*y cuando ya llegaron*
their point,	*a su punto,*
when the flavors have melded	*cuando cuajó el sabor*
into a sauce	*en una salsa*
formed by the juices	*formada por el jugo*
of the sea	*del océano*
and by the clear water	*y por el agua clara*
unleashed by the onion's light,	*que desprendió la luz de la cebolla,*
then	*entonces*
let the conger enter	*que entre el congrio*
to submerge itself in glory,	*y se sumerja en gloria,*
while there in the stewpot	*que en la olla*
it lubricates,	*se aceite,*
shrinks, and impregnates.	*se contraiga y se impregne.*
Now all that is needed	*Ya sólo es necesario*
is to allow the cream to fall	*dejar en el manjar*
into the delicacy	*caer la crema*
like a heavy rose,	*como una rosa espesa,*
and the flame	*y al fuego*
slowly	*lentamente*
delivers the treasure	*entregar el tesoro*
until inside the stewpot	*hasta que en el caldillo*
the essences of Chile	*se calienten*
are heated,	*las esencias de Chile,*
and the tastes	*y a la mesa*
from sea and land	*lleguen recién casados*
arrive newly wed	*los sabores*
to the table	*del mar y de la tierra*
so that in this dish	*para que en ese plato*
you know heaven.	*tú conozcas el cielo.*

This poem has been reproduced with the permission of the Pablo Neruda Estate.

Eel and Shellfish Soup

Paila Marina   4 servings

This is a quick dish to make if you have ample fish stock on hand. It hails from the thriving port of Valparaíso, where fresh fish and shellfish combine to make rich, memorable soups. Usually it includes one fish, such as conger eel, shored up by a variety of shellfish, and served in a greda. If you can find a few giant barnacles at your fish market, throw them into the soup. They are as succulent and prized in Chile as lobster is in the U.S.

8 cups Fish Stock (see recipe, page 132)
1 to 1½ pounds conger eel or other fish, with bones
1½ teaspoons oregano
1 pound (about 12) mussels in their shells, cleaned and scrubbed
1 pound (about 9) littleneck clams in their shells, cleaned and scrubbed
2 to 3 giant barnacles (if available)
¼ cup plus 1 tablespoon tomato sauce or tomato juice
¼ cup finely chopped fresh scallions or chives
1 teaspoon freshly squeezed lemon juice
Salt and freshly ground black pepper

1. Bring the fish broth to a boil in a large pot. When it boils, add the eel and the oregano. Cover and reduce the heat to low. Simmer until the fish is almost cooked, about 10 minutes. Remove any fat that rises to the surface.

2. Mix in the mussels, clams, barnacles, and tomato sauce. Continue cooking, covered, until the mussels and clams open, about 3 minutes.

3. Stir in the scallions, lemon juice, and salt and pepper to taste. Serve with plain white rice.

Wine Suggestion

Santa Rita Medalla Real Chardonnay

Crab Salad

Escarapachos

- - - - - *Known as* jaiba mayo *in northern Chile,* jaiba reina *in Los Vilos, and most commonly as* carapachos *or* escarapachos *in the rest of Chile, this dish is a wonderful way to eat crab cold. If buying fresh crabs in the shells, save the shells for decoration. Simply serve the crab salad in the shell, on a bed of lettuce with a lemon wedge. A caveat: Do not use sweet mayonnaise to make this dish. I found that when I tried, for example, Hellmann's Mayonnaise in the U.S., the dish was too sweet and the mayonnaise overwhelmed the flavor of the crab.*

2 pounds crabmeat
1 onion, cut in thin strips, then washed, and chopped very coarsely
$\frac{1}{3}$ cup finely chopped fresh cilantro
$\frac{1}{3}$ cup freshly squeezed lemon juice
2 tablespoons vegetable oil
$\frac{1}{3}$ cup Mayonnaise (see recipe, page 29) (approximately)
Salt

1. Place the crabmeat in a bowl and mix in the onion, cilantro, lemon juice, and vegetable oil.

2. Slowly mix in the mayonnaise until moist. Add the salt and serve cold.

Wine Suggestion - - - - - - - - - - - -

Palo Alto Sauvignon Blanc

Sea Scallops in a Spicy Butter Sauce

Ostiones al Pilpil

4 to 6 servings

Few cultures appreciate scallops as much as Chileans, and this traditional dish has all the meaty, buttery allure of a French mussel dish, but with the distinctive heat and spice of Latin America. **Pilpil** *refers to the combination of garlic and hot pepper that is used to make several Chilean dishes, particularly shellfish ones. In this recipe, the sherry and hot red pepper really bring the sea scallops to life, but be careful, as too fiery a sauce will mask the scallops' succulent flavor. Be sure to serve this with plenty of bread to soak up the delicious juices, and consider serving it as a light entree with just salad and rolls for those evenings when you want big flavor but not a heavy meal. Excellent substitutes for scallops that Chileans use are shrimp and calamari in dishes called, respectively,* **Camarones al Pilpil** *and* **Calamares al Pilpil.** *Shrimp and calamari would only need to be cooked for about 3 minutes.*

6 tablespoons butter
⅓ cup extra-virgin olive oil
1 teaspoon finely chopped dried hot pepper, such as California Chili Pods or New Mexico Chili Pods; or use red hot pepper flakes or *kirmizi biber*
4 cloves garlic, finely chopped
20 to 30 sea scallops (1 pound shelled)
Salt and freshly ground black pepper
2 teaspoons finely chopped fresh cilantro
1 teaspoon cognac

1. In a small saucepan over a medium-low flame, heat the butter along with the olive oil, hot pepper, and garlic. When the butter is melted, add the scallops and sprinkle with salt and pepper.

2. Stirring frequently, cook for 3 to 4 minutes, until the scallops become opaque and a bit firm.

3. A minute before removing the scallops from the heat, add the cilantro and cognac. Shake the pan briefly and remove from heat. Serve with fresh bread for dipping in the sauce.

Wine Suggestion
Cono Sur Visión Viognier

Razor Clams in Parmesan Sauce

Machas a la Parmesana   4 servings

- - - - - *Razor clams are far more common in Chile than in the U.S. And they are not long and rectangular, like the razor clams in the U.S., but rather are shaped like mussels. They are also three times smaller, and upon cooking take on a reddish hue. Whichever razor clams you use, you must pound the clam meat in order to tenderize it before cooking it. With these, I love a creamy sherry sauce with ample Parmesan cheese.*

8 razor clams, with shells
3 tablespoons butter, melted
1½ tablespoons sherry
5 teaspoons heavy cream
2 tablespoons Parmesan
  cheese
¼ teaspoon salt
Freshly ground black pepper

1. Preheat the oven to 450° F.

2. Remove the clams from their shells. Clean them, removing the black film or cream. Lightly pound the clam meat (I use a pestle) to make it tender. Wash the shells. Place each clam back in a half shell. (You will only need eight). Place the clams in one or two baking pans.

3. Mix the butter, sherry, cream, and salt and pepper in a small bowl. Pour 1 teaspoon of the mixture over each clam. Sprinkle the Parmesan cheese evenly over the clams.

4. Put the clams into the oven on the top rack. Remove them when the cheese turns golden after about 3 minutes.

Wine Suggestion -
Concha y Toro Trio Sauvignon Blanc

Mussels with Rice

Arroz con Cholgas

This dish is frequently eaten on the coast of southern Chile, where mussels are invariably fresh. Many people run out to the shore, roll up their pants a bit, and pan for their own mussels for the evening meal. As the fresh mussels steam, people gather around the pot to inhale the wonderful, briny aroma of the recently-collected "fruits from the sea." Mussels come in all sizes in Chile, some of them surprising. They start with the itty-bitty chuchita, *then comes the* chorito, *still larger is the* cholga, *then comes the* choro, *and finally there is the immense* choro zapato. *It's called "mussel shoe" because it's the size of a shoe: more than half of a foot long.*

3 tablespoons extra-virgin olive oil
½ medium onion, finely chopped
2 cloves garlic, finely chopped
2 cups uncooked white rice
2 teaspoons salt
10 ounces shelled mussels pure meat (about 1½ pounds mussels in shells), steamed
2 tablespoons finely chopped fresh cilantro
Freshly ground black pepper

1. Bring 7 cups of water to a boil.

2. Heat the oil in a deep skillet over a medium flame. When the oil is hot but not smoking, add the onion and garlic. When the onion is translucent, add the rice. Mix frequently so the rice does not burn. After the rice is golden brown, 3 to 5 minutes, add 5 cups of the boiling water and the salt. Cover and reduce the heat to low.

3. Continue cooking until the rice is tender, about 15 minutes. Add ½ to 1 cup of additional water to the pot if the rice is not tender after 15 minutes.

4. Mix in the mussels, cilantro, and pepper to taste, as well as additional salt, if necessary. Serve hot.

Wine Suggestion
Torrealba Sauvignon Blanc

Mussel and Clam Soup

Sopa de Cholgas y Almejas

4 to 6 servings

- - - - *Karen Silva learned how to make tantalizing shellfish soups from her grand-mother in the southern coastal town of Lota. The soups, says Karen, are full of nutrient-rich shellfish that can lift one's spirits, and even lift the dead (*levantar los muertos*). The dead, she says, might be those who are lazy, sluggish, or who have simply had a long, wine-ridden night out on the town. Such iron-laden soups can take on a cheerfully colorful hue in Chile because of the inclusion of local shellfish such as the fire engine red* piure *and the tan alga,* ulte. *These soups, bursting with a medley of shellfish are called* mariscal caliente. *This recipe is simpler, and while one can use a variety of shellfish, the soup is excellent with mussels and clams alone.*

2 tablespoons extra-virgin olive oil
1 small onion, finely chopped
1 carrot, grated
½ small red bell pepper, finely chopped
3 cloves garlic, finely chopped
¼ teaspoon ground cumin
1½ pounds boiling potatoes, peeled and cut into 1-inch cubes
8 cups (2 quarts) hot water
Salt
¼ cup uncooked rice
½ cup white wine
2 pounds mussels in shells
2 pounds littleneck clams in shells
Freshly ground black pepper
Finely chopped fresh cilantro
Lemon wedges

1. Heat the oil in a large pot over medium heat. When the oil is hot, add the onion, carrot, bell pepper, garlic, and cumin. Stir occasionally. After a few minutes, when the onions are translucent, add the potatoes, hot water, and salt to taste.

2. Cook the soup at a gentle boil, reducing the heat as necessary. After 15 minutes add the rice and wine. Cover, reduce the heat to low, and simmer for 10 to 15 more minutes. The rice and potatoes should almost be tender.

3. Add the mussels and clams, as well as 1 to 2 cups more water, cover again, and cook until the shells open, about 5 minutes.

4. Season with salt and pepper, top with the cilantro, and serve with lemon wedges for squeezing into the soup.

Wine Suggestion - - - - - - - - - - -
Luis Felipe Edwards Chardonnay

Mussels Sautéed in a Green Herb Sauce

Choritos en Salsa Verde   4 servings

This dish may reflect the strong French presence in Chile in the nineteenth and twentieth centuries. That influence continues today with French investment in Chilean wineries. Whatever the origin, who can question the pairing of mussels and wine from two of the nations that do them best? This recipe uses a salsa verde, or green sauce, which typically consists of chopped onions, lemon, and cilantro or parsley. Shellfish are sometimes served warm in this sauce, but they can also be served cold, almost like a ceviche.

3 ½ to 4 pounds mussels
¼ cup extra-virgin olive oil
1 onion, finely chopped
3 cloves garlic, finely chopped
3 tablespoons finely chopped fresh cilantro
4 tablespoons dry white wine
2 tablespoons heavy cream
Salt and freshly ground black pepper
½ to 1 teaspoon freshly squeezed lemon juice (optional)

1. Steam the mussels by putting them in a large pot with about 2 inches of water. You may have to do this in batches. Cover and cook over medium heat. When the shells have opened, remove the meat.

2. Heat the oil in a small saucepan over a medium flame. When the pan is hot but not smoking, add the onion and garlic. When the onion is translucent, add the cilantro. Gradually add the white wine and cream. Cook briefly, until you have a light, creamy sauce. Add the mussels to the saucepan with salt and pepper to taste. Stir thoroughly, mixing in a few drops of lemon juice, if desired. Serve immediately, with toasted bread for dipping into the rich sauce.

Wine Suggestion

Cremaschi Furlotti Tierra del Fuego Sauvignon Blanc

Sea Urchin Omelet

4 servings

According to Chileans, erizos (sea urchins) are an aphrodisiac. That would mean that there is quite a lot of love in Chile, since the country is one of the biggest netters of erizos in the world, accounting for about one third of global production. However, sea urchins also are found on most of the world's rocky coasts, including in California. The Japanese view sea urchins as the French do foie gras, and in Chile they are also marked up in price for the upper class.

The recipe below is viewed as one of the purest ways to enjoy the natural flavor of sea urchins, whose yellow tongues and profound odor can be either thoroughly enchanting or perturbing, depending on one's tastes. Some Chilean restaurants serve sea urchins raw, which you mix along with onions and cilantro served in a little saucer, accompanied with a few lemon wedges. Others substitute parsley for the cilantro. The foundations for this recipe come from Luzmira Quezada and her mother Mirna Gatica, who run the restaurant, El Apa. Founded in 1961, it overlooks the beautiful bay of Angelmo, in the southern port of Puerto Montt.

Vegetable oil for frying
½ cup finely chopped onion
(1 small onion)
8 eggs
4 teaspoons flour
2 tablespoons finely chopped parsley
8 sea urchins (1 cup sea urchin meat), pureed with a mortar and pestle
Salt and freshly ground black pepper

1. Heat 1 tablespoon of oil in an omelet pan over a medium flame. Add the onions and cook until translucent. Set aside.

2. In a bowl, lightly beat two of the eggs and mix with 1 teaspoon of the flour. Stir in 2 tablespoons of the cooked onions, 1½ teaspoons parsley, and salt and pepper. Add one quarter of the pureed sea urchins and stir thoroughly.

3. Heat 2 teaspoons of oil in the omelet pan over low heat. When hot, add the sea urchin mixture. Cook slowly and when firm and golden on the bottom, flip the entire *tortilla* over to brown the other side (do not fold like an omelet). I do this by having a large plate on standby and then rapidly moving the *tortilla* to the plate on its cooked side and then flipping it back to the skillet on its uncooked side. Repeat Step 2 to make three additional *tortillas*.

4. Serve immediately.

Wine Suggestion
Serve with a chardonnay or viognier.

Frogs' Legs

Anca de Rana   2 servings

Some Chileans believe that frogs' legs, like sea urchins, are an aphrodisiac. I had ample opportunity to find out in Talca, where many residents and several restaurants serve them. One restaurant has frogs encased in a glass pond, and diners select which one they would like, as American diners can sometimes elect their favorite lobster. If you drive on the local highways near Talca you might even see people selling them by the side of the road. Frogs abound in the Río Claro (Clear River) in Talca, especially in the warm months between September and March. In Talca, I decided to stop for lunch at the restaurant Las Viejas Cochinas, thanks to the recommendations of several townspeople. I later found that the restaurant had gained some notoriety due to local TV and newspaper coverage, and due to its vibrant name, which in English means roughly, "The Dirty Old Women." Of course, no restaurant would call itself that without having a tale to justify it. Briefly, here is how it goes:

> About a half century ago an elderly woman who owned a store in Talca passed away, as Marcela Orellana Yáñez, the restaurant's owner, recalls. Townspeople would walk past the woman's store and—obviously due to her reputation of being less than sanitary —would then declare, "There's the place of the dirty old woman!" The deceased woman's children, living nearby, were naturally offended and when passersby would inquire about the place of the "vieja cochina," they would point to the restaurant next door, called Restaurant El Turismo, and say, "It's over there." The restaurant, which had strong marks for the quality of its food, laughingly accepted that people call it both Restaurant El Turismo and Las Viejas Cochinas.

1½ pounds frogs' legs
Salt
⅓ teaspoon ground cumin
¾ cup flour
½ teaspoon baking soda
¼ cup dry white wine
Vegetable oil for deep-frying
Chancho en Piedra (see
 recipe, page 26)

1. If using freshly killed frogs, boil them in lightly salted water for about 30 minutes. Check the frogs for doneness by poking them with a wooden skewer, rather than a metal fork, as the latter will make the frogs hard. When the frogs' legs are tender, remove them from the water. If using frozen frogs' legs, defrost thoroughly.

2. Sprinkle salt and cumin on the frogs' legs.

3. Mix the flour, baking soda, white wine, and ½ cup water, removing any lumps of flour.

4. Dredge both sides of the cooked frogs' legs in the batter.

5. Heat the oil in a skillet over high heat. When the oil is hot, fry the frogs' legs for just a minute or two, until they are lightly browned. Serve with *Chancho en Piedra*.

Wine Suggestion –
El Huique Chardonnay Reserva

Wakame with Boiled Potatoes

Luche con Papas   6 servings

— — — — — — — *Luche is a long green seaweed that Chileans rustle away from the small rocks near the seashore. It is then sold in its moist, pre-cooked form in farmers' markets by vendors such as Fresia Muñoz in Lota. Fresia gave me the recipe below, which is the most typical use of seaweed. Potatoes are an invariable accompaniment served alongside, rather than cooked with, the* luche. *Because seaweed is purchased dry in the U.S., this recipe indicates how to moisten and cook one of Chile's long-adored sea plants.*

¼ ounce dried wakame
3 tablespoons extra-virgin olive oil, divided
Salt
1 medium onion, finely chopped
3 cloves garlic, pureed with a mortar and pestle
2 to 2½ pounds boiling potatoes, peeled, cooked in salted water, and halved

1. Let the wakame soak in water until fully moistened, 30 minutes. Heat 1 tablespoon of the olive oil in a skillet over low heat. When it is hot add the seaweed and cook, stirring frequently with a wooden spoon, until it is soft, about 5 to 10 minutes. Add salt to taste and stir in enough water to make the seaweed creamy, about 1½ cups.

2. In a separate skillet or saucepan, heat the rest of the oil over medium heat. When it is hot, add the onions and garlic and cook until translucent.

3. Stir the onion mixture into the seaweed mixture, adding salt as necessary. Cook for a few minutes to mesh flavors.

4. Serve the seaweed on a plate, with the hot potatoes.

Pollo, Aves de Corral, y Conejo

Throughout Chile's history its food has had a bewitching effect on visitors, largely because everything here comes right off the land (and out of the sea). When requesting traditional recipes from Chileans I quickly got a feel for how fresh the materials they use are. Frequently people told me to soak the recently killed rabbit or lamb overnight in salty water in order to remove its strong odor and to make it more tender. Chef Oriana Espinoza told me that if you are looking to buy a fresh rabbit, make sure that it is a young one, because the old ones are tough. (If your nails can pierce the rabbit, it is young and tender.) In Valparaíso, when I requested duck or rabbit in a market, a fellow would pluck one from a cage right before my eyes, disappear down the hall, then return moments later with the animal suspended from his left hand. While the country has changed immensely over the years—it is more developed and less isolated than ever—some Chileans would still be surprised to know that, in the U.S., all of this is conveniently ready for immediate preparation in grocery stores.

Poultry, Fowl, and Rabbit

Chicken Braised in Wine and Cumin

Pollo a la Cacerola   4 to 6 servings

This dish comes from Isabel Olivares Gallardo, one of the greatest proponents of traditional Chilean cuisine I have known. While a native of La Serena, Isabel has spent most of her life in Valparaíso, where she ran a corner food store for 22 years. In 2001, after selling her homemade empanadas, **Pan de Pascua, Cola de Mono,** *and other delights to great fanfare in the precipitous hill of Cerro Cordillera, she decided to use her cooking skills to start a restaurant opposite the pretty Parque Italia in the port city. Since the restaurant's opening, I have gone back again and again to try one of Isabel's countless homemade dishes. Like a little French bistro, her restaurant, El Parque, offers just a few specially-prepared meals each day so options are scant. But with gems like these who needs to choose?*

1 chicken (4 pounds), cut into 6 to 8 pieces
Salt and freshly ground black pepper
2 tablespoons extra-virgin olive oil
1 medium onion, coarsely chopped
3 medium tomatoes (14 ounces), peeled and coarsely chopped
2 carrots, peeled and sliced ¼-inch circles
2 large cloves garlic, finely chopped
3 bay leaves
¾ teaspoon ground cumin
1 cup dry white wine
¼ cup chopped fresh parsley

1. Wash the chicken pieces, and sprinkle salt and pepper on both sides.

2. Heat the oil in a large pot over medium heat. When the oil is hot but not smoking, add the chicken pieces. Lightly brown the chicken on both sides and set the pieces aside. You may have to do this in batches.

3. Add the onion to the pot and sauté until translucent. Remove any excess fat from the pot.

4. Return the chicken to the pot, along with the tomatoes, carrots, garlic, bay leaves, and cumin. Cover, reduce heat to medium-low, and continue cooking. After 10 minutes, add the wine. Continue to cook, covered, for about 30 more minutes over medium-low heat, or until the chicken is cooked and the carrots are tender. Stir frequently.

5. When the chicken is cooked, mix in the parsley. Add salt and pepper to taste. Serve with mashed potatoes or white rice.

Wine Suggestion

Ventisquero Grey Syrah

Poultry, Fowl, and Rabbit   149

Sautéed Chicken with Peas

Pollo Arvejado   4 to 6 servings

This was my favorite dish at Casabuela, a restaurant owned by Marta León Malbrich. While an enormous amount of Chileans end up leaving their little hometowns to find work in Santiago, Marta took the opposite path. Well, sort of, anyway. Raised in the southern city of Valdivia, Marta left for Santiago to become a professor of natural sciences. But after fifteen years, she returned home, in 1998, to open a restaurant offering typical Chilean fare. She also began to make her own jams and preserves, which she now sells under the name "Antufen," which means "fruits from the sun" in the indigenous Mapuche language. One of the reasons this dish is so tasty is because, in Chile, you can buy freshly picked peas at the farmers market, then pop them out of their pods and into the pot of chicken.

Salt and freshly ground black pepper
4 chicken thighs, 4 chicken legs (4 to 5 pounds), skin removed (optional)
2½ tablespoons extra-virgin olive oil
1 medium onion, cut in julienne strips
4 cloves garlic, finely chopped
1 large carrot, sliced into thin circles
1 cup white wine
¼ teaspoon ground cumin
¼ teaspoon dried oregano
1 cup fresh peas

1. Sprinkle salt and pepper on both sides of the chicken.

2. Heat the oil in a large pot over medium heat. When the oil is hot, add the chicken. Turn once, cooking until golden on both sides. You may have to do this in two batches.

3. Remove most of the oil from the pot. Add the onion, garlic, carrot, white wine, cumin, oregano, and ¼ cup of water. Cook on high until boiling. Cover, reduce the heat to low, and simmer for 25 to 30 minutes. Add the peas approximately 10 minutes before the chicken is cooked.

4. Add additional salt and pepper to taste, and serve with mashed potatoes or white rice.

Wine Suggestion ‑
Portal del Alto Chardonnay Reserva

Roast Chicken in Beer Sauce

Pollo Asado   4 servings

My wife Anny cooked this often when she was a little girl living in Lota. She learned it from her mother. Many people in Lota prepare this chicken dish in the same way, and accompany it with Salpicón *(see recipe, page 48).*

1 chicken (4 to 4½ pounds)
2 tablespoons extra-virgin
  olive oil
Salt
4 cloves garlic, pureed with
  a mortar and pestle
½ teaspoon ground cumin
½ chicken bouillon cube,
  broken into a powder with
  your fingers
½ cup beer, plus additional
  for gravy
2 tablespoons freshly
  squeezed lemon juice

1. Preheat the oven to 350° F.

2. Place the chicken in a roasting pan. Brush both sides of the chicken with the oil. Lightly salt both sides of the chicken.

3. In a bowl, mix together the garlic, cumin, bouillon cube, ½ cup of beer, and the lemon juice. Stir thoroughly, ensuring that the bouillon cube is well dissolved. Pour over the chicken.

4. Put the chicken in the oven.

5. Frequently baste the chicken with its own juices. Turn once. Add more beer to thin the gravy when the pan juices dry up.

6. Remove the chicken from the oven when cooked, about 50 minutes.

Serving Suggestion

Serve with mashed potatoes, *Salpicón* (see recipe, page 48), or *Arroz Chileno* (see recipe, page 46) and Cono Sur Visión Gewürztraminer.

Hot 'n Spicy Chicken

— — — — — —*Wandering in the tiny town of Huara in northern Chile, I was directed by villagers to make my way to the cozy house of Manuela. They told me that she served memorable almuerzos (large afternoon meals). When I knocked on her door, Digna Manuela Espinoza opened up and asked me if I would like to join the group eating* Picante de Pollo. *And why not? I sat and ate lunch with several youths from Iquique who attended a boarding school in Huara and who had worked out a nifty deal whereby they paid modest sums for Manuela's delectable home-cooked cuisine. Manuela has been winning over locals and foreign tourists alike in this small desert town, about an hour north of Iquique, ever since she opened her kitchen to the public in 2000. While this dish calls for* rocoto, *the hot pepper found in northern Chile, Manuela said some Chileans use the milder* ají verde. *The important thing is to add at least some spice by including a little finely chopped hot pepper. The sauce takes on a thick and rich texture when the chunky potatoes are added at the end.*

2 pounds baking potatoes, such as russets, peeled
2 tablespoons extra-virgin olive oil
Salt
1 chicken (4 pounds), cut into 8 pieces
1 onion, finely chopped
2 cloves garlic, pureed
1 teaspoon finely chopped hot red pepper, or 2 tablespoons milder hot green pepper, such as *cubanelle*
1 teaspoon paprika
1/4 teaspoon ground cumin
2 tablespoons chopped fresh cilantro

1. Boil the potatoes in lightly salted water. When cooked, remove from the water. Let the potatoes cool and break into little chunks using your fingers. Set the potatoes aside.

2. Heat the olive oil in a deep pot over a medium flame. Salt both sides of the chicken pieces. When the oil is hot, add the chicken. Cook until golden brown on both sides. You will probably have to do this in two batches. Remove the chicken pieces from the pot and set them aside.

3. Put the onion, garlic, hot pepper, paprika, and cumin into the pot and cook over medium heat for approximately 1 minute. Remove excess oil from the pot.

4. Return the chicken to the pot with 3 cups of water. Increase the heat to high and stir.

5. When the mixture comes to a boil, reduce the heat to low. Cook for approximately 20 minutes. Add salt to taste and additional water, if desired, to increase the amount of gravy.

6. Just before the chicken is fully cooked, remove about two cups of the gravy and put it into a gravy bowl, to serve with a side dish of white rice.

7. After removing some of the sauce, stir in the potatoes and chopped cilantro. Add additional salt to taste. Mix thoroughly.

Serving Suggestion –
Serve with a side dish of white rice, the gravy, and a Caliterra Syrah.

Roast Chicken in Orange and Walnut Sauce

Pollo a la Naranja   4 servings

Anita Ouellette lives in a beautiful part of the Chilean valley, Valle del Elqui, in the small peaceful village of El Molle, which is surrounded by mountains. Anita arrived in Chile from Germany at age six, and quickly adapted to her new country. After about fifteen years, she fell in love with an American naval officer who had fought in WWII and they married. Since her husband's death in the early 90's, Anita has devoted much energy to reading and experimenting with Chilean recipes, creating many of her own. She prepared the dish below in a restaurant she once owned in El Molle, called El Eden. Like the restaurant's name, I found this signature dish of Anita's to be ethereal.

1 chicken (4½ pounds)
2 tablespoons extra-virgin
    olive oil
Salt and freshly ground black
    pepper
1 onion, cut in julienne strips
⅓ cup plus 1 tablespoon
    freshly squeezed orange
    juice
7 ounces mushrooms,
    coarsely chopped
½ cup walnuts, ground

1. Preheat the oven to 375° F.

2. Brush both sides of the chicken with the olive oil and sprinkle with salt and pepper. Put the onion in a roasting pan. Place the chicken on top of the onion and pour the orange juice and ½ cup water over the chicken.

3. Place the pan in the oven and cook for approximately 1 hour, frequently basting the chicken in its juices. Add a bit of water if there are not sufficient juices in the pan to baste the chicken and to keep the onions moist.

4. Approximately 15 minutes before the chicken is fully cooked, add the mushrooms and nuts and enough water to have a sauce thin enough for basting the chicken. (Add about 1¼ cups water in total while cooking.) Continue basting the chicken often.

5. When the chicken is cooked, remove it from the pan. Put the gravy in a separate bowl and add salt and pepper, if necessary, to enhance the flavor. Serve with white rice.

Wine Suggestion

Casas Patronales Carmenère

Stuffed Chicken Breasts

Pollo Relleno   4 servings

While traveling through Chile, I came across many forms of stuffed chicken. Some were stuffed with such fruits as cherries, others with vegetables like spinach. However, I found the recipe below to be a particularly intriguing combination: shrimp and herbs in a creamy liquor sauce. It derives from Francisco Correa, a chef who has worked in much of central Chile.

3 tablespoons extra-virgin olive oil
10 ounces peeled shrimp
Salt and freshly ground black pepper
2 large whole boneless chicken breasts (2½ pounds), halved
1½ cups heavy cream
2 tablespoons finely chopped fresh chives
2 teaspoons dried tarragon
2 teaspoons dried rosemary
2 teaspoons dry gin (if unavailable, substitute whiskey or vodka)

1. Heat 1 tablespoon of the olive oil in a skillet over medium heat. When hot, add the shrimp, season with salt and pepper, and cook the shrimp for two minutes. Remove from the heat.

2. In the middle of the short end of each breast, use a knife to poke a hole through the piece of chicken. Stick your finger through the hole, to enlarge the space.

3. Stuff one quarter of the shrimp mixture into each hole. Lightly salt the chicken on both sides.

4. In a separate skillet, heat the rest of the olive oil over a medium-low flame. When hot, add the chicken and cook until golden brown on both sides and no longer pink inside, about 15 to 20 minutes.

5. Pour the cream into a saucepan over medium heat. Add the scallions, tarragon, and rosemary, stirring frequently. After 2 minutes, add the gin. Reduce the heat to low and cook for 3 more minutes, stirring frequently. Add a bit of water if the sauce is too thick. Remove from heat.

6. Cut each piece of chicken into several strips, at a slight angle. Ladle the sauce over the chicken and serve on a plate garnished with slices of bell pepper and fresh scallions.

Serving Suggestion

Serve with *Papas Duquesas* (see recipe, page 49) and a Chardonnay, such as Terra Andina Varietal.

Duck with Mixed Vegetables

Pato Papillote   4 servings

When roast ducks are falling in Chile you don't need to duck to escape injury, but instead you need to get yourself a nice cold refreshment. This is because this very Chilean expression, "están cayendo los patos asados," means it is very hot. There are many other delicious duck proverbs in Chile. To name just a few, a "pato malo" (literally "bad duck") is a delinquent, to "andar pato" (literally "to walk like a duck") is to be without money, and to "echar un pato" (literally "to throw a duck") is to make love. Chileans, in fact, use duck in everyday expressions far more than they use it in the kitchen. Many huasos, however, raise ducks and it is found throughout the country. The recipe below was inspired by a dish I tried during one of my trips in Patagonia.

1 large duck (5½ pounds)
1½ onions; 1 onion coarsely
   chopped, the other ½ finely
   chopped
4 to 5 peppercorns
½ tablespoon finely chopped
   fresh rosemary
1 tablespoon extra-virgin
   olive oil
1 tablespoon butter
½ carrot, grated
3½ ounces mushrooms,
   coarsely chopped
2 tablespoons cream
Salt and freshly ground black
   pepper
⅔ cup white wine
Fresh parsley, finely chopped

1. Put the duck in a pot of water, along with the coarsely chopped onion, the peppercorns, and the rosemary. Bring the water to a boil, cover, and simmer until the duck meat is tender, about 1 to 1½ hours. Remove the duck from the pot, let it cool, then debone and cut it into large pieces.

2. Preheat the oven to 350° F.

3. Heat the olive oil and butter in a skillet over a medium flame. When the oil is hot but not smoking, add the remaining onion, along with the carrot and mushrooms. Cook until the onions are translucent, about 3 to 4 minutes. Remove the skillet from the heat and mix in the duck meat, cream, and salt and pepper to taste.

4. Place the mixture in a baking pan (approximately 9 x 13). Pour the wine evenly over the mixture and cover with aluminum foil, sealing it well around the edges of the pan. Put the pan in the oven.

5. After 20 minutes, remove the pan from the oven and remove the foil, sprinkle with parsley, and serve, ladling the pan juices over the duck.

Wine Suggestion

Veramonte Primus (a blend of carmenère, cabernet sauvignon, and merlot)

Roast Rabbit

María Kutin is the chef of Las Chacras de Pasquito, a restaurant offering all of the traditional dishes of Mamiña, including much lamb, goat, and rabbit. Mamiña is a small town about three hours from the major northern city of Iquique. One gets there largely via dirt roads that scale high into the mountains. Due to its isolation, the town is full of residents who cook what they raise. This book includes several recipes from Mamiña, in part because as María noted, the most traditional northern dishes are found in its small towns rather than in its big cities (such as Iquique and Arica), whose food has been homogenized and fast food-ized.

Salt and freshly ground black pepper
1 rabbit (2½ to 3 pounds), whole or cut into several pieces
6 cloves garlic, pureed
2 bay leaves
½ teaspoon dried oregano
½ teaspoon ground cumin
½ to ¾ cup white wine

1. Sprinkle salt and pepper on both sides of the rabbit.

2. Mix the garlic, herbs, and white wine together and pour half of this mixture over the rabbit.

3. Set aside for 30 minutes, allowing the rabbit to absorb the flavors of the herbs.

4. Preheat the oven to 350° F.

5. Put the rabbit in the oven and cook for about 45 minutes, basting frequently. Add the rest of the wine and herb mixture, as necessary, to keep the rabbit moist and to create a gravy.

Wine Suggestion
Villard Pinot Noir

Rabbit in Sage and White Wine Sauce

Conejo Escabechado   4 servings

I tried this popular dish in El Melocotón, a part of the mountainous Cajón del Maipo, a popular resort near Santiago for skiing, water sports, and nature discovery. At the restaurant, El Montañes, owner Oriana Espinoza recommended that I have rabbit, saying that, along with nuts and almonds, this was the region's specialty. Rabbit is tasty around El Melocotón because farmers allow rabbits to eat grass, as opposed to the processed foods they're fed elsewhere. And rabbit has shown longevity in the region, unlike quail, which no longer finds its way onto menus because of its scarcity.

At El Montañes, I ate this fragrant dish in the ideal manner: by candlelight (though only because the power line had been cut at the restaurant), with French fries made from fresh potatoes, and a glass of white wine. **Conejo Escabechado** *is cooked in various ways, either with red wine, white wine, or vinegar. Rabbit and vegetable escabechados are quite common in Chile, as are chicken and fish.*

1 rabbit (2½ to 3 pounds), cut into several pieces
Salt and freshly ground black pepper
4 cloves garlic, finely chopped
¾ teaspoon dried sage
½ to 1 cup dry white wine
2 tablespoons extra-virgin olive oil
1 large onion, thinly sliced from top to bottom
1 medium carrot, thinly sliced

1. Wash the rabbit pieces and sprinkle salt and pepper on both sides. Place the rabbit in a bowl. Top with the garlic, sage, and ½ cup wine and stir to combine.

2. Allow the herbed rabbit to rest overnight. (If this is not possible, let it sit for at least 30 minutes.) The next day, remove the rabbit from the container and scrape off the herbs. Set the wine and herbs aside.

3. Heat the oil in a large skillet over medium heat. When it is hot, reduce the heat and add the rabbit. Cook over medium heat until golden brown on both sides, about 10 minutes total. You may have to cook the rabbit in batches.

4. Remove the rabbit from the skillet and add the onion and carrot. Cook for a few minutes, until the onion is translucent.

5. Return the rabbit to the skillet, along with $\frac{1}{2}$ cup water and the remaining wine and herbs. Cook over medium-low heat, covered, until the rabbit is tender, approximately 25 minutes. Add equal amounts of water and wine as you cook to create more gravy, if desired. Serve with French fries or rice.

Wine Suggestion
Serve with a crisp Chardonnay.

Rabbit in Hot Pepper and Peanut Sauce

Picante de Conejo   4 to 6 servings

Adding to the creative use of rabbit in northern Chile is Rosa Herrera. She, too, is from Mamiña, whose waters residents say have healing powers. The town's name means "The Little Girl of My Eyes" in the local Aymaran tongue, and received its name from a quaint little tale. The essence of the story is this: Hundreds of years ago, the Incas brought a blind child to this village to cure her. Upon entering the village, they found a spring and poured its waters onto her eyes. Suddenly the young girl was cured, her full vision restored. Chileans have taken that tale to heart. Townspeople believe that the mineral-rich waters flowing in Mamiña treat problems of the skin, bones, and more. Various thermal baths have reputed healing properties, and at least one of its thermal baths is believed to perform the miraculous feat: putting its water into one's eyes will ameliorate one's vision.

Salt
1 rabbit (2½ to 3 pounds), cut into several pieces
¼ cup extra-virgin olive oil
2 cloves garlic, finely chopped
½ teaspoon dried oregano
¼ teaspoon ground cumin
4 medium-size baking potatoes, such as russets, (1¼ pounds), peeled
1 medium onion, chopped finely
1 to 2 teaspoons finely chopped hot red pepper, or 1 to 2 tablespoons milder green peppers, such as *cubanelle*
¼ cup ground, unsalted peanuts

1. Salt both sides of the rabbit pieces.

2. Heat half of the oil in a large pot over a medium flame. When the oil is hot but not smoking, add the rabbit pieces. Cook until golden brown on both sides. You will probably have to do this in batches. Add the garlic, oregano, and cumin to the pot, along with 3 cups of water. Bring to a boil. When the mixture boils, reduce the heat, cover, and simmer until the rabbit is tender, about 45 minutes.

3. Meanwhile, boil the potatoes in a separate pot of water. When they are almost completely cooked, remove them from the pot and cut each potato into about 6 pieces.

4. Heat the rest of the oil in a skillet over a medium flame. Add the onion and cook until translucent. Add the hot pepper and $1\frac{1}{2}$ cups of water. Reduce the heat to low, cover, and cook for 5 minutes, stirring occasionally.

5. Add the potatoes and the onion mixture to the pot with rabbit. Cook until the flavors have mingled and the potatoes are fully cooked, about 6 to 8 minutes. If the potatoes begin to crumble into the pot that is fine; some prefer this since it creates a heartier sauce. Add more water or reduce the broth to create a rich sauce. Additionally, if the pot sits for a few minutes the sauce will thicken due to the broken potatoes.

6. Mix in the peanuts, add salt to taste, and serve hot.

Wine Suggestion

Vinsur Tres Rios Chardonnay

Sautéed Rabbit with Wheat

Patasca   4 to 6 servings

Plowing through the slopy hills of Mamiña, I bumped into the cultural center for indigenous people of the Iquique region in northern Chile. I talked shop there with Raquel Mamani, the president of the center and an avid cook. We broke bread, that is, we chatted as we nibbled on Raquel's juicy, tender corn and dried llama meat. The recipe below underlines the rich indigenous cooking found in northern Chile. In Marmiña, there is a strong influence from the indigenous Aymara and Quechua tribes, also found in neighboring Bolivia and Peru. Raquel and her husband Humberto Cautin Caqueo are no exception: the two happily share the gastronomy of their forefathers, who are Aymara and Quechua, in dishes such as the Patasca.

⅔ cup shelled wheat
1 pound boiling potatoes, peeled and cut into 1-inch cubes
Salt and freshly ground black pepper
1 rabbit (2½ to 3 pounds), cut into several pieces
3 tablespoons extra-virgin olive oil
1 medium onion, finely chopped
1 small carrot, grated
2 cloves garlic, finely chopped or ground with a mortar and pestle
1 teaspoon paprika
1 beef bouillon cube
2 tablespoons chopped fresh parsley

1. Boil the wheat in lightly salted water until it is cooked. Drain it and set it aside.

2. Boil the potato cubes in lightly salted water until they are cooked. Drain them and set them aside.

3. Meanwhile, lightly sprinkle salt and pepper on both sides of the rabbit pieces. Heat the oil in a large pot over medium heat. When the oil is hot, add the rabbit and cook until brown on both sides, about 10 minutes. You may have to do this in batches.

4. Remove the rabbit and add the onion, carrot, garlic, paprika, and beef bouillon cube to the pot. Cook until the onions are translucent. Return the rabbit to the pot, along with 2½ cups water. Reduce the heat, cover, and simmer until the rabbit is tender (about 30 minutes). Add more water, if necessary.

5. When the rabbit is cooked, add the potatoes, wheat, and parsley to the pot. Stir thoroughly, add salt to taste and remove from heat. Keep the pot covered for several minutes, so that the flavors mingle and the sauce thickens (the wheat and potatoes will absorb some of the liquid). Serve hot.

Wine Suggestion

Leyda Las Brisas Pinot Noir Reserve

Bistec, Chancho, Cordero, y Cabra

In Chile, a trip to the butcher can be an exciting experience because there are bound to be surprising new homemade meat products staring at you through glass windows. Frequently butchers prepare their own chorizos, blood sausages, salami, spiced pork (*arrollado huaso*), and head cheese (*queso de cabeza*), and offer it fresh, not frozen. Chileans also have a weakness for pâté, perhaps acquired during the 1800s when the French permeated the country. More than a few eat pâté for breakfast and then are ready to have at it again for the early evening tea (*once*), and there is no lack of choice with the number of packaged brands swelling out of grocery store refrigerators. Homemade pâté, called *paté del campo*, is also pervasive just as it is in France, but Chile's is smoother and creamier.

In southern Chile, Llanquihue has made a name for itself as a town with an exceptional knack for turning out cold cuts, sausages, and bacon. The German zeal for pork meat is present there and in other towns, where people eat leg of pork (*pernil*) and knockwurst (called *gordos*—literally "fat things"). Just several hours north of Llanquihue, Chillán is famous for its chorizos. In much of Chile, on the sidewalk outside of storefronts or at barbecues at home, people and vendors dig up excuses to cook up chorizos so that they can wolf down *choripanes*, a juicy smoked sausage shoehorned into a homemade piece of bread (*un batido*). Chileans eat all kinds of meat, from beef to goat to lamb. Sheep particularly run rampant in southern Patagonia.

Stewed Beef Laced with Vegetables

Carne Mechada

4 to 6 servings

This dish is attractive because layers of carrots, onions, garlic, and bell pepper appear upon carving the pot roast. I try to put as many of the vegetables inside the meat as possible, though it is of no great consequence if you cook some of the vegetables underneath the stuffed beef. For this dish—which is even better the following day—you can also substitute a boneless pork roast for boneless beef.

2½ to 3 pounds beef eye of round roast
2 tablespoons extra-virgin olive oil
1 small carrot, cut in julienne
1 small onion, coarsely chopped
4 cloves garlic, coarsely chopped
½ red bell pepper, coarsely chopped
Salt and freshly ground black pepper
1 pound tomatoes, peeled and coarsely chopped
½ teaspoon dried oregano
1 bay leaf

1. Use a sharp knife to cut several (about four) holes in the sides of the beef, from one side through to the other. I use my fingers to increase the size of the holes. Insert as much of the carrot, onion, garlic, and bell pepper as will fit into the holes, in equal portions. Salt and pepper both sides of the beef.

2. Heat the oil in a large pot over medium-low heat. When the pot is hot, add the beef. Cook until the meat is lightly browned on both sides.

3. Add the remaining carrots, onions, garlic, and bell pepper to the pot, along with the tomatoes, oregano, bay leaf, and ½ cup water. Bring the mixture to a boil, then reduce the heat to low and simmer, covered until the meat is tender and the vegetables inside are cooked, about 1 hour.

4. Remove the beef to a plate and keep it warm. Turn the heat up and continue cooking the sauce until it reduces to a thick gravy. Serve with white rice, mashed potatoes, or pasta. A tasty way to use leftover *Carne Mechada* is to make a sandwich out of it. A typical Chilean sandwich that uses *Carne Mechada* is called *Chacarero* (see recipe, page 55).

Wine Suggestion

Viña Errazuriz's Syrah Reserve, Don Maximiano Estate

Beef Strips in Vegetables and Pureed Calabaza

Charquicán   4 to 6 servings

This, Chileans say, is one of their foremost national dishes. It is very colorful, taking on a deep orange hue due to the carrots and Chilean pumpkin (calabaza). The two vegetables also give a nice tang to charquicán, a name that represents an antiquated form of the recipe. Initially Chileans used charquí—dried beef or even horsemeat—for the dish. However, times have changed and natives use raw beef that they then cook. When preparing charquicán, Chileans typically use a medley of seasonal vegetables, instead of a strictly defined combination, and some put a fried egg on top at the end.

2½ pounds baking potatoes, such as russets, peeled
¼ pound *calabaza* or butternut squash
3 tablespoons vegetable oil
1½ pounds boneless beef, cut in 1-inch cubes
1 small onion, finely chopped
3 to 4 fresh celery leaves
1 cup finely chopped spinach leaves
1 cup finely chopped cabbage leaves
1 cup finely chopped cauliflower
1 cup green beans cut in ½-inch slices
2 cups fresh corn kernels
2 small carrots, finely grated
1 large red bell pepper, finely chopped
4 cloves garlic, finely chopped
⅓ cup finely chopped fresh parsley
Salt and freshly ground black pepper

1. Boil the potatoes and *calabaza* in water over high heat until tender. Mash until fully pureed.

2. Meanwhile, heat the oil in a skillet over medium-high heat. When hot, add the beef. Cook until browned on both sides (about 2 minutes). Add the onion, celery, spinach, cabbage, cauliflower, green beans, corn, carrots, bell pepper, garlic, and salt to taste. Cook for 15 minutes, until the beef is tender. Mix in the chopped parsley and remove the skillet from the heat.

3. Add the warm potato mixture to the meat mixture. Mix together thoroughly, add salt and pepper to taste, and serve.

Wine Suggestion — — — — — — — — — — —
Carmen Grand Vidure Cabernet Sauvignon

Beef Brisket Marinated in Wine and Garlic

6 servings

What I love most about brisket is how moist and tender it can be. In this recipe, the brisket is marinated in vinegar overnight, and then cooked on the stovetop for more than two hours. This allows it to take on a unique character and for the wine and herbs to infuse it with flavor. The city of Talca claims authorship over this dish, but it is frequently found in Chilean restaurants nationwide.

⅓ cup red wine vinegar

7 cloves garlic, pureed with a mortar and pestle

½ teaspoon *Aliño Completo* (see recipe, page 28)

Salt and freshly ground black pepper

3¼ pounds beef brisket

¼ cup extra-virgin olive oil

2 onions (1 pound), cut into eigths

1 cup white wine

1. In a large container, combine the vinegar, garlic, *aliño completo*, salt, and pepper and rub into both sides of the meat. Cover and refrigerate 12 to 24 hours.

2. Heat the oil in a large pot over medium-high heat. Remove the meat from the marinade (reserve marinade) and cook until browned on both sides.

3. Add the reserved marinade, the onions, wine, and ½ cup of water and bring to a boil. Cover the pot and reduce the heat to low. Simmer the brisket, turning it occasionally, until it is very tender, approximately 2¼ to 2½ hours. A knife should easily pierce the meat. Add additional water as the brisket cooks, if desired, to create additional gravy. Add salt to taste and serve hot.

Wine Suggestion

Calina Cabernet Sauvignon Reserve

Beef Sautéed in Papaya Sauce

Jorge Aoun and his wife Marcela run a restaurant in El Molle, part of the picturesque Valle del Elqui, north of La Serena. One of Chile's most popular resorts, the valley attracts droves of nature lovers, hippies, and lest one not overlook them, papaya fanatics. Jorge told me about this dish served at El Cedro, the restaurant his mother owns in La Serena that offers an Arabic, Chilean, and international menu. Jorge, a classically trained chef with homegrown tastes, calls upon the local papaya to inject a Chilean flare into this dish. He recommends that the dish be accompanied by a side of garlic mushrooms, as described below.

The béchamel sauce
3 tablespoons butter
3 tablespoons flour
1½ cups milk

1. **For the béchamel sauce:** In a saucepan, melt the butter over low heat. Add the flour and continue cooking over low heat for about 3 minutes, stirring frequently. Very gradually add the milk, stirring constantly. Continue cooking over low heat, stirring continuously. After about 6 to 8 minutes, when the sauce is creamy and lightly bubbling, remove from the heat.

Wine Suggestion
Try a powerful syrah, such as Montes Folly.

The meat

Salt and freshly ground black
  pepper
2 to 2½ pounds boneless
  beef round sirloin tip steak,
  cut in four pieces
1 tablespoon vegetable oil
7 ounces papayas, peeled,
  seeded, and coarsely
  chopped
2 tablespoons cognac

The garlic mushrooms

1 tablespoon extra-virgin
  olive oil
2 cloves garlic, coarsely
  chopped
7 ounces mushrooms

2. Salt and pepper both sides of meat. Heat the oil in a wide skillet over a medium-high flame. When hot, add the meat and brown it on both sides, 3 to 4 minutes. You may have to do this in two batches or in two skillets. Remove the meat when cooked. Add the papaya to the skillet and cook them in the steak juice. After 45 seconds, add the cognac and continue cooking for an additional 30 seconds, shaking the pan occasionally.

3. Add the béchamel sauce to the skillet and add salt to taste. Cook briefly, adding water (about ¼ cup) if the sauce is too thick.

4. Return the steak to the skillet, mix it with the sauce, and cook it very briefly. Remove from heat.

5. Heat 1 tablespoon of olive oil in a skillet. When hot, add the mushrooms and garlic. Stir frequently and remove from heat when cooked.

6. Serve the steak with shoestring fries and the sautéed mushrooms.

Wine Suggestion ▬ ▬ ▬ ▬ ▬ ▬ ▬ ▬ ▬ ▬ ▬ ▬ ▬ ▬ ▬

Torrealba Carmenère Gran Reserva

Vegetables Rolled in Beef

Carne de Malaya   6 to 8 servings

In Chile, malaya *is a cut of beef that is terrific for rolling and creating tasty veg-etable combinations. This cut is difficult to find in U.S. stores, so you need to use a very long and thin piece of meat that is pliant, like* malaya. *This is because you layer several kinds of vegetables over the meat and then fold the meat, thereby enclosing—or stuffing—everything inside. In Valparaíso the epicurean greengro-cer Juan Espinoza taught me how to make* malayas *and indicated to make sure the vegetables are dry when covering the long, thin piece of meat. Exactly how many vegetables you add to the meat will vary slightly, according to the width and length of the beef. Just ensure that you fit the vegetables evenly across the meat before you roll the meat over them.*

2 to 2½ pounds thinnest piece of boneless beef available, in one large slice (about 21 x 12 x ⅓ inches), fat removed

Salt and freshly ground black pepper

1 beef bouillon cube

1 teaspoon dried oregano

1 teaspoon ground cumin

4 hard-boiled eggs, halved

2 medium carrots, julienned

10 green beans, whole

1 green bell pepper, julienned

1 red bell pepper, julienned

7 cloves garlic, each halved

5 ounces raw spinach leaves

Kitchen string

1. Bring 12 cups (3 quarts) of lightly salted water to a boil in a large pot.

2. Meanwhile, wash and dry the meat and lay it out flat. Salt and pepper the meat. Crumble the beef bouillon cube into a small bowl and mix in the oregano and cumin. Sprinkle evenly over the meat.

3. Place the egg halves yolk-side down, in a line down the center of the meat, leaving ½ inch between them. Line the carrots along each side of the eggs and place the beans next to the carrots. Add the green and red peppers, overlapping the beans, carrots, and eggs. You now are overlapping because you want to keep the vegetables in the cen-ter of the meat, so that you can wrap them easily. Lay the garlic on top of the vegetables. Then, from one length to the other, cover everything with the spinach leaves (there will be several layers of spinach leaves).

4. Take the side of the meat closest to you and roll it over the vegetables and eggs resting in the middle. When rolling, push the vegetables tightly under the meat so that you are able to enclose all the vegetables in the meat. Continue rolling until you reach the other side of the meat. The meat should now be shaped like a 2-foot-long submarine sandwich. Its width should be $3\frac{1}{2}$ to 4 inches.

5. Use a long string to tie the meat, securing it lengthwise and widthwise. Tie tightly because the filling will force the meat open if not properly tied. Tie the ends shut, pushing in the vegetables so nothing escapes while cooking. Bend the meat into a circular shape and tie it again so that it can fit snugly and securely in a large pot.

6. Submerge the meat into the boiling water. It should be covered by about 2 inches of water; add additional water if necessary. Cook, covered, over medium-high heat for 2 hours. Occasionally add more water to maintain the water level. After 2 hours, remove the meat and refrigerate it. Continue on to Step 9 if you do not intend on using the broth for a soup.

7. The broth that remains after cooking the stuffed beef is tasty and can be used as stock or made into a noodle soup. To make the latter, test the broth for flavor. If it is too strong, add a bit more water. If the flavors are not strong enough, cook the broth until some of the water dissipates. When it is the right concentration, add $\frac{1}{2}$ cup of angel hair noodles, wheels or other pasta. Remove the pot from the heat when the noodles are cooked.

8. When the meat has chilled, discard the string. Cut the meat into $1\frac{1}{4}$-inch slices.

9. Serve the meat cold on individual plates, which can include potato or tomato salad or chopped lettuce. Include a dollop of mayonnaise, which many Chileans eat with the meat. Serve the meat as a main course, with the noodle soup, or as an appetizer.

Spinach and Cabbage Sewn in Beef

Cima de Malaya

*If you're patient enough to do some sewing while you cook, this dish will reward you handsomely. Made at fiestas in Chile, **Cima de Malaya** is packed with aromatic herbs and vegetables that cook inside the beef. Patience is needed because you use a thread and needle to sew the beef shut. Be careful though, since the meat can develop small holes, which you need to sew up before boiling the meat so the filling does not escape. While **malayas** like this can be a full meal, they are often eaten as appetizers.*

1. In a large bowl, mix the ground spinach, chopped spinach, cabbage, peas, garlic, raw eggs, beef bouillon cube, cumin, oregano, and salt (about 1 teaspoon) and pepper to taste. Mix thoroughly.

2. Wash and dry the beef thoroughly and lay it out flat. Liberally season the meat with salt and pepper.

3. Lay it out and fold the two longer sides towards one another, so that one of the long sides is sealed, the other long side is partially open, and the two short sides are open. Now stitch shut one of the short sides and the long side that is open, creating a single open pocket on one short side through which to stuff the ingredients. Thread a large-eyed, sterilized sewing needle with kitchen string. Start on one of the shorter ends, where the closed side ends, by tying the top and bottom parts of the meat together. Use the needle to sew the meat, gradually sealing three sides shut. Work your way from the top of the meat to the bottom from one of the shorter ends towards the longer end that remains open. Then sew the longer end shut and leave the needle and thread dangling on the corner of that end. After stuffing the meat, you will sew the final open pocket shut.

4. Stuff the meat through the open pocket, evenly distributing each ingredient. Put each ingredient next to or on top of the previous ingredient. I start by first adding the bacon, then the green beans, carrots, celery, green onions, bell peppers, spinach mixture, and lastly the whole eggs. It is correct to see the eggs bulging through the meat. The julienned vegetables should be parallel with the longer side of the meat.

1 pound raw spinach leaves; half ground in a food processor, the other half finely chopped
4 cups finely chopped cabbage
1 cup green peas
6 garlic cloves, quartered
3 eggs, lightly beaten
1 beef bouillon cube, crumbled
$\frac{1}{2}$ teaspoon ground cumin
$\frac{1}{2}$ teaspoon dried oregano
Salt and freshly ground black pepper
$2\frac{1}{2}$ to 3 pounds thinnest piece of boneless beef available, in one large slice (about 21 by 12 inches), fat removed
6 ounces bacon, lightly fried
7 ounces green beans, cut in julienne
6 ounces carrots, cut in julienne
$3\frac{1}{2}$ ounces celery stalks, cut in julienne
5 to 6 ounces green onions, cut in julienne
5 to 6 ounces red bell peppers, each cut into 8 pieces
6 hard-boiled eggs
Kitchen string

5. Heat, but do not boil, a very large pot of lightly salted water over a medium flame.

6. Sew the open side shut with the needle and kitchen string that is dangling on the corner of the meat. The meat will now be 1 foot long by $\frac{1}{2}$ foot wide. Check the meat to make sure that it is completely closed. It may have puncture wounds, meaning that in one or two places there is a small hole through which the stuffed vegetables could escape upon cooking. In that case, you need to sew the wound shut with the needle and additional kitchen string.

7. Add the meat to the hot water. It should be fully submerged. Cover and cook over medium heat, boiling robustly, for 1 hour 30 minutes. As the meat cooks remove any fat (which will be spinach-colored, so don't be alarmed by the green fuzz) from the surface. Also, the meat should always be fully submerged so add water as it cooks, when necessary.

8. Remove the meat. The broth that remains is tasty, and can become a full-fledged soup: Simply stir in salt, pepper, cilantro, and two raw eggs.

9. Serve the meat lukewarm or put it in the refrigerator and serve it chilled. When serving, cut 1-inch pieces from one long side to the other. Serve with a lettuce salad and a dollop of mayonnaise.

Bacon-Wrapped Beef Medallions

Medallón de Lomo   4 servings

*The mushroom sauce in this dish is made with toasted flour and called a black sauce (**salsa negra**). Ladled over the bacon-wrapped beef medallions, it makes for a rich dish that demands a good, hearty wine.*

¼ cup flour
Salt and freshly ground black pepper
4 beef medallions that are ½ pound each (2 pounds total)
4 long strips (4 to 6 ounces) bacon or panceta
3 to 4 tablespoons extra-virgin olive oil
3 cloves garlic, finely chopped
7 ounces mushrooms, coarsely chopped
Kitchen string

1. Put the flour in a saucepan and cook over medium heat, stirring constantly so that it does not burn. Mix until light brown, about 3 to 4 minutes. Remove and allow to cool.

2. Sprinkle salt and pepper on both sides of the medallions, wrap a slice of bacon around each medallion, and tie a string around the bacon.

3. Heat 1 to 2 tablespoons of the oil in a wide skillet over medium heat. When the oil is hot but not smoking, add the beef. Cover and cook until browned on both sides, and cooked to the desired degree of doneness.

4. Meanwhile, in a small bowl mix the browned flour with 1 cup water. Stir thoroughly.

5. Heat the rest of the oil in a medium skillet over medium heat. When hot, add the garlic. After about 2 minutes, when the garlic is golden, increase the heat to high and add the mushrooms. Cook for about 2 minutes, shaking the pan frequently. Then slowly add the flour mixture. Add a bit more water (about ½ cup) to lighten the sauce and sprinkle on a touch of salt. Pour the mushroom sauce over the beef medallions and serve.

Serving Suggestion

Serve with white rice or *Papas Duquesas* (see recipe, page 49) and a full-bodied wine such as De Martino's Enigma Cabernet Sauvignon.

Herbed Pork

Arrollado Huaso

▬ ▬ ▬ ▬ ▬ *Driving from Santiago to Rancagua, you can't help but be drawn to a restaurant in Machalí with a sign bearing a large, hat-wearing pig, called* **El Chancho con Chupalla,** *or "The Pig with the Straw Cowboy Hat." When I stumbled upon it, I opted for pork, and to my enormous pleasure I was able to feast on delicious ribs and a succulent, rolled pork made by the chef, Jorge Sandoval. This dish, described below, is known as* **Arrollado Huaso,** *which means "A Farmers Roll-up." A* huaso *is someone from the country, though it usually refers to a person rather than to a friendly pig on a sign. In central and southern Chile, people also eat* arrollado *sandwiches. When served this dish, also known as* **Arrollado de Campo,** *many people choose not to eat the pigskin, which is rich and fatty. But it is tender and tasty and makes the nonfat meat interior moister, so I indulge. Pigskin can be found in Latin or Asian stores.*

2 to 2½ pounds pork loin
½ cup white wine
3 cloves garlic, pureed with a mortar and pestle
1 teaspoon dried oregano
1 teaspoon hot red pepper salsa (see recipe, page 25), or purchase a similar sauce in Latin or Asian stores
2 to 2½ pounds pigskin
Kitchen string

1. Marinate the pork in the white wine, garlic, and the herbs overnight. Turn the pork a few times to ensure the flavors soak in completely.

2. The next day, bring a quart of salted water to a boil.

3. Remove the pork from the marinade. Reserve the marinade. Salt the pork and arrange the meat so that you have something similar to a large pork loin.

4. Wrap the skin around the pork, fully covering it (except for its two ends). Tie a string tightly around the pigskin. If you have small pigskin strips instead of one large strip, tie each piece individually.

5. Put the pork in the water, add the marinade, and boil over medium-high heat until the pigskin is tender and the pork is cooked, about 20 to 25 minutes.

Serving Suggestion ▬ ▬ ▬ ▬ ▬ ▬ ▬ ▬ ▬ ▬ ▬ ▬ ▬ ▬ ▬ ▬
Serve with mashed potatoes and *Salsa de Ají Rojo* (see recipe, page 25), along with a Carmenère, such as TerraNoble Carmenère.

Blood Sausage

Prietas

18 blood sausages

When Chileans have barbecues they throw lots of chorizos and blood sausage on the grill. Called morcillas in Argentina, as well as in Spain, from where they originate, these sausages are called prietas ("blacks") in Chile due to the color they take on when cooked. Blood sausages are largely a winter food, especially if you are making them from scratch. In central Chile one can obtain pigs' blood only when the winter months begin because it is only then that slaughterhouses sell blood to butchers, when the demand for this comfort food arises.

Few in Chile are squeamish when it comes to eating this dish, and many tell of having drank ñachi, which is warm blood fresh from a slaughtered animal, mixed with herbs and consumed with a glass of red wine. Victor Vega, my local butcher in Santiago who makes his own blood sausages, spicy sausages, and other meat products, gave me the basic outline for this recipe. Victor learned the meat trade from his father and he stores bottles and bottles of his mother's homemade wine from southern Chile. So from the family's soil and sweat alone he has all the ingredients necessary to make a sterling barbecue. It is important that you check your state's safety standards before purchasing pig's blood.

5 cups pig's blood
4 to 4½ pounds onions, finely chopped
1½ teaspoons sugar
7 ounces cooked bacon, finely chopped
⅓ cup finely chopped walnuts
5 cloves garlic, finely chopped
1 teaspoon ground cumin
1 teaspoon dried oregano
1 cup whole milk
1¾ tablespoons salt
Freshly ground black pepper
6½ feet of sausage casing (about 7 ounces)

1. Make sure that the blood is clean by removing all impurities and lumps.

2. Fry the onions in a large pot, covered, over medium heat. Stir frequently, cooking until the onions no longer have a strong odor, about 20 minutes. Discard any liquid that remains. Stir the sugar into the onions. Remove the onions from the pot and set aside.

3. Bring a large pot of water to a boil.

4. Heat the oil over a medium flame in the same pot you were using for the onions. When the oil is hot but not smoking, return the onions to the pot, with the bacon, walnuts, garlic, cumin, oregano, milk, salt, and pepper to taste. Cook the mixture for a few minutes, stirring constantly. Remove from heat. Taste the filling and adjust the seasoning.

5. Mix the blood into the pot, cook for several minutes, and again try the mixture for taste, adding more salt, if desired.

6. Cut the sausage casing into thirds so it will be easier to fill (three roughly 2-foot-long strips). Tie one end of a piece of casing, then blow into the casing to expand it. Put a funnel into the open end. Gradually ladle the sausage mixture through the funnel into the casing. Press the filling down to reach the bottom. When the casing is about 4½ inches full of the mixture, tie it shut at that point with kitchen string. Continue adding the mixture, tying every 4½ inches until the casing is full, and tie off the end. You should have six sausages. Repeat with the other two strips of casing, using up all of the mixture.

7. Submerge the sausages in the boiling water. Do this in stages, if necessary. Cook over medium heat, covered, until blood does not come out when a knife pierces the sausages. This should take about 30 minutes.

8. Remove the sausages and cut them at the points where they are tied. Serve immediately. Alternatively, you can store cooked sausages in the freezer and reheat them by boiling, frying, or baking them in the oven.

Serving Suggestion – – – – – – – – – – – – – – – – – – –
Serve with boiled potatoes, *pebre* (see recipe, page 23), or a salad, such as *Ensalada a la Chilena* (see recipe, page 33). Accompany it with a hearty red wine, such as El Aromo Dogma Cabernet Sauvignon.

Pork Shanks with Red Cabbage

Guiso de Repollo Morado

I met the elderly Ema Ortiz at the blocks-long street market on Avenida Argentina in Valparaíso, where she was selling lettuce, carrots, and many other vegetables. Pointing to her red cabbage, she offered me the recipe below, which she says is a classic porteño *dish (that is, a dish from the port of Valparaíso). Like many Chilean market vendors, if you start talking cuisine with Ema, it's difficult to end the conversation. In the recipe below, rather than halving the cabbage, you can chop it coarsely to cook it more quickly.*

½ large or 1 small red cabbage (2 pounds), halved
Salt and freshly ground black pepper
2 to 2½ pounds pork shank, cut in several pieces
2 tablespoons extra-virgin olive oil
1 small onion, cut in julienne strips
3 cloves garlic, finely chopped
1 teaspoon dried oregano
Dash ground cumin
¼ cup finely chopped fresh parsley
2 eggs

1. Put the cabbage in a deep pot. Add water to reach approximately half the height of the cabbage. Cover and cook on high. Turn the cabbage occasionally to cook evenly. When the cabbage is tender, after about 20 to 30 minutes, remove from the heat. A sharp knife should pierce the cabbage easily. Set the cabbage aside, and when it is cool enough to touch, finely chop it. This makes about 4 cups of chopped cabbage.

2. Salt and pepper the pork. Heat the oil in a large skillet over a medium flame. When hot, add the pork. Do this in two batches, if necessary. Lightly brown the pork on both sides, about 15 to 20 minutes total. Stir in the onion, garlic, oregano, and cumin. Reduce the heat to medium-low and continue to cook, stirring frequently, until the pork is fully cooked inside—that is, when it is no longer pink about 10 to 15 minutes. Remove the pork from the skillet.

3. Place the cooked cabbage, parsley, and eggs in the skillet and stir, while cooking over medium heat. Cook for about 2 minutes, adding salt and pepper to taste. Return the pork to the skillet with the cabbage mixture. Mix thoroughly. Serve hot, placing some of the cabbage mixture on top of and around the pieces of pork.

Serving Suggestion

Serve with fried, cubed potatoes and a Montes Alpha Merlot.

Pork Chops with Cabbage and Stewed Apples

Chuletas con Repollo y Manzanas   4 servings

The German influence in Chile is undeniable, as underscored by the tones of this dish. The pork chops and the hot cabbage are cooked separately, but are served together on a single plate. Both are steeped in white wine and you can dip the pork chops in the stewed cabbage for additional juices. One way to cook the dish to save olive oil and intertwine the two mixtures is to first fry the bacon, then fry the pork chops in the leftover bacon grease.

The pork

Salt and finely ground black pepper
4 large pork chops (2½ pounds)
2 tablespoons extra-virgin olive oil
4 cloves garlic, pureed with a mortar and pestle
½ cup dry white wine
½ teaspoon finely chopped dried rosemary

The cabbage

3½ ounces bacon, coarsely chopped
1 small red or green cabbage (1½ pounds), chopped into thin strips
2 green (such as Granny Smith) apples (7 ounces), peeled and thinly sliced into rings, from top to bottom
1½ cups white wine
12 whole black olives
Salt

1. Salt and pepper the pork. Heat the oil in a large skillet over medium heat. When hot, add the pork chops. Fry until browned on both sides, about 15 minutes. You may have to do this in batches. Remove the pork from the skillet. Add the garlic and cook until golden brown. Add ¼ cup of the wine and the rosemary to the hot skillet and stir thoroughly. After a minute, return the pork to the skillet, add another ¼ cup of wine, and reduce the heat to medium low. Continue cooking the pork chops until they are fully cooked and the wine has reduced, about 5 minutes.

2. Fry the bacon in a small skillet. Remove the bacon and set on paper towels to absorb excess grease.

3. Put the cabbage, apples, and 1 cup of the wine into a large pot and cook over a medium flame, covered. After 15 minutes add the bacon, olives, and an additional ½ cup of wine. Reduce the heat to low and continue cooking, covered, until the cabbage and apples are tender, about 10 more minutes. If the mixture becomes too dry, add a bit more wine. Add salt to taste and serve the hot cabbage mixture with the pork chops.

Wine Suggestion

Viu Manent Semillon

Spicy Pork Spareribs

Costillar de Cerdo 4 to 6 servings

Pomaire, just an hour southwest of Santiago, has developed a bit of a reputation in Chile for its hearty, country-style cuisine. In fact, this town is little more than one very long street riddled with restaurants and pottery, its two attractions. While its inexpensive earthenware bowls, pots, mugs, and other kitchenware drove me to Pomaire, the rich, traditional cooking of its restaurants has led me back again and again. Pastel de Choclo, spareribs, and Mote con Huesillo are just a few of the items in high demand here, as are its empanadas, which come in all shapes and sizes. In fact, Pomaire has found a place in The Guinness Book of World Records for creating the world's biggest empanada, which bolstered the town's notoriety as one preoccupied with gastronomical feats. With these ribs—which come from Luis Jara, of the restaurant Los Naranjos—so rich, spicy, and succulent, I usually see no need to hunt down mammoth empanadas when in Pomaire.

3½ to 4 pounds pork
   spareribs
½ cup red wine vinegar
Salt
½ cup extra-virgin olive oil
5 cloves garlic, finely
   chopped
¾ teaspoon red pepper
   flakes
½ teaspoon ground cumin
Freshly ground black pepper

1. Preheat oven to 400° F.

2. Rinse the spareribs with water. Rub the vinegar into the ribs and let them marinate for 1 to 2 hours.

3. Remove the ribs from the vinegar. Salt both sides of the ribs.

4. Mix the oil with the garlic, red pepper flakes, cumin, and a pinch of black pepper in a bowl. Brush the mixture on both sides of the ribs.

5. Bake the ribs in the oven for 45 to 50 minutes, until cooked, turning once. While the ribs are baking, occasionally baste them with their juices to keep them moist.

Serving Suggestion

Serve with mashed potatoes and a simple tomato salad, along with a Cabernet Sauvignon, such as such as Gracia, de Chile, Ocasión Merlot, Reserva Superior.

Kidneys in Sherry Sauce

*Sherry comes from Spain and is often used for cooking in Chile, as well for the occasional mixed drink, such as **Vaina** (see recipe, page 233). Here it provides a tasty sauce for kidneys.*

2 tablespoons butter
1 small onion, finely chopped
1 carrot, grated
3 garlic cloves, finely chopped
2 to 2½ pounds kidneys, chopped into 1 to ½ inch strips
½ teaspoons ground cumin
Salt and freshly ground black pepper
½ cup dry sherry
Fresh parsley, finely chopped

1. Melt the butter in a medium-size pot over a medium flame. Add the onion, carrot, and garlic.

2. When the onion is translucent, add the kidneys, cumin, and salt and pepper to taste. Continue cooking the mixture, stirring frequently, until the kidneys have browned, about 5 minutes.

3. Add the sherry, reduce the heat to medium-low, and continue cooking until the kidneys are tender, about 20 minutes.

4. Remove the pot from the stove, mix in the parsley, and serve immediately.

Serving Suggestion

Serve with *Arroz Chileno* (see recipe, page 46) and a full-bodied wine, such as Tarapacá Milenium Cabernet Sauvignon.

Roast Lamb

Cordero al Horno 4 to 6 servings

In Chile, lamb is most commonly eaten in the cold, verdant south. Lidia Fuentealba found that out when she realized that one of the few dishes that didn't sell like hotcakes in her restaurant, Hijuelas, in central Chile, is lamb. In Temuco where Lidia is from, in southern Chile, lamb is snapped up quickly. Especially in the far south in Patagonia, natives delight in eating lamb because it is so fresh, while tourists who pass through can't miss the sheep because they may well be blocking traffic. In southern Chile, lamb is often prepared without many herbs, but simply cooked "al palo"— twirled on a spit over hot coals. Lidia learned the recipe below from her mother and offered it to me.

Salt
1 teaspoon ground dried
  rosemary
2½ to 3 pounds lamb (ribs or
  chops)
1 cup whole milk

1. Sprinkle salt and rosemary on both sides of the lamb. Place the lamb in a container, pour the milk over it, and let it marinate overnight.

2. Preheat the oven to 300° F.

3. Place the lamb with the milk in a roasting pan and put in the oven. Let the lamb cook slowly, about 1 hour, until it is tender and glazed. Turn it once and baste it with its juices from time to time. Put the pan on the top rack during the last 10 to 15 minutes of cooking if the lamb is not glazing sufficiently.

Serving Suggestion

Serve with boiled potatoes or *Papas Salteadas* (see recipe, page 52) and a Cabernet Sauvignon, such as Carpe Diem Cabernet Sauvignon Gran Reserva.

Sautéed Lamb

*Uberlinda Valdes and husband Armando are natives of Mamiña, where they raise rabbits, chickens, ducks, and pigs for their own consumption. In the early '90s they left Mamiña to live in Santiago, but the tranquil, peaceful life of Mamiña brought them back to this small mountain town. Since then, they have established a small bed and breakfast, and according to natives in the town, they serve up the best food in Mamiña. One of Uberlinda's home-cooked meals is this **Cordero al Jugo**, which is literally translated as "Lamb in Juice." It is as moist and tasty as its name suggests, and goes well with mashed potatoes or rice.*

Salt
2½ pounds lamb (leg or other meat-on-the-bone), cut into 6 pieces
2 tablespoons extra-virgin olive oil
1 medium onion, finely chopped
2 tomatoes (1 pound), peeled and quartered
1 cup white wine
½ cup boiling water
¼ cup finely chopped fresh parsley

1. Salt both sides of the lamb pieces.

2. Heat the oil in a deep cooking pot over medium heat. When the oil is hot, add the lamb pieces and cook them until golden brown on both sides, about 10 minutes total. Do this in two batches, if necessary. Remove the lamb from the pot.

3. Add the onions to the pot and cook until translucent.

4. Return the lamb to the pot, along with the tomatoes and the wine. Bring to a boil, then reduce the heat to low and cover.

5. After 20 minutes add the boiling water. Continue cooking the lamb until it is tender, about 30 more minutes. Add more water while cooking, if necessary. Add salt to taste and mix in the parsley.

Wine Suggestion
Miguel Torres Cordillera, a blend of Carignan, Syrah, and Merlot.

Braised Goat

Goat is not that easy to come by in most of Chile, save in the north. Yet, every Independence Day (September 18th) and at midnight on December 31st—in order to usher in the New Year—many Chileans, including the inhabitants of the town of Tiltil, get their hands on goat for the big fiesta. The recipe below is typical, nice, and simple. It comes from Grecia Vargas, who told me that in Tiltil, people typically add only a few herbs to goat because they believe it masks the delicious flavor. Cultural mores have certainly changed over the years more than has Chilean cuisine: Grecia has been happily married to Armando for more than a half-century, a long time since their wedding day when she was fourteen years old and he was twenty-seven. The two share cooking duties.

4 cloves garlic, finely
   chopped
1 teaspoon dried oregano
1/3 cup white wine vinegar
Salt and freshly ground black
   pepper
1 1/2 to 2 pounds goat meat

1. Combine the garlic, oregano, and vinegar and mix thoroughly.

2. Salt and pepper both sides of the meat.

3. Brush the vinegar sauce on both sides of the meat and marinate for at least two hours.

4. Preheat the oven to 350° F.

5. Put the meat and its marinade in a roasting pan and put it in the oven. Baste the meat in its own juices frequently, turning once. Cook for approximately 35 to 40 minutes.

Wine Suggestion
MontGras Ninquén Cabernet Sauvignon

Pan

Chileans are gluttons for good bread. Perhaps this is primarily due to the German and French influence on the nation. In the eighteenth and nineteenth centuries many French arrived in Chile and quickly put their imprint on the world of bread. In fact, prior to the arrival of the French, Chileans prepared bread at home. The waves of French who arrived on Chilean shores began to install bakeries throughout the country, and in doing so pioneered the commercialization of bread in their adopted nation. Previously, Chileans largely consumed corn and wheat *tortillas*, which are of indigenous origin. This no longer is the case as the French mode prevails today: Chile's most common bread arose from the French *baguette*, though it is much smaller. It is called *pan francés* (French bread) by many, while others call it by the Spanish words, *marraqueta* or *batido*. Some would argue that the French are again revolutioning the bread tastes of Chile. The bakery Le Fournil, run by the Frenchman Jerome Reynes, opened in the late '90s and has seen great success by introducing a wide variety of fresh breads to Chile. With more than 30 types of bread, it has met with rave reviews and is expanding throughout the nation.

Unlike other countries, Chile is not known to have a great variety of breads. Rather, they have perfected the few that they bake down to a science. Mom and pop stores on every corner of most neighborhoods provide several rounds of fresh bread daily, as Chileans demand fresh bread for every meal of the day. At grocery stores, people mill anxiously in front of the bread section, frequently shunning hours' old bread in order to be the first to pounce on piping hot bread as soon as it is put out. For these reasons there is no doubt that such bread rarely needs an accompaniment. There are those, however, who make one demand when they see their waiter for the first time: "*Pan y pebre, por favor.*" When bread and this hot sauce arrives at their table, they are able to rest in peace and patiently await the remainder of the meal.

Fruitcake

*This Chilean fruitcake, which means Christmas bread in English, is typically made during the Christmas season, but it can be found in Chile year-round. While Pascua refers to Easter in much of the Spanish-speaking world, in Chile it means Christmas. Chileans call Easter Day "Pascua de los Conejos" or "Pascua de Resurrección." La Isla de Pascua (Easter Island) also is the name of an island owned by Chile that holds shrines, statues, tombs, and other ancient treasures. For the below recipe, another longtime Chilean treasure, the bread cooks very slowly so maintain the oven at low heat. Chancaca helps give Pan de Pascua its brown color, but as it can be hard to find in the U.S. (where it is called **panela**), I use brown sugar. Or, like some Chileans, you can add some coffee to the mixture, which will dye it deep brown.*

1 cup raisins
2 cups mixed candied fruit (1 pound)
⅓ cup rum
5 cups flour
2 cups granulated sugar
1 cup dark brown sugar
1 tablespoon baking powder
1 teaspoon baking soda
1 teaspoon ground cinnamon
1 teaspoon ground nutmeg
½ teaspoon ground cloves
1 pound butter, melted and cooled; plus additional for greasing pans
6 eggs, lightly beaten
2 tablespoons white wine vinegar
1 cup shelled walnuts, halved

1. Soak the raisins and candied fruit mix in the rum for 1½ to 2 hours. Stir the mixture a couple of times so the fruit absorbs the maximum amount of rum.

2. Preheat the oven to 300° F. Grease two round 7-inch pans.

3. Put the flour, and both sugars into a very large bowl. Make a well in the middle and add the baking powder, baking soda, cinnamon, nutmeg, cloves, and moistened fruits. Mix thoroughly with a wooden spoon.

4. Slowly add the butter, eggs, and vinegar, using a wooden spoon to mix the ingredients together. Add the nuts and use your hands to fully mix the ingredients. You should have a batter that is thick and heavy but moist. It should barely fall from the wooden spoon.

5. Put the mixture in the pans, filling them only halfway since the bread will rise considerably.

6. Put the pans in the oven. Bake for about 1½ hours. The bread is done when a knife inserted into the center of the bread comes out clean.

Fried Calabaza Bread

Sopaipillas   Sixty to sixty-five 3 x 3-inch sopaipillas

These moist little fritters are customarily served in Chile as appetizers with hot salsa or as an afternoon or evening snack. While found throughout Chile in bakeries, farmers' markets, and restaurants, sopaipillas are arguably most delicious in the south, where they are made with a bit of pureed calabaza. If you do not have calabaza or a substitute such as butternut squash, increase the amount of water, as calabaza is somewhat watery. Sopaipillas, whose origin traces back to the 1700s with the Arabs, can also be enjoyed sweet by dusting them with a bit of powdered sugar or serving them with jam. Their sweetest manifestation is Sopaipillas Pasadas, in which they are steeped in a sauce with a brown sugar base (see recipe, page 213). The recipe below calls for 3-inch sopaipillas, which is the ideal size if you are eating them as an appetizer. However, in Chile they are often 5-inches in diameter, so simply use a cookie cutter that meets your needs.

7 ounces *calabaza* or butternut squash, cut into small chunks
6½ cups flour
1½ teaspoons yeast
⅓ cup vegetable shortening (3½ ounces), melted and cooled
2½ teaspoons salt
2 cups vegetable oil for deep frying

1. Boil the *calabaza* in a pot of water over high heat until soft, about 15 minutes. Drain and mash the *calabaza* thoroughly, creating a puree. Let it cool.

2. Put the flour in a large bowl. Shape it like a volcano, creating a well in the middle. Put the *calabaza*, yeast, vegetable shortening, and salt into the well. Mix it with a wooden spoon. Slowly add enough water to form a dough (about 1¼ cups). As you work, you will need to begin mixing with your hands. Combine until thoroughly mixed and the dough comes together. It should be a bit moist but should not stick to your hands.

3. Knead the dough for about 15 minutes. To do this more manageably, you may have to cut the dough into two pieces and work with one piece at a time.

4. Place the dough on a floured board. With a rolling pin, flatten it to about ¼-inch thickness.

5. Cut the dough into rounds using a circular cookie cutter, about 3 inches in diameter. Use the tips of two fingers to make 2 small indentations in the center of each *sopaipilla* (like 2 little eyes). Do not break through the dough. Cover the dough with cloth and allow to rest for 30 minutes. You can also store the dough for 48 hours in a plastic bag in the refrigerator.

6. Heat the vegetable oil in a large skillet over a low flame. When the oil is hot but not smoking, add several fritters. Do not crowd them. Cook until they are golden brown on both sides, 2 to 3 minutes total. Remove the fritters and place them on paper towels to absorb excess oil. They should be crisp on the outside and tender on the inside. Serve hot.

Ash-cooked Bread
with Mussels

Tortilla de Rescoldo con Choritos

4 loaves of bread
(the mussels alone make 6 to 8 servings)

As with curanto, Chileans start digging when they get ready to make this dish. First, they make a pit and build a fire. After the fire has died down and burning ashes remain, dough is placed in the pit. It is then covered with ashes, which seal in the dough, allow it to bake, and give it a unique smoky flavor. When the bread is ready, the ashes are dusted off and a fresh mussel salad placed on top. Or the bread is eaten alongside the mussel mixture that rests in individual mussel shells.

The dough
10½ cups flour
2 tablespoons salt
1½ teaspoons baking soda
¾ cup vegetable oil or melted
   vegetable shortening

The filling
6½ pounds mussels, cleaned
   and scrubbed
3 tablespoons finely chopped
   onion
3 tablespoons freshly
   squeezed lemon juice
2 tablespoons finely chopped
   fresh cilantro
1 tablespoon extra-virgin
   olive oil
Salt and freshly ground black
   pepper

1.Dig a pit about 3-feet in diameter. Using ample firewood, build a fire in the pit. Allow the fire to burn for at least an hour so that it generates intense heat. Do not fan the flames.

2. Mix the flour, salt, and baking soda in a large bowl. Mix in the vegetable oil or the melted short-ening and 3 cups of water to make a dough. Knead the dough for about about 10 minutes, until it is smooth and the ingredients are thoroughly blended.

3. Cut the dough into four pieces. Make smooth balls out of each, then press them down to create flat circles about 8 inches in diameter.

4. When there are no flames but the coals are hot, brush some of the ashes aside and set the dough in the pit. Sweep the hot ashes back over the dough. After about 25 minutes, scrape the ashes off the dough. If they are hard and golden on the side that is face up, flip them; otherwise, sweep the ashes back over them. When thoroughly cooked, after about 45 to 50 minutes, remove them from the ashes and brush off the ashes.

5. Steam the mussels by adding them to a large pot with about 2 inches of water. You may have to do this in batches. Cover and cook over medium heat. When the shells have opened, remove the meat and place it in a medium-size bowl. Add the onion, lemon juice, cilantro, olive oil, and salt and pepper to taste. Mix thoroughly.

6. Slice a loaf of bread into four pieces and put each on a plate. Place spoonfuls of the mussels on top of each piece of bread and serve. Repeat for the rest of the loaves of bread and mussel mixture.

Country Rolls

Throughout the countryside and small towns of Chile there is one mainstay: pan amasado, *or homemade rolls. Some of the best rolls I have tried come from a family-owned bakery called Amasandería Panche, nestled in the looping hills of Valparaíso. It is tucked in the corner of Plaza Bismarck, a park that draws numerous tourists because of its spectacular view of the Pacific Ocean and the hip beach towns nearby. As you watch the barges drifting in the distance and the kaleidoscope of houses around, beneath, and above you, the waft of fresh baked bread from the Rivera family magnetically lures you in like a bake from the sea below.*

The dough

3 tablespoons vegetable shortening
2 tablespoons lard
About 6 cups flour, plus extra (for flouring the baking pan)
1½ tablespoons yeast
2 teaspoons salt

The glaze

½ teaspoon sugar

1. Melt the vegetable shortening and lard. Let the mixture cool, but not so much that it begins to harden.

2. In a large bowl, mix the flour, yeast, and salt. Make a well in the mixture by pushing the flour to the bowl's edges.

3. Put the shortening, lard, and 1¼ cups water in the well and mix, at first with a wooden spoon, and then with your hands, to form a dough. Add a bit more flour or water to make a dough that does not stick to your hands.

4. Knead the dough with your hands for about 10 to 15 minutes.

5. Cut the dough into 10 equal pieces. Form each piece of dough into a ball, and then press each piece down to create patties that are about 4 inches wide and 1 inch thick.

6. Cover the rolls with a cloth and let them rise in a warm place until almost doubled in size, about 45 minutes to 1 hour.

7. Preheat the oven to 350° F.

8. Prick four to six little holes in the center of each roll.

9. Mix $\frac{1}{2}$ cup water and the sugar, and brush over the rolls.

10. Lightly flour a baking pan. Put the rolls on the baking pan and put the pan into the oven.

11. Bake the rolls until they are golden brown, about 20 to 25 minutes.

Custard-Filled Donuts

Berlines con Crema Pastelera   10 donuts

Chile is a long way from Berlin, Germany, where President John F. Kennedy memorably declared in 1961 before hundreds of thousands of Germans, "Ich bin ein Berliner," meaning "I am a jelly donut." Yet, his comment, which also can mean, "I am a citizen of Berlin," had resonance all the way to Latin America. One of the customs that waves of German immigrants have inculcated in the Chilean culture is a passion for morning donuts. In Chile, the donuts, aptly called **Berlines**, *take on an indigenous flavor when filled with* **manjar** *(see recipe, page 200), local fruit jams, as well as a pastry cream filling called* **Crema Pastelera**. *This delicious cream compliments many other Chilean sweets, commonly found in La Ligua and Curacaví. Since the dough does not have a strong personality, the creams and jams make the donut. María Burgos told me the recipe below calls for a lot of yeast because these donuts are meant to swell.*

The donuts

6 cups flour
2 tablespoons sugar
1 tablespoon yeast
Dash salt
3 eggs, lightly beaten
2 tablespoons powdered milk
2½ tablespoons butter or margarine
Vegetable oil for deep frying

For the donuts

1. Put the flour in a large bowl. Form a well in the center of the flour. Put the sugar, yeast, salt, eggs, powdered milk, and butter into the well. Use your hands to form a dough. Gradually add about 1 cup water to form a dough that is not sticky. This is a stiff dough at first, so you will have to work hard to knead it thoroughly with your hands until it is smooth and fairly light. Knead the dough for 10 to 15 minutes.

2. Cut the dough in two pieces and stretch each piece into a long rope. Cut each of these into five additional pieces. Form each piece into a smooth ball. You will have ten balls, each about 2½ inches. Let the balls rest in a warm place, covered by a cloth, until almost doubled in size, about 1 hour.

3. Heat the vegetable oil in a deep pot over low heat until hot. Add enough oil to enable the donuts to float. If you use a narrow pot you will need less oil, but you will have more batches to cook. When the oil is hot, add one or two donuts. Cook very slowly, covered, until they are golden brown on both sides, about 15 to 20 minutes total. A knife should come out clean when inserted into the donut.

4. Remove the donuts and place on paper towels to absorb excess oil. Let cool. When cool, make a cut about ⅔ of the way around the donut. You will insert the filling into this "mouth" of the donut.

The pastry cream filling

4 cups milk
¾ cup plus 1 tablespoon sugar
½ cup cornstarch
2 teaspoons vanilla extract
2 egg yolks, lightly beaten

For the filling ━ ━ ━ ━ ━ ━ ━ ━ ━ ━ ━ ━ ━

1. Mix the milk and ¾ cup sugar in a medium saucepan over a low flame. Dissolve the cornstarch into the milk mixture.

2. After a few minutes, mix in the vanilla extract and egg yolks. Continue mixing constantly until the raw smell has dissipated and you have a creamy consistency, about 15 minutes total. It will be like a sweet béchamel sauce. Remove it from the heat.

3. Sprinkle the remaining tablespoon of sugar over the mixture (do not stir), and let cool. When it has cooled, mix in the sugar. The yield will be 3½ to 4 cups cream.

4. Spread a bit less than ¼ cup of the cream into each donut and serve warm or at room temperature. Store any leftover cream in the refrigerator.

Postres y Dulces

N o food seems to stir Chilean youths and adults alike as much as *manjar*. This cream, the color of light coffee and a trifle similar to toffee, is no doubt ideal for those of us born with a sweet tooth. Literally translated to mean "delicacy," *manjar* is also the fuel that drives bustling pastry industries in cities such as Curacaví and La Ligua in central Chile. Vendors of these pastries pop up everywhere in sight, and I am always eager to see what they will have hidden inside those baskets of theirs. What a cheerful sight for tired eyes they are when waiting at the tollbooth on the highway from Santiago to Valparaíso! Myriad brands of *manjar* can be found in stores in Chile, so there is no shortage of options for tickling your tongue. And of course it can be prepared at home as well, where it is particularly *sabroso* (delicious). Many of the recipes in this section are based on *manjar*, and you will often find it packaged in grocery stores (especially Latin ones) in the U.S. as *dulce de leche*. Egg-based pastries with creamy fillings are the rule in Chile, and the variations of delicious *dulces* (sweets) are endless.

Desserts and Sweets

Sweet Dough Crisps

Calzones Rotos y Roscas   About 40 crisps

It's not every day that you hope to see underwear on the kitchen table. However, that is what Chileans frequently long for. Sweet underwear, that is. **Calzones Rotos** *means "ripped underwear," and the name is not of scandalous origin. The dough is cut in small rectangular pieces, a hole is poked in the middle, and one end is pulled through the hole and back until the piece looks like a torn undergarment. For those at your table who find this tale far from amusing, serve them* **Roscas.** *It is made of the exact same dough, but the form is one of a penny-thin doughnut.*

7 ounces (2 sticks less 2
  tablespoons) margarine
1 cup granulated sugar
3 eggs
6½ cups flour (approximately)
Vegetable oil for deep-frying
Confectioners' sugar

1. Cream the margarine in a large bowl, slowly adding the granulated sugar. Beat in the eggs.

2. Stir in 6 cups of flour. Use your hands to form a bread-like dough, adding more flour, if necessary.

3. Sprinkle flour on a board. Put a few tablespoons of dough on the board and roll it flat with a rolling pin.

4. Now, form either *Calzones Rotos* and/or *Roscas*. They are identical, except for their different names and shapes.

For calzones rotos

Make a rectangular shape with the dough and cut a little rectangular slit in the center of the rectangle. Trim the sides to make it even. Tuck one of the short ends through the hole in the middle and pull it through. Pull it gently so that the dough does not tear.

For roscas

Use a round cookie cutter to cut out a circle of dough. Cut out a smaller circle of dough from the center.

  Heat about 1½ cups of vegetable oil in a skillet (enough to submerge the piece of dough) over a medium flame. When the oil is hot but not smoking, add the *Calzones Rotos* or *Roscas* without crowding them. Cook until golden brown on both sides, about 2 minutes total. Place them on paper towels to absorb excess oil. Let them cool and sprinkle with confectioners' sugar. Repeat the procedure with the remaining dough. Serve the goodies at room temperature.

Caramel Cream

Manjar   1 cup

The sweetest of delicacies requires patience so do not try to speed up the process of making manjar. *Chileans cook the ingredients over minimum heat by putting a mini-grill device called a* tostador de pan *below the saucepan to reduce the flame's heat. At the end of the cooking process, as the cream begins to really form, some people, such as Valesca Tercilla of Punta Arenas, use a hair dryer to further reduce the heat. In Chile, unlike in other Latin American countries, vanilla is generally not included in* manjar.

4 cups milk
1 cup sugar
Dash baking soda

1. Put the milk and sugar in a small saucepan and cook, uncovered, over minimum heat so that it is just simmering. Stir the mixture frequently, scraping not only the bottom of the pan but also the sides. The mixture will slowly begin to reduce and become creamy. It is ready when it has reduced to almost half of its original volume and it becomes thick like syrup. It should fall from a wooden spoon like a light syrup, rather than like honey or molasses. It will take on a light brown color, similar to that of coffee with milk (*café con leche*). This will take about 2 hours. Just as the mixture becomes creamy, mix in the baking soda.

2. Store refrigerated in a sealed container. The *manjar* will become thicker and creamier upon cooling.

Chilean Crepes with Caramel Cream

Panqueques con Manjar (Panqueques Celestino) About 8 crepes

Panqueques *are like crepes. In Santiago, Cynthia Vargas explained to me the simple but flawless way to prepare* **panqueques**, *which make a terrific dessert, but can also be eaten as a snack, for breakfast, or for the Chilean once (evening tea). The fillings vary by region, and not only include fruits and liquors, but also cheese, tomatoes, and mixed vegetables. The most cherished filling, however, is* **manjar**. *This adds to the dish's unique identity, and gives it a sweet and creamy taste. In parts of Chile (especially Patagonia), such a combination is called* **Panqueque Celestino**, *which also includes confectioners' sugar sprinkled on top.* **Manjar** *is generally added cold, rather than hot, to* **panqueques**. *You can also make a lighter* **manjar** *by mixing it with a bit of water.*

1 cup whole milk
¾ cup flour
2 eggs
Manjar (see recipe, page 200)
Confectioners' sugar (optional)

1. Combine the milk, flour, and eggs. Whisk thoroughly to make a batter free of lumps.

2. Heat a small nonstick skillet over medium-low heat. If you do not have a nonstick skillet, add just enough vegetable oil to coat the skillet. When the skillet is hot, add enough batter to cover the pan. Cook the *panqueque* until golden brown on both sides. If you only put a very thin layer of batter in the pan, the *panqueque* should cook in about 3 minutes.

3. Remove the *panqueque* and set it aside. Repeat with the remaining batter.

4. Serve the *panqueques* hot or cold. When serving, lay a *panqueque* flat on a plate and spread with a thin layer of jam or *manjar*. Roll up the *panqueque*. Sprinkle confectioners' sugar on top, if desired. Two or three crepes per diner are recommended.

Caramel Cream Sponge Cake

Brazo de Reina   2 cakes

▪ ▪ ▪ ▪ ▪ ▪ ▪ **Manjar** *is central in this regal dish known as* **Brazo de Reina** *(literally, "the Arm of a Queen"). The dish owes its name to its shape, which is also similar to that of a bûche de Noël, or small log. The recipe comes from María Burgos, who cooks both frequently and quickly. For María is used to a lot of heat in the kitchen, whenever her husband comes home for a quick bite. He is a fireman and the couple literally live in the backyard of a fire station. For a while María prepared dishes for all of the hungry firemen at the firehouse. These firehouses, which are sometimes open to the public, can be hotbeds of typical cuisine in Chile since mothers and friends of firemen are in the firehouse kitchens preparing their home-cooked specialties. María explained the chief ingredients of the* **Brazo de Reina** *in terms of tens, which is an easy way to remember the recipe and pass it on to others.* **Brazo de Reina** *is usually eaten as a dessert and accompanied by a cup of tea.*

10 eggs, separated
1¼ cups granulated sugar
1¼ cups flour
Manjar (see recipe, page 200)
3 tablespoons flaked or
  shredded coconut
2 tablespoons coarsely
  chopped walnuts
Butter for wax paper

1. Preheat the oven to 300° F. Grease a strip of wax paper (about 39 x 31 inches). You may have to use more than one piece of paper. Lay the wax paper on a large baking sheet. You may have to lay it over 2 baking sheets.

2. Put the egg yolks in a medium bowl. Gradually beat the yolks, slowly adding half the sugar. Beat thoroughly until the mixture is thick and creamy (like mayonnaise). It is ready when bubbles begin to form on the surface.

3. In a separate bowl, beat the egg whites, gradually adding the remaining sugar. Beat until stiff peaks form.

4. Gradually fold the egg yolk mixture into the egg white mixture, using sweeping strokes. Continue until it is thoroughly mixed and bubbles appear on the surface. Gradually mix in the flour so that lumps do not form. Divide the batter into two equal amounts by placing half of it into the bowl you used for the egg yolks.

5. Pour one batch of the mixture on to the waxed paper and place in the oven.

6. Bake the cake for about 10 minutes. Remove the cake from the oven as soon as the surface is lightly golden and the corners are golden brown. Do not overbake. The cake will have a sponge-like consistency. Immediately after you have removed the cake from the oven, use a knife or a spatula to carefully remove it from the pan onto a clean, flat surface; otherwise, it will continue to cook and stick to the wax paper.

7. Spread a thin layer of *manjar* over the surface of the cake. Starting from one of the short sides, roll the cake gently away from you, "jellyroll style," folding it over the *manjar* in several rolls. You now will have something shaped like an arm. It will be about 11 inches long, 3 inches wide, and 2 inches thick.

8. Spread another thin layer of manjar over the surface of the cake. Sprinkle 1½ tablespoons of coconut over the top (and along the sides, if desired). Layer 1 tablespoon of the walnuts across the center of the cake.

9. Repeat with the remaining batter to make a second *Brazo de Reina*.

10. Cut into individual pieces and serve at room temperature.

Multilayer Cake

Torta de Mil Hojas   1 cake

The literal name of the dish, "Cake of 1,000 Leaves," suggests a truly daunting task for the brave soul who will tackle it in the kitchen. However, it is only about fifteen layers and the preparation is fairly simple. The cake is similar in ingredients to Brazo de Reina, but its consistency and result are markedly different. While it is somewhat reminiscent of a Middle Eastern sweet, with fine layers of dough like phyllo, the use of manjar helps give it its Latin signature. This recipe comes from Olga Rodriguez, who says that some make the layers of this cake in square rather than circular shapes. Olga also makes a range of cakes and jams using native foods, such as those of alcayota and rosa mosqueta, and she fills the panqueques that she makes with her homemade quince jam.

10 egg yolks
½ cup butter, melted
2½ cups flour (approximately)
3 tablespoons white wine
4 cups *Manjar* (approximately)
  (see recipe, page 200)
½ cup coconut flakes
  (approximately)

1. Blend the egg yolks and melted butter in a blender. Gradually add ½ cup flour. Pour the mixture into a bowl.

2. Mix in 2 tablespoons of water and, gradually, another 1½ cups flour. Form a dough with your hands, adding more flour, if necessary. Use your hands to knead the dough until it is smooth.

3. Preheat the oven to 350° F.

4. Roll out the dough on both sides on a lightly-floured surface. Cut the dough into about eleven pieces. Form each piece into a smooth ball.

5. Use a rolling pin to roll each ball into a pancake, making them as thin as possible without breaking them—paper-thin is ideal.

6. Put a large plate (about 9 inches in diameter) face down over one of the sheets of dough. Use a knife to cut around the plate. Repeat this procedure for the rest of the dough. Re-roll the leftover dough scraps to make additional circles. You should end up with about fourteen circles.

7. Use a fork to gently prick all over the surface of each circle.

8. Place the circles of dough on large baking sheets (without overlapping) and put as many into the oven as comfortably fit on one or two racks. Bake until they are golden brown on both sides (turning once), about 5 minutes. Immediately brush the circles of dough very lightly on both sides with white wine. Repeat with the remaining layers of dough. Let the layers cool.

9. Put one layer on a large plate. With a brush, spread just enough *manjar* to cover the surface. Then for each additional layer, spread just enough *manjar* to cover both sides of the layer. Do it gently so that the cake does not break. Sprinkle coconut flakes on one side. Put that layer on top of the layer on the cake plate and repeat this procedure until you have layered all the circles onto one another. Spread *manjar* on the top of the cake as well as around its sides. Use a straw to blow coconut flakes off of a flat dish, onto the cake's sides.

Stewed Peaches and Shelled Wheat

Mote con Huesillo   10 to 12 servings

If you wander around in the wonderful farmers' markets in any city or town of Chile you'll likely bump into an ambulating **Mote con Huesillo** *vendor. Men and women stroll wheeled carts through the market year-round in order to peddle their homemade juice of peach nectar and shelled wheat. While it may sound quaint, indulging in this sweet and satisfying drink will become second nature to you if you spend a bit of time in Chile. It can be served well-chilled in a glass as a drink to cool you off on a hot day, in place of dessert. Some Latin stores in the U.S. carry dried peaches; the larger the peach, the better.*

1 pound dried peaches, with pits (approximately 22 dried peaches)
1 to 1¼ cups sugar
1 cup (7 ounces) shelled wheat

1. Submerge the dried peaches in 3 quarts of water and soak overnight.

2. The next day, cook the peaches in the soaking water over high heat. When it comes to a boil, add 1 cup sugar and reduce the heat to low. As it simmers add more sugar or water, if necessary, to create a tasty juice.

3. The peaches are cooked when they are soft and tender and the peaches have doubled in size, about 25 to 30 minutes. Remove from the heat and chill the peaches and sweetened water in the refrigerator.

4. Meanwhile, rinse the wheat and place in a medium-size pot with 8 cups (2 quarts) of water. Bring to a boil over high heat. Continue boiling over high heat until the wheat is tender, like cooked rice, about 25 to 30 minutes, and then drain it. You should have approximately 3 cups of wheat. Chill the wheat in the refrigerator, in a separate container from the peach mixture. (The wheat would become soggy if left in the peach mixture.)

5. When all the ingredients are cold, put approximately ¼ cup wheat in a drinking glass. Add two of the peaches and about ½ cup of the sweetened water. Repeat with remaining ingredients. Serve with a spoon.

Kuchen de Manzana

Apple Cake 1 cake

- - - - The south of Chile is replete with Germans, many of whom have been in towns
like Valdivia and Frutillar for 200 years. Consequently, the German influence on
Chilean food, particularly its sweets, has been profound. Over the years, Chileans
have adopted desserts such as kuchen as their own and are often unaware of their
German origin. The recipe below comes from Jeanette Silva Peña, a non-German
Chilean who makes pear, banana, walnut, raspberry, and other kuchens for the
lodgers of her bed-and-breakfast Hostal Anwandter in Valdivia. Kuchen means
"cake" in German, and among the most traditional varieties is that filled with
apples. Kuchen is filling and one way to lighten it, if desired, is by halving the
amount of crumbs layered over the apples.

The apples
6 apples (3½ pounds),
   peeled
2 tablespoons butter
⅓ cup sugar

The dough
3 eggs
1 cup sugar
1 cup butter, softened
1½ teaspoons baking powder
4 cups flour

The crumbs
¼ cup butter, softened
¼ teaspoon vanilla extract
¼ cup sugar
½ cup plus 2 tablespoons flour

1. Preheat the oven to 350°F and grease a 9 x 9-inch pan.

2. **For the apples:** Chop the apples coarsely. Place them in a medium saucepan with the butter. Heat over a medium flame, covered, stirring frequently until the apples are tender, about 40 minutes. Mix in the sugar and set aside.

3. **For the dough:** In a large bowl, lightly whisk the eggs and mix in the sugar. Add the butter and baking powder and whisk briefly to remove any lumps. Mix in the flour with a spoon, and then with your hands, to make a soft dough.

4. **For the crumbs:** In a medium bowl, mix the butter, vanilla, and sugar. Gradually mix in the flour with a spoon, and then with your hands. Use your fingers and the palms of your hands to break the mixture into small crumbs.

5. Press the dough into the pan. Spread the apple mixture evenly over the dough. Spoon the crumbs evenly over the apple mixture.

6. Put the pan into the oven. Cook until the cake rises and is golden on the surface, about 35 minutes.

Creamy Coffee Boat

Corazón de Café

With all of the ports lining coastal Chile the sight of boats going in and out becomes part of the everyday panorama. The boat produced by this recipe that I learned from Jorge Aoun goes into your mouth. Chileans do not as a habit devour coffee, opting instead for tea (they are one of the world's greatest tea consumers). And café life is meager, apart from the ubiquitous cafés con piernas *(cafes with legs), in which scantily-clad women serve espresso in establishments that are sometimes barely legal. On occasion, however, coffee finds a place in haute cuisine. In this dish, I find the sweet coffee taste of these floating vessels to be delectable.*

1 quart cold whole milk
2 tablespoons vanilla extract
Peel from one orange
3 eggs, separated
1 tablespoon cornstarch
1½ cups sugar
1½ tablespoons ground coffee

1. Preheat the oven to 350° F.

2. Put the milk, vanilla extract, and orange peel in a saucepan. Bring to a boil over high heat, then turn off the heat and discard the orange peel. Let cool.

3. Meanwhile, whisk the egg yolks thoroughly in a medium-size bowl. Add the cornstarch and continue whisking until creamy, removing any lumps. When the milk mixture has cooled, gradually whisk it into the bowl of egg yolks. Set aside.

4. Beat the egg whites in another bowl until soft peaks form. Put the sugar, coffee, and 2 tablespoons of water in a medium-size saucepan and cook over medium heat. Stir occasionally with a wooden spoon. The mixture is ready when the sugar caramelizes and the caramel falls very slowly from a spoon like molasses, about 4 to 5 minutes. Remove the saucepan from a stove and immediately add the egg whites, mixing them in rapidly. Do not wait to mix in the egg whites, or the caramel will become too hard and begin to crystallize. Stir the egg whites and caramel together until they are thoroughly combined and you have a beige cream.

5. Fill a large rectangular baking pan, about 9 x 13 inches, $\frac{1}{3}$ full with water. Set it in the hot oven.

6. Pour the mixture into a smaller rectangular baking pan that fits inside the larger pan, about 8 x 2 inches. When the water in the larger pan is boiling, reduce the oven temperature to 250° F, and place the smaller baking pan into the larger pan. It should float in the water like a boat. Bake until it doubles in size and a knife inserted comes out clean, about 25 minutes. Turn off the heat and remove the smaller pan. Let the mixture cool.

7. Use a funnel to poke a hole in one of the corners of the cooled mixture in the pan. Add all of the milk mixture from Step 3, so that it flows under the cake, lifting it up. Again, you will have a kind of floating boat. If the cake does not lift when you pour in the milk, remove the entire cake from its pan and place it in a separate pan of the milk mixture.

8. Refrigerate and serve cold.

Papayas and Cream

Claudia Charlin calls La Serena, the "City of Papayas." She should know. The septuagenarian mother of six is in perfect health, largely, she says due to her heavy consumption of papayas. Indeed, according to Claudia, papaya is good for the body in twenty ways, including that it helps digestion, breaks down meats in the body, makes nails hard, gives hair life and shine, and cleans the skin. Claudia, who eats entire papayas (skin, pits, and all), says the seeds of very ripe papayas cleanse the stomach.

1½ pounds fresh papayas
Ice
½ cup sugar, plus additional
5 cups water
½ cup whipping cream
  (approximately)

1. Chill the papayas on ice and set aside for ½ hour.

2. Use a knife to peel the chilled papayas and use a spoon to remove the seeds.

3. Put the papayas in a pot and cover with 5 cups of water. Bring to a boil and cover.

4. When the papayas are soft, after about 5 minutes, add ½ cup sugar to sweeten the liquid. Boil for 3 to 4 more minutes, mixing thoroughly. Add more sugar if desired and remove from the heat.

5. Refrigerate the cooked papaya in its juice. When it has chilled, serve it in a champagne glass or a bowl, and cover with cream.

Sweet Meringue Pudding

– – – – *Chile is known for glorious snow-capped mountain peaks that attract the most adventuresome of skiers. In the dish below, the highest altitudes are brought to life. This dish is called* **Leche Nevada,** *or "Snowy Milk," for a reason: the fluffy egg whites float on the hot milk like snowballs.*

6½ cups whole milk
1 cup plus 3 tablespoons
   sugar
2 to 3 cinnamon sticks
2 eggs, separated
2 tablespoons cornstarch
Dash salt
Ground cinnamon

1. Put 6 cups of the milk, 1 cup of the sugar, and the cinnamon sticks into a large pot. Stir thoroughly. Bring to a boil, then immediately reduce the heat to simmer.

2. Meanwhile, beat the egg whites and a dash of salt with an electric mixer until foamy. Add the remaining sugar and continue beating until it is thick and stands in soft peaks, about 5 minutes. Here you are creating *"la nieve,"* or "the snow," for the dessert.

3. Drop about ¼ to ½ cup of the egg whites into the simmering milk mixture. Ladle some of the hot milk over the egg whites. (If the egg whites begin to bubble and inflate on the surface of the hot milk, briefly remove the pot from the heat.) After ladling the hot milk over the egg white mixture for about 2 minutes, use a spoon to transfer them to a large bowl. Repeat with remaining egg whites. Continue to simmer the milk.

4. Pour off all but ½ cup of milk from the bowl with the egg whites. Whisk the cornstarch into the remaining ½ cup of milk. Add this mixture to the pot and stir for 5 minutes. Discard the cinnamon sticks.

5. Put the egg yolks in the bowl and lightly beat them. Whisk in ⅔ cup of the hot milk mixture. Stir constantly. Repeat with another ⅔ cup of hot milk. Gradually add this mixture to the hot milk. As you add the egg yolk mixture to the pot of hot milk, stir vigorously to maintain a light consistency. After about 30 seconds, when the egg yolk mixture is mixed into the hot milk mixture, pour it over the egg whites. You should see thick, creamy white fluff floating upon a milky liquid, resembling melted marshmallows adrift a pale yellow pool.

6. Let the mixture cool, then put it in the refrigerator. When it has chilled thoroughly, serve in individual bowls, sprinkled with a bit of cinnamon.

Caramel Pudding

Leche Asada

One of the doormen to my apartment in Valparaíso became intrigued by the constant scents drifting from above. We soon began talking about cuisine and he introduced me to the caramel pudding of his mother, Luisa Cabrera. Similar to flan, it can be put together in a matter of minutes, yet it provides an afternoon of satisfaction.

The caramel:
1 cup sugar

The pudding:
8 eggs
6 cups whole milk
1 cup sugar

1. Preheat the oven to 350° F.

2. **For the caramel:** Place the sugar in a saucepan and cook over low heat. Stir it when it begins to bubble and take on a light brown color. Continue stirring until it is light brown throughout and there are no lumps of sugar. Gradually add ⅓ cup of water, stirring constantly, and remove from the heat after about two minutes. You should have a light syrup that falls from a spoon. It will thicken upon cooling.

3. **For the pudding:** Use an electric beater to mix the eggs at medium speed, about 1 minute. Gradually add the milk and sugar and continue beating for another 4 minutes. The ingredients should now be thoroughly combined and the mixture should be slightly foamy.

4. Brush a thin layer of caramel on the bottom and sides of a 9 x 13 inch pan. This is done not only to add sweetness to the dish, but also to ensure that the milk mixture does not stick to the pan. You will probably use about ⅔ of the caramel. Set the rest of the caramel aside.

5. Pour the milk mixture into the pan and put the pan into the oven. Bake until the surface turns golden and a knife comes out clean when inserted into the pudding. This should take 45 minutes to 1 hour.

6. Remove the pan from the oven, let cool and place in the refrigerator. When it is thoroughly chilled, ladle the rest of the caramel over the pudding. Cut into individual slices and serve.

Calabaza Fritters in Molasses Sauce

Sopaipillas Pasadas

2¼ cups or sauce for thirty-five to forty
3 x 3-inch fritters

In this recipe, you can use the sopaipillas *that you made for a salty snack to make a delicious dessert or an afternoon tea. At the heart of the recipe is chancaca, which is sweet like molasses but is a solid form made of sugar and cane juice; it is dissolved in water to produce a syrupy liquid. Chancaca is so hard that Chileans hammer a knife into it to break off small amounts for cooking. Chancaca can be found in Latin stores in the U.S., usually under the name panela. In this recipe, you simply pass the fritter in the hot syrup to enable it to heat and absorb the rich flavors. Thus the dish's surname,* Pasadas, *meaning "passed." The end result is something that is perhaps slightly redolent of French toast in taste.*

35 to 40 (3-inch) *Sopaipillas*
(see recipe, page 187)
10 ounces *panela* or, if
unavailable, 1½ cups
brown sugar
2 cinnamon sticks
2 whole cloves
Peel of ¼ orange
2 tablespoons cornstarch

1. Put the *panela* in a medium-size saucepan. Add 4 cups of water, the cinnamon, cloves, and orange peel. Bring to a boil, stirring constantly to dissolve the *panela*.

2. Dissolve the cornstarch in ¼ cup of water.

3. When the *panela* mixture is boiling, add the cornstarch mixture and reduce the heat to medium. As the liquid bubbles, continue stirring until it has reduced to a light syrup, about 30 minutes (though you can add more cornstarch to thicken the liquid more quickly). The mixture should be lighter than molasses but thicker than water. Remove the cinnamon stick, cloves, and orange peel.

4. Submerge 2 *sopaipillas* in the syrup, cover and continue cooking over very low heat. Turn them occasionally with a wooden spoon. They are ready when they are hot and have absorbed the flavors of the syrup, 4 to 5 minutes. Do not cook the sopaipillas in the syrup for too long because they will overcook and become soggy.

5. Remove the sopaipillas from the pot, put them on a plate, and drizzle 1 to 2 tablespoons of the syrup over them. Repeat with the remaining *sopaipillas*, two at a time. Serve hot.

Calabaza Fritters in Sweet Broth

Picarones   8 to 10 servings

Mainly found in southern Chile, picarones are like little pumpkin donuts that soak up the flavors of a sweet soup. They are generally eaten as a snack or light evening meal, rather than as a dessert, and are ideal for consuming by the fire during winter. The picarones that Chileans eat are said to have originated in Lima, Peru, with a woman called Rosalía. Around 1825 she fell in love with a Chilean soldier, and they married and moved to Santiago. She began selling her sweets to great fanfare, and the concept of picarones spread. Yet in Chillán, Chileans were making similar fritters of flour, yeast, and calabaza even before Rosalía's business boomed, though they were called Furundungos. Although the precise form of the picarones is not of dire importance, in Chile they sell equipment that carves perfectly cylindrical picarones. Literally, a picarón is a flirtatious man, so picarones means flirtatious men. Here, though, they are fried pumpkin fritters, or properly, fried pumpkin bread fritters.

The calabaza fritters

9 ounces *calabaza* or
  butternut squash,
  cut in small slices
2 to 2½ cups flour
½ cup sugar
2 teaspoons dry yeast

For the calabaza fritters

1. Boil the *calabaza* in water over high heat until tender. Strain and mash the calabaza until creamy. Let cool.

2. Put the *calabaza* in a large bowl with the flour, sugar, and yeast. Mix thoroughly. Use your hands to make a dough that is like a somewhat moist bread dough, adding more flour if necessary. It should be a bit sticky and very light. (about 2½ cups) Cover with a cloth and set in a warm place to rise until almost doubled in size, about 1½ hours.

3. Heat the vegetable oil in a skillet over high heat. When it is hot, reduce the heat to medium. Moisten fingers in a glass of water, take a piece of dough—about 1 heaping tablespoon—and form 2-inch circles, with a small hole in the middle (like a small donut). Add the *picarones* to the skillet without crowding them. Cook each *picarón* briefly until golden brown on both sides, about 1 to 2 minutes. Remove them to paper towels to absorb excess oil and set aside. Repeat with the remaining dough. For a treat, you can sprinkle powdered sugar on a couple of *picarones* and eat them warm.

The broth

1¾ cups sugar, divided
5 tablespoons cornstarch
Peel of ¼ orange
10 whole cloves
1 cinnamon stick

2 cups vegetable oil for
   deep-frying

For the broth

1. Bring 10 cups (2½ quarts) of water to a boil in a large pot.

2. Dissolve the cornstarch in an additional ½ cup water. Set aside.

3. When the water in the pot is boiling, add the orange peel, cloves, and cinnamon stick, along with the cornstarch mixture. Mix thoroughly. Reduce the heat and simmer.

4. In a small saucepan, caramelize 1 cup of sugar (for instructions on caramelizing, see recipe, page 216, *Plátanos en Almíbar*). When the caramel is ready, after about 5 minutes, gradually add it to the pot. Do this carefully because bubbles will leap up from the pot. Mix thoroughly. Continue simmering an additional 10 minutes, while adding more sugar (about ¾ cup) to create a sweet, satisfying broth. Remove from heat.

For the assembly

1. Immediately add the number of fritters that you plan to serve to the pot of hot broth, cover, and set aside for 5 to 10 minutes so the fritters absorb the sweet flavors. If you are serving some of the fritters later, store them separate from the soup, then bring the soup to a boil and add the fritters.

2. Serve each person a bowl with a bit of the hot broth and a few fried calabaza pieces. Serve 2 *picarones* per 1 cup of broth.

Bananas in Caramel

This dish smacks of Arab origins with its name and flavor. Whenever I am running short of time for dessert, this is what I turn to since guests are never disappointed.

1 cup sugar
6 fresh bananas, sliced into
  chips

1. Put the sugar in a saucepan and heat it over low heat. Do not stir it until it begins to bubble and turn brown underneath. Gradually stir until all of the sugar granules have completely dissolved and you have a clear brown syrup, about 5 minutes.

2. Immediately add a bit of water, stirring constantly. Continue adding water (about ⅓ cup in total) gradually and stirring until you have a light syrup. It will thicken upon cooling. You will have about ¾ cup of caramel.

3. Divide the bananas between six bowls and drizzle the syrup over each.

Fig Jam

*Many people in Chile have their own fig trees and pick figs before they mature. They boil them and are left with whole juicy figs, which they stuff with chestnuts and serve in a sweet sauce (**Higos Rellenos con Castañas en Almíbar**). Others make fig pie, or the fig jam described below. Decades ago, Chileans regularly prepared their own jams, taking advantage of some of the world's most exquisite strawberries, cherries, grapes, and other fruits. With a variety of jams now bursting off supermarket shelves and the growing trend of two parents working long hours, this custom has fallen by the wayside. However, delectable jams such as alcayota (a melon-shaped native fruit) and walnut can still be discovered when driving in the countryside. Fig jam too is popular, using either of the two fruits that grace the fig trees of Chile: **higos**, which are figs like our own, and **brevas**, which are almost twice the size. Use powdered fruit pectin or liquid fruit pectin if you plan to preserve the jam.*

2 to 2½ pounds fresh figs, stems removed
¾ cup sugar
1 cinnamon stick

1. Chop the figs finely or briefly blend them in a food processor.

2. Put the figs in a pot with ¼ cup of water and bring to a boil.

3. Add the sugar and the cinnamon stick and reduce heat to low. Add additional sugar if you like very sweet jam. Simmer on low heat, stirring constantly with a wooden spoon.

4. Cook for approximately 20 minutes, until the jam thickens and clings to the spoon.

5. Remove the cinnamon stick and let the jam cool. Pack in sterile jars and refrigerate.

Rhubarb Mousse

A trip to Los Ganaderos, a restaurant in Punta Arenas, says a lot about the cuisine in the southern reaches of Chile. When traveling deep south from central Chile you finally arrive in Patagonia, where hordes and hordes of sheep greet you. Suddenly lamb festoons tables at home and graces restaurant menus, including at barbecues, or parrilladas, where chorizo, blood sausage, and beef grill away. The same transformation is true about rhubarb. While rhubarb was nowhere to be seen in the rest of Chile, in Punta Arenas it is readily available at grocery stores, and merchants offer up their own rhubarb creations, such as rhubarb and fig jam. Rhubarb thrives in Punta Arenas because it is happiest in extreme climates like Patagonia. Delicious when sweetened with sugar, rhubarb is composed of 95 percent water, though it does provide a decent source of potassium. The source of this recipe is John Mattson, the owner of Los Ganaderos. I added a bit of shaved chocolate to really bring out the flavor of the rhubarb. While Patagonian lamb is what leads many to Los Ganaderos, intriguing desserts such as this rhubarb mousse helps bring them back.

2 pounds fresh rhubarb
1⅔ cups sugar
½ envelope (½ tablespoon) vegetable-based plain gelatin
1 cup heavy cream
Semisweet chocolate, shaved

1. Bring the rhubarb to a boil in 2 cups of water. Reduce the heat, cover, and simmer slowly to draw out the the intense flavor of the rhubarb, stirring frequently. Mix in 1⅓ cups of the sugar. Total cooking time for the rhubarb is approximately 2 hours. Let cool and then mix in the gelatin.

2. Whip the cream with the remaining ⅓ cup of sugar. Mix thoroughly into the rhubarb mixture. Spoon into individual glasses and chill. Sprinkle the chocolate shavings over each glass and serve cold.

Bebidas y Tragos

Pisco Sour has finally started making a splash in the U.S., finding its way into fashionable bars on both coasts. On the other hand, in Chile Piscomania is nothing new. Unless you're a teetotaler you can't go to Chile without having a Pisco Sour. The country's national mixed drink, it is wonderful as a cocktail before dinner or as a cooler during a hot day. Piscola, the simple mixture of *Pisco* and coke, is also a national favorite.

There is a fierce debate, however, over the grape brandy called *Pisco* that pits Chile against its northern neighbor. Peru claims *Pisco* as its own because *Pisco* Sours are also wildly popular there and there is a city in Peru named Pisco. However, Chile has a place bearing the name Pisco as well—Pisco Elqui, in the northern valley of Elqui—which is the heart of Pisco country. At times the debate between the countries intensifies, and they badmouth each other a bit or show their superior allegiance to the grape liqueur by instituting national *Pisco* days and going through their government to fight for their case.

While they are the world's two *Pisco* producers, Chile far outranks Peru in terms of exports, and personal experience suggests the Chileans will not back down from their claim to or love for Pisco any time soon. Just as well, since they are coming up with new and delicious recipes at a time when more and more Chilean companies are looking to sell Pisco in the U.S. market. The most popular of those recipes follow. *Pisco* is increasingly available in U.S. wine and liquor stores, particularly in states with large Latin populations such as California, Florida, Texas, and New York, with the major brands of Capel and Pisco Control dominating. I have recommended *Pisco* that is 40 proof, since it is quite common, but bottles of 35 proof are also available. Many of these drinks call for egg yolks; those wary of consuming raw eggs can substitute a bit of heavy cream.

Those who shun alcohol would be equally delighted with the fruit juices available in Chile. Freshly squeezed mangos and papayas in the north make two of the most unforgettable juices, though there are many others such as passion fruit and cactus fruit. Or, in the south you can warm up with a cup of *mate*, an all-natural herbal tea.

Traditional Pisco Sour

Pisco Sour   4 servings

The purest Pisco drink is a simple mix of Pisco, sugar, lemon, and ice, though in the north, key limes stand in for lemons. The town of Pica has gained particular renown for key limes: The Chilean term for these is "limón de Pica," literally meaning "lemon from Pica." In Chile, unlike in Peru, whisked egg whites are rarely added to the surface of the glass of Pisco to provide foam. Typically, Chileans use confectioners' sugar when making mixed drinks with Pisco.

½ cup freshly squeezed
  lemon or key lime juice
1½ cups Pisco (40 proof)
⅓ to ½ cup confectioners'
  sugar
1½ cups crushed ice

Mix the lemon juice, Pisco, sugar, and ice. Or use a cocktail shaker to blend the ingredients.

Pisco Sour with Mango and Lime Juice

Mango Sour   4 servings

Mango is principally found in northern Chile and, since lime replaces lemon there, it was only a matter of time before this recipe evolved.

1½ cups Pisco (40 proof)
1 cup mango juice
2 tablespoons freshly
   squeezed lime juice
1½ to 2 cups crushed ice
Confectioners' sugar (optional)

Thoroughly blend the Pisco, mango juice, lime juice, and crushed ice. Try the mixture. If it is tart, add confectioners' sugar. The amount of sugar you add will depend on the sweetness of your mango juice.

Papaya Pisco Sour

Serena Libre   4 servings

Papaya is at its richest and most fragrant in La Serena and El Valle del Elqui. In Chile it is all to easy too enjoy papayas because they are sold fresh in markets and grocery stores and in bottles with their sweet natural juices. Water is added to the recipe below because otherwise the drink is very thick. If you buy extra papayas, you can make homemade papaya juice (see recipe, page 230) and replace the water with the papaya juice, reducing the sugar.

10 ounces fresh papaya
   (about 4 papayas), peeled
   and seeded
1⅓ cups Pisco (40 proof)
1½ cups crushed ice
⅔ cup confectioners' sugar
   (approximately)

Mix the papaya, Pisco, ice, sugar, and ⅔ cup of water in a blender until the papaya is pureed. Add papaya juice or sugar if you prefer the drink sweeter.

Banana and Papaya Twist

La Primavera   4 servings

La Primavera *is a popular drink in Chile that includes Pisco and a few types of fruit. Other countries often use vodka in their* Primavera *recipes. Like the word* primavera, *which means "springtime," it is refreshing, as is the non-alcoholic version made without Pisco.*

½ pound fresh papayas
2 bananas
¼ cup chopped pineapple
⅓ cup confectioners' sugar
1 cup Fresh Papaya Juice (see recipe, page 230 or use water and additional sugar)
1½ cups crushed ice
1½ cups Pisco (40 proof)

Blend all the ingredients together until fully pureed, and serve.

Pisco and Vermouth

Pichuncho   4 servings

Pichuncho *provides instant warmth on a cold day.*

1 cup vermouth
1 cup Pisco (40 proof)
4 thin slices of lemon

Mix the vermouth and Pisco and pour into 4 glasses. Place a lemon slice on the rim of each glass and serve.

Chilean Caipirinha

Every time I think of Brazil I envision lazing away on one of the beaches with the sun burning down and a Caipirinha in my hand. That sensation can be felt in a way in Chile with the Pisquiriña, which calls for Pisco rather than the Brazilian liquor, cachaça. Use ordinary or key limes.

1 lime, quartered
3 tablespoons Pisco (40 proof)
2 tablespoons confectioners' sugar
½ cup finely crushed ice

1. Place the lime quarters in a glass. Crush the limes with a pestle or the handle of a spoon until they are well-squashed and have released most of their juices.

2. Add the Pisco, sugar, and ice. Stir thoroughly with a spoon, continuing to press down on the limes to release more juice.

Piscrewdriver

Canario 4 servings

In Chile, orange juice and vodka combined are not called screwdrivers, but they are quite popular. I named this drink "Piscrewdriver" because it is the same as a screwdriver except that Pisco stands in for vodka. The amount of sugar you need depends on the sweetness of your orange juice.

½ cup plus 2 tablespoons orange juice
1 cup Pisco (40 proof)
1½ cups crushed ice
A few tablespoons confectioners' sugar (optional)

Thoroughly blend all the ingredients. If the mixture is lacking in sweetness, add additional confectioners' sugar.

Cinnamon Shooter

Canelita

This is one of my favorite mistelas, *which are drinks made by boiling a fruit or vegetable in water with sugar, and later adding* aguardiente. *This is a cane alcohol that is usually 50 proof found in Chile and other Latin countries. At your liquor store you may find it under a Colombian label. There are quite a number of varieties of* mistelas, *including* Mistela Mandarina *(with mandarin orange),* Mistela Beterraga *(with beets),* Apiado *(with celery leaves), and* Enguindado *(with cherries).* Mistelas *are generally drunk as a* bajativo, *or after-dinner drink, and are served in shot glasses.*

---

7 cinnamon sticks
3 whole cloves
½ to ¾ cup sugar
6 cups water
1½ cups *aguardiente* (50 proof) (approximately)

1. Boil the cinnamon sticks, cloves, and sugar in a pot with 6 cups of water, over high heat. The liquid will reduce considerably and gradually take on a brownish-red color. When it has taken on this color and there is a pronounced cinnamon taste to the liquid, after 40 to 45 minutes, remove the pot from the stove. There should be approximately 3 cups of liquid. Let the mixture cool.

2. When it has cooled, strain the liquid and discard the cinnamon sticks and cloves. Add *aguardiente* according to how strong you want the drink.

3. Mix thoroughly and refrigerate until chilled. Serve cold.

Celery Leaf Shooter

Apiado   4½ cups

One day in San Felipe, a typical restaurant called La Ruca, I became very inquisitive about traditional Chilean drinks. The waiter, Victor Sabando, put me in his hands and let me sample several mistelas, including this one that uses celery leaves, a staple in the Chilean kitchen. Below is one way of giving the drink its required green hue, though to make it still deeper-colored one can also put numerous celery leaves in a full bottle of aguardiente for a couple of weeks in a place where it soaks in sun, or use a bit of green coloring.

½ cup fresh celery leaves
½ to ¾ cup sugar
1½ cups aguardiente (50 proof) (approximately)

1. Bring the celery leaves, sugar, and 6 cups of water to a boil, over high heat. The liquid will reduce considerably and gradually take on a yellowish-green color. When it has taken on this color and there is a pronounced celery taste to the liquid, after about 30 to 35 minutes, remove the pot from the stove. There should be approximately 3 cups of liquid in the pot. Let the mixture cool.

2. When it has cooled strain the liquid, discarding the leaves. Add *aguardiente* according to how strong you want the drink.

3. Mix thoroughly and refrigerate. Serve cold. You do not need to store *Apiado* in the refrigerator, and it keeps for more than 1 year.

Cherry Shooter

Hortensia Mora and her husband Hernan run a small bar, where they offer many home-brewed concoctions. This includes ample **mistelas**, *one of which is made from* **mutilla**, *a very small red fruit found in southern Chile. Another is this widely consumed cherry* **mistela**, *often pronounced "en-geen-dow-oo," as Chileans frequently omit the last "d." Don't be bashful about trying the cherries after they soak for several days, as they go from dry and tart to moist and sweet. When you prepare this drink several times you will learn to adjust the sugar amount in accordance with the tartness of the cherries you purchase.*

1⅓ cups (½ pound) dried cherries
2 cups full-bodied red wine (such as Cabernet Sauvignon)
¼ cup granulated sugar
2 large cinnamon sticks
2 whole cloves
2½ cups aguardiente (50 proof)

1. Put the cherries, red wine, sugar, cinnamon sticks, and cloves in a medium saucepan. Mix thoroughly. Set aside overnight.

2. The next day, bring the mixture to a boil in the saucepan. When the mixture boils reduce the heat to low. Continue cooking until the liquid thickens, the red-wine flavor dissipates, and the alcohol burns away, about 15 minutes. There will be about 1 cup of liquid remaining. Remove the pot from the heat and let the mixture cool.

3. Mix in the *aguardiente*. Do not remove the spices. There is no need to refrigerate it, as it does not go bad. Over time you may want to remove the spices as the drink may become too "spicy."

Chilean "Irish Coffee"

Cola de Mono *is typically enjoyed over the holidays, especially on Christmas and New Year's Eve. On these special days, Chileans wander from house to house, knocking on doors and sharing* Cola de Mono *with a slice of* Pan de Pascua *(see recipe, page 187). The creamy drink, which is very popular in central Chile, contains several spices and packs a punch.*

There may be as many different origins for the drink's name, which is trans-lated "Monkey's Tail," as there are recipes. Some Chileans suggest the name owes itself to the drink's color, which is brown like that of a monkey's tail. Others argue that bottles of the concoction were sent to Chile from Spain with a monkey embossed on the labels. However, the more colorful and bandied about theories lie with a storied Chilean called Pedro Montt.

Those who want to make Montt look like a bit of a monkey claim that the drink's name stems from the presidential election he lost in 1901. When one loses something Chileans say that they are left con cola, *or "with a tail." The followers of Germán Riesco, who vanquished Montt for the presidency, celebrated the victory at a bar where they were served a drink that they dubbed "Cola de Montt." The nomencla-ture soon metamorphosed into something a bit more animated, combining as such perhaps because Montt's complexion was dark like a monkey's and the Riesco camp was calling him a "cola," which is pejorative in Chile for homosexual.*

Yet, in another version, Montt saved face—when he became the proud president of Chile (1906-1910). Here we find President Montt at the party of the widow Filomena Cortés, who titillated many a bachelor's stomach with her cuisine, along with her four single daughters, who charmed many an ear with their heavenly gui-tar and harp playing. When Pedro finally decided to turn in for the night, he asked someone to fetch his Colt revolver. However, attendees, concerned by the blis-tering downpour that evening, pretended not to be able to find the revolver so that the party would go merrily on. With most of the wine and liquor already down the hatch, they could only muster up milk, coffee, aguardiente, and sugar. But how well they blended together! The frolickers called their new serendipitous master-piece, "Colt de Montt."

5 cups whole milk
2 cinnamon sticks
5 whole cloves
$\frac{1}{2}$ cup sugar
$2\frac{1}{2}$ teaspoons instant coffee
$1\frac{1}{2}$ cups *aguardiente*
  (50 proof)
1 egg yolk, lightly beaten
2 teaspoons vanilla extract

1. Put the milk, cinnamon sticks, and cloves in a medium-size saucepan and bring to a boil. Reduce the heat to low and simmer, stirring frequently. Continue to simmer until the milk takes on a pronounced flavor from the cinnamon and cloves, 15 to 20 minutes. Mix in the sugar and coffee, and then let the mixture cool.

2. When it has cooled, discard the cinnamon sticks and cloves. Mix in the *aguardiente*, egg yolk, and vanilla extract.

3. Pour the mixture into bottles and keep refrigerated. The drink stays good for a couple of weeks. Shake it thoroughly before serving.

Banana Milk Shake

Leche con Plátano   5 cups

Bananas, which in Chile are called plátanos, are frequently served with almíbar sauce (see recipe, page 216), or in kuchen (see recipe, page 207). In this popular breakfast drink, they are combined with milk and a bit of sugar. To make this frothy drink, both the milk and bananas should be refrigerated because ice is not used.

3 small bananas, chilled
3 cups milk
¼ cup sugar

Cut the bananas into several pieces. Place the bananas, milk, and sugar in a blender. Blend in several rapid motions, for 10 to 20 seconds, or until the bananas are almost pureed. Serve cold.

Fresh Papaya Juice

Jugo de Papaya Crudo   Yield: 3 cups

Chile has a wonderful variety of fresh juices sold throughout the country in small restaurants, sandwich establishments, and markets. The sight of mango juice in the central market of Iquique or papaya juice in the little shops of La Serena invariably lures me in. Some make papaya juice not only with the pulp, but also use the skin due to its rich nutrients.

7 ounces papaya
¼ cup sugar (approximately)
½ cup ground ice

1. Cut off the ends of the papaya and discard. Also discard the seeds.

2. Finely chop the papaya including its peel. Put the papaya, sugar, 2 cups of water, and ice in a blender or juice machine. Blend thoroughly and serve.

Warm Orange-scented Red Wine

As legend has it, years ago Chilean winemakers had a major shipment of wine destined for Europe. The only problem was that the Europeans demanded 750-milliliter bottles, and what they received from Chile were 700-milliliter bottles. It seemed as though a few Chilean winemakers were trying to pull a fast one on those exacting Europeans. The Europeans, understandably upset, sent the wine back to its thrifty makers, so the wine, in Spanish terms, had "navegado"— "navigated"—all the way back to Chile. The distraught Chilean wine exporters decided to make the most of that wine and invented this tasty, warming drink. It is somewhat akin to Spain's sangría, though it is seasoned somewhat differently and heated. Be careful not to overcook it or you will burn away the alcohol. The recipe comes from Patricio Gonzalez, who runs his own restaurant in Olmué, in central Chile, but who spends the summers cooking in a restaurant on Martha's Vineyard.

1 bottle red wine, preferably
   Cabernet Sauvignon
1/2 cup sugar
1/4 cup freshly squeezed
   orange juice (about
   1 orange)
A few slices of orange
2 cinnamon sticks
1 teaspoon cognac

1. Put the red wine, sugar, orange juice, orange slices, and cinnamon sticks in a medium-sized pot. Cook over medium heat. Stir occasionally.

2. When the mixture begins to boil, mix in the cognac. Cook for 30 seconds and remove from heat.

3. Serve warm. If you plan to let it sit for a long period of time, remove the orange slices immediately so that the drink does not become bitter and dominated by orange.

Sweet Shellfish Punch

There is so much terrific fresh shellfish in Chile extracted from the country's vast coastline that some creative, eclectic recipes were bound to spring up. One of the ways to enjoy shellfish is to actually drink them before or during a meal. Shellfish punches, come in numerous variations, but always contain wine and a pureed shellfish. There are sea urchin, mussel, shrimp, and mixed shellfish punches, as well as a giant barnacle variety, described here. If you can't find large barnacles, use another shellfish. Only a bit of cooked shellfish meat is blended into the drink so that they add only a subtle flavor. The recipe below comes from Do Brasil, one of the restaurants in the central market of Concepción. The name means "From Brazil," but the restaurant is "Chilean as beans," as the saying goes. Chileans are fond of giving foreign names to their children, their restaurants, and much else, even when they are 100% Chilean.

At Chilean parties, less racy punches are also quite commonly served, including **Borgoña**, *which is berries (typically strawberries) mixed with red wine and powdered sugar. Another punch is called* **Cleri**, *which has a white wine base and combines powdered sugar and fruits such as fresh peaches, melon, and chirimoya.*

2 giant barnacles, or
   3 mussels
2 cups white wine, well-chilled
1 tablespoon cognac
1 tablespoon rum
¼ teaspoon vanilla extract
1 egg yolk, lightly beaten
Sugar
Ground cinnamon

1. Steam the shellfish by putting it in a pot with about 2 inches of water. Cover and cook over medium heat. When the shells have opened, remove the meat. Discard the shells and chop the meat coarsely.

2. Put the meat in a blender or juicer, along with the white wine, cognac, rum, and vanilla extract. Blend until liquefied.

3. Mix in the egg yolk and add sugar to taste. The amount of sugar will depend on how dry your wine is.

4. Pour into 4 glasses and sprinkle a touch of cinnamon over each. Serve cold, with a spoon for stirring.

Creamy Sherry and Cocoa Liqueur

Vaina   4 servings

*Vaina incorporates liquors from other countries, but the concoction is fully Chilean. In Chile, **Vaina** sometimes includes **vino añejo**, which is aged red wine, but both sherry and port are delicious as well. Although **Vaina** is often served in Chile as a pre-dinner cocktail, most Americans would likely find it more to their tastes as an after-dinner drink.*

⅓ cup cacao liqueur
⅓ cup dry sherry or port
¼ cup cognac
1 cup well-crushed ice
1 tablespoon confectioners'
    sugar
2 egg yolks
Ground cinnamon for topping

Briefly blend all the ingredients in a blender, or use a cocktail shaker and shake the ingredients briefly. Don't blend or shake the drink for too long, or it will take on too much foam. Pour into 4 glasses, sprinkle a bit of cinnamon on each, and serve.

Los Vinos Chilenos

The grapes of Chile are no longer a secret: They are creating some of the world's best wine. From the well-known grape varieties of Cabernet Sauvignon and Sauvignon Blanc to its own vintage grape, Carmenère, Chile is no longer overlooked on the world stage of wine.

That Chile offers excellent low-end wines is a surprise to no one. However, in recent years the nation has shaken the simplistic and sometimes pejorative label of "value" to prove that it also can produce wines that compete with the fine wines of France, Italy, and California. Dozens of Chilean winemakers are proving that Latin America, too, can make outstanding wines (neighboring Argentina is doing its part through its rich Malbec wines grown in the Mendoza region).

Indeed, Chile is in the midst of a wine frenzy—or a wine reawakening, if you will. It is like a slumbering David stirred from his sleep, only now ready to take on Goliath. Certainly the nation has been awake for centuries to the fact that its soil and climate are ideal for winemaking and that grapes are one of its most prized natural resources. However, apart from the exceptional few winemakers that were far ahead of the field, the wine industry on a whole has only recently discovered how it can win over the more demanding palates worldwide. This not only includes enhancing its wines by improving technology and concentrating on low-yield—and thus high-quality—vineyards, but also by working together as an industry to try to boost exports and create a wine tourism industry at home.

A Privileged Heritage

Wine has become a vital national industry for Chile and its importance is only increasing. The explosion in the number of Chilean winemakers attests to the passion for wine in the country, and to the fierce competition that has ensued. In 1989 there were only 12 major Chilean wine companies with vineyards and export channels, whereas in 2003 that figure reached almost 110, according to the Chilean wine association, Chilevid. Furthermore, exports have soared, increasing five-fold in just a decade, to US$606 million in 2002 from US$119 million in 1992. This has allowed Chilean wine to venture far deeper into the markets of the U.S., Europe, and Asia.

In Chile one can see the unbridled energy in the wine industry and the excitement as its bottles fare well in national competitions. Often viewed as stratified and divided, Chile is a nation where love for wine transcends class and age. The way some youths whip around terms like "oak" and "chocolate" and debate the merits of various labels is akin to the way those of other cultures assess their favorite soda or candy bar.

While such passion is usually put to responsible, temperate use, other times the savoring of irresistible wine becomes less than restrained. Many a time I was surprised to sit down with a table of people and see someone give a toast just moments after the toast that announced the beginning of the meal. And then another toast would follow, then another, and still another. I was told this is *la brindis a la flamenca* (toasting Flamenco-style). How could a guest complain? The wine was delicious and the practice ingrained. Chile inherited the custom hundreds of years ago, when Spanish colonialists gave innumerable toasts, paying their sodden respects to whoever leaped into their memory.

The Spaniards' predilections converted wine into the national drink of Chile, and under the Conquistadors' thumb, Chile quickly began to export it. Or people came to the source itself. Full of ports that saw waves of opportunistic Europeans, Chile mesmerized more than a few foreigners with its grapes. To think that the French took but did not give to Chile could not be further from the truth. In the late 1800s, French oenologists came to Chile and inculcated the locals with the best practices and techniques from back home. They also brought the Carmenère grape, something they did not expect to become a source of envy at any time down the road. Even today, French and Chileans with French ancestry are forceful players in the Chilean wine industry. The prestigious company Casa Lapostolle proudly boasts that it is "Chilean by Nature, French by Design."

Natural Strength

While the Spanish, French, and of course the Chileans themselves have played vital roles to help establish the nation's important position in the wine field, Chile is also blessed with a myriad of natural gifts. It is a country, some say, tailor-made for winemaking—"a viticultural paradise." The winemaker is armed with all that he needs. Perched along the Pacific Ocean, the rich grape-growing valleys benefit from the cool sea breezes that moderate the hot summer days. The vast difference between the day and evening temperatures is ideal for the growth of grapes, as are dry summers counterbalanced by steady rain in Chile's winter months. For most of the year, the grapes are bathed in rich light, and they flourish over Chile's four pronounced seasons. Chile's location, too, is ideal from a global perspective. The ideal latitude for winemaking in the Southern Hemisphere is considered to be between the thirtieth and fortieth parallels; Chile falls between the thirty-second and thirty-eighth.

Lurking above the country's numerous valleys are the towering Andes Mountains, majestic to the traveler and nothing short of a godsend to the wine-grower, who treasures the crystal-clear waters that cascade down onto his vines. At the same time, these mountains and Chile's relative remoteness from the rest of the world protect the budding grapes. With the driest desert on earth, the Atacama, on the wine valleys' northern front, the Andes mountain range to the east, the Pacific to the west, and the glacial Antarctica on the country's southern extreme, Chile is shielded from the plagues and insects that feed on grapes elsewhere.

Nothing makes this more emphatically clear than the Carmenère grape, which originated in Bordeaux. In the 1850s, the vine-loving bug, the phyllox-era, ravaged French grapes and went on to wreak havoc throughout European vineyards. However, at the "end of the earth" in Chile, the bug was nowhere to be seen, as it mercifully reserved its feast for the Old Country. The problem was that no one in Chile realized that its Carmenère had survived, so it grew alongside similar-looking Merlot grapes for years. Until 1994, that is, when Chilean winemakers scurried to take advantage of the fact that they were the only major wine-producing country with bountiful Carmenère stocks.

Types of Grapes Cultivated

Those efforts have reaped excellent dividends, as wine experts often heap praise on Chile's Carmenère wines, with their low tannins and big, bright blackberry-color fruit. Some of Chile's best wines lean on the Carmenère grape for creative blends with Cabernet Sauvignon, Merlot, or Syrah. However, the wine lover should hardly focus on Chile's signature grape alone. Historically the country concentrated on Cabernet Sauvignon and Merlot, among reds, and Chardonnay and Sauvignon Blanc, among whites. And with each of these grapes it has made enormous strides. The hot dry heat beating down on Chile's wine-producing valleys has given the country its reputation for full-bodied reds, particularly Cabernet Sauvignons. The awards won tend to fall to this grape variety, especially since Merlots have often been a disappointment.

However, Merlots are improving, in part because with the distinction made between these and Carmenère grapes, winegrowers are now picking the two when properly ripened (before, both Carmenère and Merlot suffered, since they mature at different rates but were picked together). Chilean winemakers are also diversifying their red wine offerings, cultivating Syrah grapes that Australia is famous for (called Shiraz), as well as Malbec, which Argentina has produced en masse. Pinot Noir, Sangiovese, and Cabernet Franc also are popping up more frequently with Chilean labels.

Though Chile's reds have snared most of the attention abroad over the years, the country also has been gaining an important name for itself with its white wines, especially Chardonnays and Sauvignon Blancs. What better wines to leap in popularity in tandem with the Chilean sea bass? Some of the most exciting white wine production centers in the valley of Curicó, but also in the younger wine valley of Casablanca. Just a half-hour east of the port of Valparaíso, Casablanca is ideal for the cultivation of white grapes, with the cool sea breezes and a morning fog that keeps the hot summer temperatures at bay. Perhaps that is why it wasn't a surprise that, in 2002, it became the sister city to Napa Valley.

Casablanca and Curicó are but two of the grape-rich valleys of Chile, which can at times appear to be a vast swathe of grapes when you travel from the northern Limarí Valley to Chillán in the south. The northern valley of Limarí is so hot and dry that it is home not only to robust wine production, but also that of the grape brandy, Pisco. In the southern reaches of wine country, the climate is perfect for the production of white wines such as Gewürztraminer, and the dessert wines called "Late Harvest" in Chile.

Chilean Wine Prices

Despite the great climatic advantages and the lofty advances made by Chilean winemakers in recent years, there is room for improvement, and indiscriminately purchasing a Chilean wine is not a recipe for guaranteed enjoyment. Some Chilean winemakers continue to focus on quantity over quality. On the other hand, dismissing Chilean wines as subpar when you see their inexpensive price is equally hasty. You would be passing up countless gems.

There are important reasons why good Chilean wines are frequently so affordable in the U.S. and Europe. Partly it is due to the low cost of land and labor in Chile compared to other winemaking countries. And if you think Chilean wine is inexpensive where you live, come to Chile. You can drink a pretty good bottle of wine for just a few dollars. A French company that sells wines for $8 to $10 a bottle will complain that the money does not go a long way back at home in France, whereas for a Chilean winery, relatively speaking, this is a substantial amount for a bottle.

Further, while Chile is competing in world markets against the inveterate wine country titans, its competitors are largely emerging-market wine nations, such as South Africa, Argentina, Australia, and New Zealand, so prices should not be expected to regularly approximate those of France and Italy. Nor should Chile be expected to be on France's level overnight. France has had a multi-century head start over Chile in the production of wine.

Lastly, Chile historically concentrated on the lower-tier market, and some Chilean wineries still do go after that niche. However, Chilean wineries are now winning awards and earning special distinctions at the highest level. Foreign investment, including from Spain and France, pours into the wineries, auguring an even more auspicious future for Chilean wine.

While the awards are piling up, Chilean wineries are banding together to present a united front and are creating opportunities to boost their exposure both at home and abroad. In 1999, when I arrived in Chile, several vineyard representatives raised a brow when I asked about wine tours, as if I were requesting that they disrobe. Even today, most of the small vineyards do not offer tours on their own. However, larger wineries do offer tours of their vineyards, and smaller firms are visited and their wines sampled via valley tours.

Most of the wine-producing valleys of Chile now enable you to take a tour of the beautiful countryside in their region. They include tours of the vineyard, wine tastings, and sometimes meals. People who enjoy the exquisite traditional cuisine of Chile will finally be able to get an intimate look at some of the best and most exciting wines on the world stage today.

Addresses of Wine Companies in Chile

In the list that follows, you will find contact numbers for the wineries of Chile, as well as an indication of the valley in which they are producing wines. Many wineries have their business and administration headquarters in Santiago, and of course their vineyards elsewhere.

Remember to add the country name after the name of the city—e.g., "Santiago, Chile"—if sending correspondence from outside of Chile to a Chilean company. If telephoning or faxing from outside of Chile, Chile's country code, 56 should precede all telephone and fax numbers provided below. The first digit in the list indicates the city code (e.g., Santiago's city code is 2), and the subsequent six or seven digits constitute the local exchange and number. Finally, the abbreviation "NA" means the information was not made available.

Because Chile's wine market is very fluid and fast-growing, this list can not be all-inclusive; however, the major players and dozens upon dozens of others are listed here.

Agustinos
Vitacura 4380
Piso 18
Santiago
Tel: 2-206 7868
Fax: 2-206 7862
info@agustinos.cl
www.agustinos.cl
Valley: Cachapoal, Aconcagua, Maipo
Available in U.S.

Almaviva
Av. Santa Rosa 821
Puente Alto
Casilla 274
Santiago
Tel: 2-852 9300
Fax: 2-852 5405
almaviva@rdc.cl
www.bphr.com
Valley: Maipo
Available in U.S.

AltaCima
Casilla 70
Lontue
Tel: 75-47 1034
Fax: 75-47 1118
enokathaklaus@terra.cl
Valley: Curicó

Anakena
Alónso de Córdova 5151
Of. 1103
Las Condes
Santiago
Tel: 2-426 0608
Fax: 2-426 0609
info@anakenawines.cl
www.anakenawines.cl
Valleys: Cachapoal, Colchagua, Casablanca
Available in U.S.

Aquitania
Avenida Consistorial 5090
Peñalolén
Casilla 213-12
Santiago
Tel: 2-284 5470
Fax: 2-284 5469
info@aquitania.cl
www.aquitania.cl
Valley: Maipo
Available in U.S.

Aresti
Tucapel 3140
Santiago
Tel: 2-680 6771
Fax: 2-683 5630
www.arestichile.cl
Valley: Curicó
Available in U.S.

Balduzzi
Av. Balmaceda 1189
San Javier
Tel: 73-32 2138
Fax: 73-32 2416
www.balduzzi.cl
Valley: Maule
Available in U.S.

Bisquertt
El Comendador 2264
Providencia
Santiago
Tel: 2-233 6681, 2-422 0650
Fax: 2-231 9137
www.bisquertt.cl
Valley: Colchagua
Available in U.S.

Calina
Av. Nueva Tajamar 481
Torre Norte
Of. 501
Las Condes
Santiago
Tel: 2-339 7166
Fax: 2-339 7168
vinos@calina.cl
www.calina.com
Valley: Maule
Available in U.S.

Camino Real
Camino La Punta S/N
San Francisco de Mostazal
Tel: 72-491 014
Fax: 72-492 218
www.caminoreal.cl
Valleys: Cachapoal
Available in U.S.

Canepa
Lo Sierra 1500
Camino Lo Espejo
Casilla 2098
Santiago
Tel: 2-870 7131, 870 7100
Fax: 2-557 9186
josecanepa@canepa.cl
www.canepa.cl
Valleys: Colchagua, Maipo
Available in U.S.

Cantera
Eduardo Marquina 3937
Of. 84
Vitacura
Santiago
Tel: 2-245 7062
Fax: 2-249 7377
Valley: Colchagua
Available in U.S.: Negligible amount

Carmen (includes the brand
Terra Andina)
Apoquindo 3669
Piso 16
Las Condes
Santiago
Tel: 2-362 2122
Fax: 2-263 1599
info@carmen.cl
www.carmen.com
Valleys: Casablanca, Maipo, Colchagua,
Maule
Available in U.S.

Casa Donoso (includes the brand
Domaine Oriental)
Av. Vitacura 2909
Suite 1101
Las Condes
Santiago
Tel: 2-233 1056
Fax: 2-233 1117
info@casadonoso.com
www.casadonoso.cl
Valley: Maule
Available in U.S.

Casa Lapostolle
Benjamín 2935
Of. 801
Las Condes
Santiago
Tel: 2-242 9774/75
Fax: 2-234 4536
info@casalapostolle.cl
www.casalapostolle.com
Valleys: Casablanca, Cachapoal,
Colchagua
Available in U.S.

Casa Marín
Las Peñas 3101
Las Condes
Santiago
Tel: 2-334 2986
Fax: 2-334 9723
vinacasamarin@xpovin.cl
www.casamarin.cl
Valley: San Antonio

Casa Rivas
Pedro de Valdivia 555
Of. 512
Providencia
Santiago
Tel: 2-225 4506
Fax: 2-274 4125
mariajosebrowne@casarivas.cl
www.casarivas.cl
Valley: Maipo
Available in U.S.

Casa Silva
Hijuela Norte
Angostura
Casilla 97
San Fernando
Tel: 72-71 6519
Fax: 72-71 0204
www.casasilva.cl
Valley: Colchagua

Casa Tamaya
Concordia 2247
Providencia
Santiago
Tel: 2-650 8490
Fax: 2-362 0161
vina@tamaya.cl
www.tamaya.cl
Valley: Limarí
Available in U.S.

Casas del Bosque
Alonso de Córdova 5151
Of. 1501
Las Condes
Santiago
Tel: 2-378 5544
Fax: 2-378 5495
info_cdb@entelchile.net
www.casasdelbosque.cl
Valley: Casablanca
Available in U.S.

Casas Patronales
Av. Américo Vespucio
No. 1821
Huechuraba
Tel: 2-624 9219
Fax: 2-623 9732
comercial@casaspatronales.com
www.casaspatronales.com
Valley: Maule
Available in U.S.

Chateau Los Boldos
Camino Los Boldos s/n
Requínoa
Tel: 72-55 1230
Fax: 72-55 1202
boldos@clb.cl
www.chateaulosboldos.com
Valley: Cachapoal
Available in U.S.

Clos Quebrada de Macul
Av. Consistorial 5900
Peñalolén
Santiago
Tel: 2-298 2374
Fax: 2-284 8271
isabellezaeta@terra.cl
Valley: Maipo
Available in U.S.

Concha y Toro
Av. Nueva Tajamar 481
Torre Norte
Piso 15 y 16
Las Condes
Santiago
Tel: 2-821 7300
Fax: 2-203 6740
www.conchaytoro.com
Valleys: Casablanca, Maipo, Cachapoal,
Colchagua, Curicó, Maule
Available in U.S.

Cono Sur
Av. Nueva Tajamar 481
Piso 16
Torre Sur
Las Condes
Santiago
Tel: 2-203 6100
Fax: 2-203 6732
query@conosur.com
www.conosur.com
Valleys: Casablanca, Colchagua, Maipo,
Bío Bío
Available in U.S.

Correa Albano
Santa Rosa s/n
Sagrada Familia
Curicó
Tel: 75-47 1081
Fax: 75-47 1305
inform@correalbano.cl
www.correalbano.cl
Valley: Curicó

Cousiño Macul
Av. Quilín 7100
Peñalolén
Santiago
Tel: 2-284 1011
Fax: 2-284 1509
info@cousinomacul.cl
www.cousinomacul.cl
Valley: Maipo
Available in U.S.

Cremaschi Furlotti
Estado 359
Piso 4
Santiago
Tel: 2-632 9442
Fax: 2-632 7346
informaciones@cremaschifurlotti.cl
www.cremaschifurlotti.cl
Valley: Maule
Available in U.S.

De Larose
Casilla 249
Rengo
Tel: 72-55 1568
Fax: 72-55 1568
www.vinadelarose.cl
Valley: Cachapoal
Available in U.S.

Doña Javiera
Luis Thayer Ojeda 073
Of. 1001
Providencia
Santiago
Tel: 2-232 5538, 2-244 3038
Fax: 2-233 6253
t_global@entelchile.net
Valley: Maipo
Available in U.S.

Echeverría
Malaga 115
Of. 1006
Las Condes
Santiago
Tel: 2-207 4327
Fax: 2-207 4328
info@echewine.com
www.echewine.com
Valley: Curicó
Available in U.S.

El Aromo
17 Oriente 931
3 y 4 Sur
Talca
Tel: 71-24 2438
Fax: 71-24 5533
www.elaromo.cl
Valley: Maule
Available in U.S.

El Huique
Alcántara 200
Of. 306
Las Condes
Santiago
Tel: 2-207 8410
Fax: 2-206 4305
info@elhuique.com
www.vinoselhuique.cl
Valley: Colchagua
Available in U.S.

El Principal
Napoleón 3037
Of. 81
Las Condes
Santiago
Tel/Fax: 2-242 9800
vinaep@ctcinternet.cl
Valley: Maipo
Available in U.S.

Errázuriz (includes the brands **Seña**, **Viñedo Chadwick**, **Errázuriz**, **Arboleda**, and **Caliterra**)
Av. Nueva Tajamar 481
Of. 503
Torre Sur
Las Condes
Santiago
Tel: 2-203 6688
Fax: 2-203 6690
wine.report@errazuriz.cl
www.errazuriz.com
Valleys: Aconcagua (Seña wines), Maipo
(Viñedo Chadwick), Curicó
Available in U.S.

Estampa
Av. Kennedy 5735
Of. 606
Las Condes
Santiago
Tel: 2-426 5410, 426 5417
Fax: 2-426 5419
info@estampa.com
www.estampa.com
Valley: Colchagua

Francisco de Aguirre
Carrion 1586
Independencia
Santiago
Tel: 2-462 2000
Fax: 2-777 7154
www.vinafranciscodeaguirre.cl
Valley: Limarí
Available in U.S.

Gracia
Av. Vitacura 4380
Piso 18
Vitacura
Santiago
Tel: 2-206 7868
Fax: 2-206 7862
www.gracia.cl
Valley: Aconcagua
Available in U.S.

Haras de Pirque
Fundo La Rochuela
Camino San Vicente s/n
Sector Macul
Casilla 247
Pirque
Tel: 2-854 7910
Fax: 2-854 9309
www.harasdepirque.com
Valley: Maipo
Available in U.S.: NA

Huelquén
Camino Paine a Huelquén s/n
Casilla 185 Buin
Santiago
Tel: 2-822 1264
Fax: 2-822 1264
www.huelquen.com
Valley: Maipo
Available in U.S.: NA

Hugo Casanova
Casilla 82
Talca
Tel: 71-26 6540
Fax: 71-26 6539
vcasanov@ctcinternet.cl
www.hugocasanova.cl
Valley: Maule
Available in U.S.

Indómita Wine
Casilla 162
Casablanca
Tel: 32-75 4403
Fax: 32-75 4401
c_munozg@123mail.cl
www.indomita.cl
Valley: Casablanca
Available in U.S.: NA

J. Bouchon
Evaristo Lillo 178
Of. 21
Las Condes
Santiago
Tel: 2-246 9778
Fax: 2-246 9707
julio@jbouchon.cl
www.jbouchon.cl
Valley: Maule
Available in U.S.: Negligible amount

La Arboleda Estate and Winery
(includes **Arboleda** and **Caliterra** wines)
Contact is:
Robert Mondavi
PO Box 106
Oakville, CA 94562
Tel: (707) 226-1395
Fax: (707) 251-4386
info@robertmondavi.com
www.caliterra.com,
www.robertmondavi.com
Valley: For Arboleda, primarily the
valleys of Maipo and Colchagua; for
Caliterra, the valleys of Maipo,
Cachapoal, Curicó, Casablanca
Available in U.S.

La Fortuna
Tabancura 1515
Suite 316
Vitacura
Santiago
Tel: 2-954 2829
Fax: 2-954 2631
bodega@lafortuna.cl
www.lafortuna.cl
Valley: Curicó
Available in U.S.

La Posada
Rafael Casanova 570
Santa Cruz
Tel/Fax: 72-82 2448, 72-82 2589
laposada@entelchile.net
Valley: Colchagua
Available in U.S.

La Roncière
Rancagua
Tel: 72-23 0136
Fax: 72-23 3534
www.laronciere.com
Valleys: Colchagua, Cachapoal
Available in U.S.

La Rosa
Coyancura 2283
Ed. Paseo Las Palmas
Providencia
Santiago
Fax: 2-233 0353
vinalarosa@larosa.cl
www.larosa.cl
Valleys: Colchagua, Cachapoal
Available in U.S.

Las Pitras
Casilla 326
Curicó
Tel: 75-44 1697
Fax: 75-44 1091
pitras@entelchile.net
www.laspitras.cl
Valley: Curicó

Leyda
Isidora Goyenechea 3642
Piso 5
Santiago
Tel: 2-234 0002
Fax: 2-231 2510
info@leyda.cl
www.leyda.cl
Valleys: Leyda, Colchagua, Maipo
Available in U.S.

Linderos
Vina Linderos s/n
Linderos
Buin
Tel: 2-821 0390
Fax: 2-821 0385
www.linderos.cl
Valley: Maipo

Lomas de Cauquenes
Casilla 157
Cauquenes
Tel: 73-51 2026
Fax: 73-51 2274
mmolina@lomasdecauquenes.cl
www.covica.cl
Valley: Maule
Available in U.S.: NA

Los Robles
Luis Thayer Ojeda 0130
Of. 212
Santiago
Tel: 2-334 8856
Fax: 2-334 4185
robles@uva.cl
www.losrobles.cl
Valley: Curicó
Available in U.S.

Los Vascos
Benjamín 2944
Of. 31
Las Condes
Santiago
Tel: 2-232 6633
Fax: 2-231 4373
mpce@losvascos.cl
Valley: Colchagua
Available in U.S.

Luis Felipe Edwards
Av. Vitacura 4130
Vitacura
Santiago
Tel: 2-208 6819
Fax: 2-208 7775
vinalfedwards@entelchile.net
www.lfewines.com
Valley: Colchagua
Available in U.S.

Manquehue (includes the brands
Casal de Gorchs and **Domaine Rabat**)
Av. Vicuña Mackenna 2289
Santiago
Tel: 2-750 4000
Fax: 2-750 4068
info@manquehue.com
info@casaldegorchs.com
www.manquehue.com
Valleys: Colchagua, Casablanca, Maipo
Available in U.S.

Martínez de Salinas
San Francisco 470
Cauquenes
Tel: 73-51 2505
Fax: 73-51 1787
mmayo@entelchile.net
www.martinezdesalinas.cl
Valley: Maule
Available in U.S.

Miguel Torres
Av. Portugal 1968
Santiago
Tel: 2-233 4422
Fax: 2-555 6627
ventas@migueltorres.cl
www.torreswines.com
Valley: Curicó
Available in U.S.

Montes
Av. Del Valle 945, Of. 2611
Ciudad Empresarial
Huechuraba
Santiago
Tel: 2-248 4805
Fax: 2-248 4790
montes@monteswines.com
www.monteswines.com
Valleys: Curicó, Colchagua
Available in U.S.

MontGras
Av. Eliodoro Yáñez 2962
Providencia
Santiago
Tel: 2-520 4355
Fax: 2-520 4354
www.montgras.cl
Valley: Colchagua
Available in U.S.

Morandé
Av. Del Valle 601 Of. 12
Ciudad Empresarial
Huechuraba
Santiago
Tel: 2-270 8900
Fax: 2-443 1022
morande@morande.cl
www.morande.cl
Valley: Casablanca
Available in U.S.

Odfjell Vineyards
Casilla 23
Correo Padre Hurtado
Santiago
Tel: 2-811 1530
Fax: 2-811 1245
www.odfjellvineyards.cl
Valley: Maipo
Available in U.S.

Porta
Vitacura 4380
Piso 18
Santiago
Te: 2-206 7868
Fax: 2-206 7862
www.portawinery.cl
Valleys: Aconcagua, Cachapoal, Maipo,
Bío Bío, Casablanca
Available in U.S.

Portal del Alto
Camino el Arpa S/N
Alto Jahuel
Casilla 182
Buín
Tel: 2-821 2059, 821 3363
Fax: 2-821 3371
www.portaldelalto.cl
Valley: Maipo
Available in U.S.

Pueblo Antiguo
Florencio Valdes 236
Nancagua
Tel: 72-85 8296
Fax: 72-92 3712
ftorretti@puebloantiguo.cl
www.torretti.cl
Valley: Colchagua
Available in U.S.

Ravanal
Los Conquistadores 2595
Piso 2
Providencia
Santiago
Tel: 2-474 4074
Fax: 2-474 4075
info@ravanal.cl
www.ravanal.cl
Valley: Colchagua
Available in U.S.: Negligible amount

Requingua
Estado 337
9th floor
Santiago
Tel: 2-632 7984
Fax: 2-638 7584
info@requingua.cl
www.requingua.cl
Valley: Curicó
Available in U.S.

San Esteban
Federico Froebel 1583
Providencia
Santiago
Tel: 2-650 9793, 650 9794
Fax: 2-264 1764
sanesteban@vse.cl
www.vse.cl
Valley: Aconcagua
Available in U.S.

San Pedro
Vitacura 4380
Piso 6
Santiago
Tel: 2-477 5300
Fax: 2-477 5438
www.sanpedro.cl
Valley: Curicó
Available in U.S.

Santa Carolina (includes the brand **Casablanca**)
Tiltil 2228
Macul
Santiago
Tel: 2-450 3000
Fax: 2-238 0307
www.santacarolina.com
Valleys: Casablanca, Maipo, Colchagua, Lontué, Maule
Available in U.S.

Santa Ema
Izaga 1096
Casilla 17
Isla de Maipo
Tel: 2-819 2996
Fax: 2-819 2811
santaema@entelchile.net
www.santaema.cl
Valley: Maipo
Available in U.S.

Santa Emiliana
Av. Nueva Tajamar 481
Torre Sur
Of. 701
Las Condes
Santiago
Tel: 2-353 9130, 353 9141
Fax: 2-203 6936
www.santaemiliana.cl
Valleys: Casablanca, Maipo, Cachapoal, Colchagua
Available in U.S.

Santa Helena
La Concepción 266
Piso 6
Providencia
Santiago
Tel: 2-362 1526
Fax: 2-362 1527
www.santahelena.cl
Valley: Colchagua
Available in U.S.

Santa Inés de Martino (includes the brand **De Martino**)
Av. Manuel Rodríguez 229
Casilla 247
Isla de Maipo
Tel: 2-819 2959
Fax: 2-819 2986
www.santainesvineyards.com,
www.demartino.cl
Valley: Maipo
Available in U.S.

Santa Mónica
Camino a Donihue km 5
Rancagua
Tel: 72-22 4951
Fax: 72-23 8802
www.santamonica.cl
Valley: Cachapoal

Santa Rita
Av. Apoquindo 3669
Of. 601
Las Condes
Santiago
Tel: 2-362 2000
Fax: 2-228 6335
www.santarita.cl
Valleys: Maipo, Casablanca, Colchagua
Available in U.S.

Segú
Fundo Mirador Melozal s/n
San Javier
Casilla 72
Linares
Tel: 73-21 0078
Fax: 73-37 2383
vinosegu@entelchile.net
www.vinosegu.com
Valley: Maule
Available in U.S.: NA

Siegel
Fundo La Laguna s/n
San Fernando
Casilla 202
San Fernando
Tel/Fax: 72-71 1229
info@siegelvinos.com
www.siegelvinos.com
Valley: Colchagua
Available in U.S.

Tabontinaja (includes the
brand **Gillmore**)
Av. Vitacura 2909
Of. 805
Las Condes
Santiago
Tel: 2-231 7694
Fax: 2-946 2227
www.gillmore.cl
Valley: Maule
Available in U.S.

Tarapacá (includes the brand
Misiones de Rengo)
Los Conquistadores 1700
Torre Santa María
Piso 15
Providencia
Santiago
Tel: 2-707 6200
Fax: 2-233 3162
vinos@tarapaca.cl
www.tarapaca.cl
Valley: Maipo
Available in U.S.

Terramater (includes the
brand **Millaman**)
Luis Thayer Ojeda 236
Piso 6
Providencia
Santiago
Tel: 2-233 1311
Fax: 2-231 6391
www.terramater.cl
Valley: Maipo
Available in U.S.

Terranoble
Av. Andres Bello 2777
Of. 901
Las Condes
Santiago
Tel: 2-203 3628
Fax: 2-203 3620
terranoble@terranoble.cl
www.terranoble.cl
Valley: Maule
Available in U.S.

Torrealba
Longitudinal Sur km 204
Curicó
Tel/Fax: 75-47 1332
www.torrealbawines.cl
Valley: Curicó
Available in U.S.

Torreón de Paredes
Av. Apoquindo 5500
Las Condes
Santiago
Tel: 2-211 5323, 201 1823
Fax: 2-246 2684
torreon@torreon.cl
www.torreon.cl
Valley: Cachapoal
Available in U.S.

Tuniche
Camino a Tuniche s/n
Rancagua
Tel: 72-25 0818
Fax: 72-25 0833
info@tuniche.com
www.tuniche.com
Valley: Cachapoal

Undurraga
Vitacura 2939
Piso 21
Las Condes
Santiago
Tel: 2-372 2900
Fax: 2-372 2946
www.undurraga.cl
Valley: Maipo
Available in U.S.

Valdivieso
Juan Mitjans 200
Macul
Paradero 2 Vicuna MacKenna
Santiago
Tel: 2-381 9200
Fax: 2-238 2383
www.vinavaldivieso.cl
Valley: Curicó
Available in U.S.

Ventisquero
Camino La Estrella 401
Of. 5
Sector Punta de Cortes
Rancagua
Tel: 72-20 1240
Fax: 72-20 1244
www.vinaventisquero.com
Valleys: Casablanca, Colchagua, Maipo
Available in U.S.

Veramonte
Ruta 68
Km 66
Casablanca
Tel: 32-74 2421
Fax: 32-74 2420
www.veramonte.cl
Valley: Casablanca
Available in U.S.

Villard Estate
La Concepción 165
Of. 506
Providencia
Santiago
Tel: 2-235 7857, 235 7715
Fax: 2-235 7671
info@villard.cl
www.villard.cl
Valley: Casablanca
Available in U.S.

Viñedos Sutil
Av. 11 de Septiembre 1860
Of. 92
Providencia
Santiago
Tel: 2-362 1929
Fax: 2-371 3461
www.vinedossutil.com
Valley: Colchagua
Available in U.S.

Vinos del Sur (VINSUR) (Includes the
brand **Carpe Diem**)
Alsacia 57
Of. 2
Las Condes
Santiago
Tel: 2-228 9342, 9315
Fax: 2-207 0967
vinsur@fundacionchile.org
www.vinosdelsur.cl
Valleys: Itata, Maule
Available in U.S.

Viu Manent
Antonio Varas 2740
Ñuñoa
Santiago
Tel: 2-379 0020
Fax: 2-379 0439
www.viumanent.cl
Valley: Colchagua
Available in U.S.

William Fèvre
Huelén 56
Of. B
Providencia
Santiago
Tel: 2-235 1919
Fax: 2-235 4525
wfchile@wfchile.cl
www.wfchile.cl
Valley: Maipo
Available in U.S.

Wine Valley Tour Contacts

For those of you interesting in seeing Chile, one of the best ways is via a wine tour. Most of the wine regions of Chile now have organized routes that pass through numerous wineries. They are the valleys of Casablanca, Cachapoal, Colchagua, Curicó, and Maule. Here is a list of companies running wine tours in those valleys:

Casablanca Valley Wine Route
Constitucion 252
Of. A
Piso 3
Casablanca
Tel: 32-743 755
Fax: 32-743 933
wineroute@casablancavalley.cl
www.casablancavalley.cl

La Ruta del Vino del Valle de Cachapoal
Casilla 151
Requinoa
Tel/Fax: 72-553 684
info@cachapoalwineroute.com,
mhagel@agi.cl
www.cachapoalwineroute.com

Ruta del Vino del Valle de Colchagua
Plaza de Armas 140
Of. 6
Santa Cruz
Sexta Región
info@rutadelvino.cl
www.rutadelvino.cl

Ruta del Vino Valles de Curicó S.A.
Merced 341
Piso 2
Curicó
Tel: 75-328 972
Fax: 75-328 967
info@rvvc.cl
www.rvvc.cl

Maule Valley Wine Route
Villa Cultural Huiquilemu
Km. 7 near to San Clemente
Talca
Maule Region
Tel/Fax: 71-24 6460
wineroute@entelchile.net
www.chilewineroute.cl

Contacting Chilean Wine Exporters

If you are interested in Chilean wine imports and exports, the following two associations group together winemakers that represent the lion's share of Chile's total export sales volume. They are commonly known, respectively, as ChileVid and Viñas de Chile.

Asociación de Productores de Vinos
Finos de Exportación A.G.
Providencía 2330
Of. 63
Santiago
Tel: 2-232 9849, 335 9112, 335 4623,
335 4624
Fax: 2-232 7743, 232 5949
chilevid@chilevid.cl
www.chilevid.cl

Asociación de Viñas de Chile A.G.
Edificio World Trade Center
Av. Nueva Tajamar 481
Torre Sur
Of. 804
Las Condes
Santiago
Tel: 2-203 6353
Fax: 2-203 6356
info@vinasdechile.com
www.vinasdechile.com

C hile has among the most diverse selection of fish in the world. The following is a list of those fish and shellfish most frequently found in Chile, with their English translations. Some Chilean fish are not found in the U.S., nor can one find something similar to them in the U.S. Some of the translations for those Chilean fish below are for fish found in the U.S. that approximate their Chilean cousins.

Español	English
Albacora	Swordfish
Almeja	Littleneck clam
Anchoa	Anchovy
Atún	Tuna
Bacalao de Profundidad	Chilean sea bass
Calamar	Squid
Camarón de río	Crayfish
Camarón	Prawn, shrimp
Cangrejo	Crab
Caracol	Snail
Centolla	King crab
Cholga	Large mussel
Chorito	Medium mussel
Choro zapato	Very large mussel
Chuchita	Small mussel
Cochayuyo	Kelp, brown alga, rockweed
Cojinova	Silver warehou, white warehou
Congrio	Conger eel
Corvina	Croaker, grouper, Southern grunt
Erizo	Sea urchin
Gamba	Shrimp
Jaiba	Crab
Jibia	Cuttlefish
Jurel	Yellow mackerel
Langosta	Lobster
Lapa	Keyhole limpet
Lenguado	Flounder, sole, flatfish
Loco	Abalone

Luche	Wakame
Macha	Razor clam
Merluza	Hake
Ostión	Sea scallop
Ostra	Oyster
Pancora	Crab
Pejegallo	Elephant fish
Pejesapo	Anglerfish, monkfish, goosefish
Pejeyrrey	Smelt, silverside
Picoroco	Large barnacle
Piure	Shellfish not found in the U.S.
Pulpo	Octopus
Reineta	Pomfret
Róbalo	Sea bass
Salmón	Salmon
Sierra	Pacific sierra, mackerel
Trucha	Trout
Turbo	Turbot
Ulte	Alga not found in the U.S.

Index

FROM HIPPOCRENE'S
LATIN AMERICAN COOKBOOK
LIBRARY

APROVECHO

A Mexican-American Border Cookbook
Teresa Cordero Cordell and Robert Cordell

This cookbook celebrates the food and culture found along the Mexican Border. It offers more than 250 recipes from appetizers and beverages to entrees and desserts, combining a tantalizing array of ingredients from both sides of the border. Easy-to-follow instructions enable cooks to create a special dish or an entire fiesta in no time. The book contains informative sections ranging from how tequila is made, making tamales, and a guide to Mexican beer.

400 PAGES • 7 X 10 • 0-7818-1026-4 • $24.95HC • (554)

ARGENTINA COOKS!

Treasured Recipes from the Nine Regions of Argentina (Expanded Edition)
Shirley Lomax Brooks

Argentine cuisine is one of the world's best-kept culinary secrets. The country's expansive landscape includes tropical jungles, vast grasslands with sheep and cattle, alpine lakes and glacier-studded mountains. As a result, a great variety of foods are available—game, lamb, an incredible assortment of fish and seafood, exotic fruits and prime quality beef. This cookbook highlights the food from Argentina's nine regions in 190 recipes, including signature dishes from Five Star chefs, along with the best recipes from the author and other talented home chefs. Along with insight into Argentina's landscape, history, traditions and culture, this cookbook includes a section on Argentine wines.

314 PAGES • 6 X 9 • 0-7818-0997-5 • $24.95HC • (384)

ART OF BRAZILIAN COOKERY

Dolores Botafogo

In the 40 years since its original publication, *The Art of Brazilian Cookery* has been a trusted source for home cooks. This authentic cookbook of Brazilian food, the first of its kind to be published in the U.S., includes over 300 recipes, both savory and sweet, as well as a vivid historical-geographic and culinary picture of Brazil.

240 PAGES • 5$^{1}/_{2}$ X 8$^{1}/_{4}$ • 0-7818-0130-3 • $11.95PB • (250)

ART OF SOUTH AMERICAN COOKERY

Myra Waldo

This cookbook offers delicious recipes for the typical South American meal, with specialties from all countries. The recipes included in the book reflect the influence of both Spanish and Portuguese cuisines, but are enhanced by the use of locally available ingredients.

272 PAGES • 5 X 8$^{1}/_{2}$ • 0-7818-0485-X • $12.95PB • (423)

CUISINES OF PORTUGUESE ENCOUNTERS
Cherie Hamilton

This fascinating collection of 225 authentic recipes is the first cookbook to encompass the entire Portuguese-speaking world and explain how Portugal and its former colonies influenced each other's culinary traditions. The cookbook includes dishes containing Asian, South American, African, and European flavors, along with varied ingredients such as piripiri pepper, coconut milk, cilantro, manioc root, bananas, and dried fish. The recipes range from appetizers like *Pastel com o Diabo Dentro* (Pastry with the Devil Inside) from Cape Verde, to entrees such as *Frango à Africana* (Grilled Chicken African Style) from Mozambique and *Cuscuz de Camarão* (Shrimp Couscous) from Brazil, to desserts like *Pudim de Côco* (Coconut Pudding) from Timor. Menus for religious holidays and festive occasions, a glossary, a section on mail-order sources, a brief history of the cuisines, and a bilingual index assist the home chef in creating meals that celebrate the rich, diverse, and delicious culinary legacy of this old empire.

378 PAGES • 6 X 9 • 0-7818-0831-6 • $24.95HC • (91)

FRENCH CARIBBEAN CUISINE
Stéphanie Ovide
Preface by Maryse Condé

This marvelous cookbook contains over 150 authentic recipes from the French islands of Guadeloupe and Martinique. Favorites such as Avocado Charlotte, Pumpkin and Coconut Soup, Fish Crêpes Saintoise, and Fish Court Bouillon will beckon everyone to the table. The author has spent many hours traveling, researching, and cooking throughout the French Caribbean to give readers a real taste and appreciation of what French Creole cuisine entails.

The book would not be complete without a chapter on favorite drinks, featuring the famous Ti Punch. Also included are an extensive glossary of culinary terms that familiarize home cooks with exotic fruits, vegetables, and fish, as well as a list of resources for Caribbean products and spices.

232 PAGES • 6 X 9 • 0-7818-0925-8 • $24.95HC • (3)

MAYAN COOKING
RECIPES FROM THE SUN KINGDOMS OF MEXICO
Cherry Hamman

Take a culinary journey into the Mexican Yucatan and unravel the mysteries of ancient Mayan cuisine! This book contains over 150 traditional recipes that date back several centuries, as well as contemporary creations that represent Maya ingenuity and imagination in borrowing new foods and ideas.

275 PAGES • 6 X 9 • DRAWINGS • 0-7818-0580-5 • $24.95HC • (680)

OLD HAVANA COOKBOOK

Cuban Recipes in Spanish and English

Cuban cuisine, though derived from its mother country, Spain, has been modified and refined by locally available foods and the requirements of a tropical climate. Gulf Stream fish, crabs and lobsters, and an almost infinite variety of vegetables and luscious, tropical fruits have an important place on the Cuban table. This cookbook includes over 50 recipes, each in Spanish with side-by-side English translation—all of them classic Cuban fare and old Havana specialties adapted for the North American kitchen. Among the recipes included are: *Ajiaco* (famous Cuban Stew), Boiled Red Snapper with Avocado Sauce, Lobster Havanaise, *Tamal en Cazuela* (Soft Tamal), *Quimbombó* (okra), *Picadillo*, Roast Suckling Pig, and Boniatillo (Sweet Potato Dulce), along with a chapter on famous Cuban cocktails and beverages.

123 PAGES • 5 X 7 • LINE DRAWINGS • 0-7818-0767-0 • $11.95HC • (590)

SECRETS OF COLOMBIAN COOKING

Patricia McCausland-Gallo

From the coffee and cacao grown high in the Andes Mountains to the many tropical fruits of the Caribbean and Amazonian regions, the great cattle farms on the plains, and bountiful seafood from the Pacific Ocean and the Caribbean Sea, Colombia is a country of vast and exotic culinary creations. Secrets of Colombian Cooking presents the wide spectrum of Colombian cuisine to home cooks in more than 175 inviting recipes from simple, hearty *sancochos* (soups and stews prepared differently in every region) to more exotic fare such as *Langosta al Coco* (lobster in coconut sauce) and *Ají de Uchuvas* (Yellow Gooseberry Sauce).

270 PAGES • 6 X 9 • 0-7818-1025-6 • $24.95HC • (560)

A TASTE OF HAITI (EXPANDED EDITION)

Mirta Yurnet-Thomas & The Thomas Family

African, French, Arabic and Amerindian influences make the food and culture of Haiti fascinating subjects to explore. From the days of slavery to present times, traditional Haitian cuisine has relied upon staples such as root vegetables, pork, fish, and flavor enhancers like *Pikliz* (picklese, or hot pepper vinegar) and *Zepis* (ground spices). This cookbook presents more than 100 traditional Haitian recipes, which are complemented by information on Haiti's history, holidays and celebrations, staple foods, and cooking methods. Recipe titles are presented in English, Creole, and French.

180 PAGES • 5^1/$_2$ X 8^1/$_2$ • 0-7818-0998-3 • $24.95HC • (588)

SPANISH AND LATIN AMERICAN INTEREST
TITLES FROM HIPPOCRENE BOOKS...

HISTORY AND CULTURE
SPAIN: AN ILLUSTRATED HISTORY
Spain has had a remarkable history. It was a thriving center of Islamic civilization for many centuries until its conquest by Christian kings. Before long, this country had expanded to become one of the world's greatest empires, leaving traces of its culture, language, and religion throughout the world. This narrative provides a survey of Spanish history that is perfect for the student, traveler, or generally curious reader.
176 PAGES • 5 X 7 • 50 B/W PHOTOS./ILLUS/MAPS • 0-7818-0874-X • $12.95PB • (339)

MEXICO: AN ILLUSTRATED HISTORY
This historical guide traces Mexico's growth from the days of the Olmecs to the present. With the aid of over 50 illustrations, photos, and maps, the reader will discover how events of Mexico's past have left an indelible mark on the politics, economy, culture, and spirit of this country and its people. The author explores issues of social class, power, dependency, conquest, and the fortitude of this remarkable country.
150 PAGES • 5 X 7 • 50 B/W PHOTOS./ILLUS/MAPS • 0-7818-0690-9 • $11.95HC • (585)

LITERATURE
TREASURY OF CLASSIC SPANISH LOVE SHORT STORIES
In Spanish and English
A perfect gift for a loved one, this volume features side-by-side Spanish and English.
157 PAGES • 5 X 7 • 0-7818-0512-0 • $11.95 • (604)

TREASURY OF SPANISH LOVE POEMS, QUOTATIONS & PROVERBS
In Spanish and English
This classic collection features great Spanish poems and characteristic sayings on the subject of romance. It spans 1500 years of Spanish literature and folklore. Many authors are featured, including Miguel de Cervantes. All works appear in Spanish with facing English translations.
128 PAGES • 5 X 7 • 0-7818-0358-6 • $11.95 • (589)
2 CASSETTES: CA. 2 HOURS • $12.95 • (584) • 0-7818-0365-9

TREASURY OF MEXICAN LOVE POEMS, QUOTATIONS & PROVERBS

In Spanish and English

This beautiful anthology captures the many varieties of love in Mexican literature. Its selections include passionate works by Sor Juana de la Cruz, postmodern verse by Ramón López Velarde, and the contemporary poetry of Rosario Castellanos. All works appear in Spanish with facing English translations.

150 PAGES • 5 X 7 • 0-7818-0985-1 • $11.95HC • (495)

FOLK TALES FROM CHILE

These classic stories will delight young and old readers. This unique collection of fifteen folk tales represents a fusion of two cultures—the Old World culture of the Spanish soldiers and priests, and the native culture of Chile's original inhabitants.

121 PAGES • 5 X 8 • 15 ILLUSTRATIONS • 0-7818-0712-3 • $12.50HC • (785)

DICTIONARY OF 1,000 SPANISH PROVERBS

Organized alphabetically by key words, this bilingual reference book is a guide to and information source for a key element of Spanish.

131 PAGES • $5^{1}/_{2}$ X $8^{1}/_{2}$ • 0-7818-0412-4 • $11.95PB • (254)

LANGUAGE GUIDES

SPANISH-ENGLISH/ENGLISH-SPANISH PRACTICAL DICTIONARY

35,000 ENTRIES • 338 PAGES • $5^{1}/_{2}$ X $8^{1}/_{2}$ • 0-7818-0179-6 • $9.95PB • (211)

SPANISH-ENGLISH/ENGLISH-SPANISH DICTIONARY & PHRASEBOOK (LATIN AMERICAN)

2,000 ENTRIES • 250 PAGES • $3^{3}/_{4}$ X $7^{1}/_{2}$ • 0-7818-0773-5 • $11.95PB • (261)

EMERGENCY SPANISH PHRASEBOOK

80 PAGES • $7^{1}/_{2}$ X $4^{1}/_{8}$ • 0-7818-0977-0 • $5.95PB • (460)

HIPPOCRENE CHILDREN'S ILLUSTRATED SPANISH DICTIONARY

English-Spanish/Spanish-English

• for ages 5 and up
• 500 entries with color pictures
• commonsense pronunciation for each Spanish word
• Spanish-English index

500 ENTRIES • 94 PAGES • 8 X 11 • 0-7818-0889-8 • $11.95PB • (181)

BEGINNER'S SPANISH

313 PAGES • 5^1/2 X 8^1/2 • 0-7818-0840-5 • $14.95PB • (225)

MASTERING ADVANCED SPANISH

326 PAGES • 5^1/2 X 8^1/2 • 0-7818-0081-1 • $14.95PB • (413)

2 CASSETTES: CA. 2 HOURS • 0-7818-0089-7 • $12.95 • (426)

SPANISH GRAMMAR

224 PAGES • 5^1/2 X 8^1/2 • 0-87052-893-9 • $12.95PB • (273)

SPANISH VERBS: SER AND ESTAR

220 PAGES • 5^1/2 X 8^1/2 • 0-7818-0024-2 • $8.95PB • (292)

DICTIONARY OF LATIN AMERICAN SPANISH PHRASES AND EXPRESSIONS

1,900 ENTRIES • 178 PAGES • 5^1/2 X 8^1/2 • 0-7818-0865-0 • $14.95 • (286)

SPANISH PROVERBS, IDIOMS AND SLANG

350 PAGES • 6 X 9 • 0-7818-0675-5 • $14.95PB • (760)

Prices subject to change without prior notice. **TO PURCHASE HIPPOCRENE BOOKS** contact your local bookstore, call (718) 454-2366, or write to: HIPPOCRENE BOOKS, 171 Madison Avenue, New York, NY 10016. Please enclose check or money order, adding $5.00 shipping (UPS) for the first book, and $.50 for each additional book.